SONG OF THE HILL

Life, Love, Legacy

Ralph Proctor, Jr., Ph.D.

Far End of Herron Avenue Looking toward Centre Avenue (c. 1940s)

**WITH PHOTOGRAPHS BY
CHARLES "TEENIE" HARRIS**

Wisdom of Life Series
Learning Moments Press
Pittsburgh, PA

Song of The Hill: Life, Love, Legacy
Ralph Proctor, Jr., Ph.D.

Learning Moments Press
Publishing Arm of Scholar Practitioner Nexus
Oakmont, PA 15139
scholarpractitionernexus.com

*Self-portrait of Charles "Teenie" Harris with son,
Charles A. "Little Teenie" Harris (c. 1937)*

BISAC Subject: History/Social History (HIS 054000)
Social Science/Ethnic Studies/American/
African American & Black Studies (SOC 001000)
Social Science/Discrimination (SOC 031000)
Social Science/Race & Ethnic Relations (SOC 070000)
Education/Multicultural Education (EDU 020000)
Political Science/Civil Rights (POL 004000)
Biography & Autobiography/Cultural, Ethnic & Regional/
African American & Black (BIO 002010)
Biography & Autobiography/Personal Memoirs (BIO 026000)
Onix Audience Code: 01 General Trade; 06 Professional & Scholarly

Book Layout: Mike Murray, pearhouse.com
Photographs courtesy of the Carnegie Museum of Art,
Charles "Teenie" Harris Archive © 2014

Table of Contents

Songs of The Hill[1]

I hear a song of
> ...sorrow for lost love sung by a blues singer or played by B.B. King on his magic guitar...
> ...weariness pounded out by a Black steelmaker or Pittsburgh drummer Art Blakey...
> ...frustration in the Broadway performance of an August Wilson play...
> ...laughter as White and Black children played together...
> ....joy and redemption raised by a rousing gospel choir...

This song I hear
> ...flows in the smooth love ballads of Billy Eckstein or Lena Horne...
> ...offers the comfort of a mother's embracing arms...
> ...vibrates in anticipation of a father's coming home...
> ...shouts—from the top of our lungs and the bottom of our souls—in defiance of injustice...
> ...wails from the depths of grief for another Black life lost...

I hear this song
> ...of safety...
> ...of knowing I am home at last...
> ...of hope when all seems lost...
> ...of my people...

I hear this song that can never die as
> It echoes across the years gone by and
> Floats forever forward as
> We sing it to the end of time—

This song of my people's enduring strength.

I am a son of The Hill. Its people call to me. Its way of life shaped
me. None of what I have accomplished would have been possible
had it not been for the people in the vibrant, resilient community
in which I was raised. Its songs infuse my soul. In the sunshine
of a glorious summer day, in the quiet stillness of the night, I
hear its song whisper to me.

---

1 Author's Note: This poem took shape as Maria Piantanida and I engaged in a collaborative exchange. I want to acknowledge her contribution to its creation.

Prologue

One year, I received a call from a very large church in East Liberty that was planning a week-long Jazz festival. After reviewing the list of jazz groups scheduled to appear as requested, I called the festival director, and asked, "I'm wondering why no Black groups are playing?" Without hesitation she responded, "Oh, are there any *Black* jazz groups?" While biting my tongue, I explained that Jazz had been invented by Black folks and yes, I did happen to know a few Black groups."

...

One year, a White teacher in Pittsburgh asked for my help with a young Black student. "He denies he is African American," she explained. "We're working on an art project that requires each student to make a mask reflecting a specific culture. He is working on an 'Indian' mask because he says he is an *Indian Prince*. He refuses to participate in any discussions about Africa. He'll participate when we start talking about *his* people."

...

When I was studying at The University of Pittsburgh, one professor said, "Oh, I'm surprised you're from The Hill. Judging from the way you speak, we all thought you were from some mixed-race, middle class neighborhood. I responded: "I am; it is called THE HILL."

These three anecdotes serve to illustrate the ignorance I have encountered throughout my life—ignorance of Black culture, ignorance of African American history, and ignorance of an exceptional Black community.

I write this book against the background of racism in America. That racism exists—has existed since the founding of our nation—cannot be denied. That millions of my people have suffered and died at the hands of madmen and women is evident. So, too, is the indelible, bloody stain that slavery and racism have left on the nation's collective history.

In telling the cultural stories of racism, many authors from doctoral candidates to esteemed sociologists to Negro-ologists[2] have cast all Blacks in one of two stereotypical roles: one of villain to be feared; the other of victim to be pitied. I am tired of those stories. Thus, the story I want to tell is about a remarkable place called The Hill, a nationally known Black enclave that flourished in the early decades of the 20th century. I knew this place intimately, for it is where I grew up, and I hope my memories of this special time and place will resonate with others of my generation. At the same time, this is not merely a nostalgic story of an idealized past. For me and others, our memories also carry pain and anger about what our lives could and should have been if discrimination hadn't stacked the deck against us.

I am also writing for the younger generations of Blacks who grew up after the civil rights movement removed some barriers that limited our options and opportunities. Too often I meet young men and women who know far too little of past struggles against the racist culture and the ways this culture persists today. We live in dangerous times and cannot take for granted any of the rights gained through the sacrifice of many courageous men, women, teenagers, and children.

Many people, especially Whites, may be surprised by my contention that we live in dangerous times. True, the killing of George Floyd and many other innocent Black men and women has brought national attention to *racist incidents*. Those who see themselves as "enlightened," who would never perpetrate acts of violence against Blacks, who would never use the word *nigger*, who strive to avoid micro-aggressions[3] in their daily interactions with Blacks can still remain oblivious to the *institutionalized racism* to which Blacks are still subjected.

Even as this is being written, Republicans are leading racist charges to take away many of the voting rights gained through the Civil Rights Movement. These rights were won through spilled blood and lost lives. As was the case of southern Jim Crow laws, these latest attempts to make voting more difficult stand against the intent of the 15th Amendment to the Constitution that states:

> The right of citizens of the United States to vote shall not be denied or abridged by the United States or any State on account of race, color, or previous condition of servitude.

Even though these new assaults are couched in terms of "preventing voter fraud," they will create barriers that will disproportionately prevent people of color and those in poor communities from exercising their right to vote. Although study after study has found NO

---

2   NEGRO-OLOGIST is a White person who often has received a grant to study the thinking, feelings, and behaviors of Negroes. Some were social workers, who like anthropologist Margaret Meade, should have known better than to write about cultures they could never understand as outside observers.

3   "Micro aggression" is a current buzz word used to connote words or actions that are consciously or unconsciously insulting and hurtful. Those who use the term to describe or criticize the behavior of others tend to assume that everyone understands what the term means and why it is an important concept. That is a somewhat simplistic assumption. When I first began hearing the word, I had no idea what it meant, beyond the literal meaning of "small aggressions." To see if I was alone in not understanding the term, I called 20 individuals I consider to be extremely knowledgeable and asked what "micro-aggressions" meant to them. Like me, some understood the literal meaning, but could offer no examples. I have come to regard the term as a bit of a "trigger" word that impedes rather than encourages mutual understanding. I return to this issue in Chapter 20 when I discuss differences in conversational style between Blacks and Whites.

evidence of voter fraud, some of the most powerful Republican leaders continue to parrot Donald Trump's claim that the 2020 election was stolen. In attacking the lawful and peaceful transition of power, these leaders (ironically in the party of Abraham Lincoln) are threatening the foundation of democracy. Are they so devoted to retaining their party's power (and their own) that they will enact the equivalent of Jim Crow laws that for decades disenfranchised Black voters in the southern States?

Residents of The Hill Exercising Their Right to Vote. Legislation currently being proposed or passed threatens this fundamental democratic right.

It's trite to say "if you are not part of the solution, you are part of the problem." But trite sayings still carry a truth, and the truth is that willful ignorance of systemic racism creates conditions for oppression. If my grandparents' and parents' generation lived with regrets about what could have and should have been, my generation has lived with the fury that Whites could have and should have understood how their society suppressed ours. I have no doubt the course of my life would have been different had I not been Black. Still, as I look back on my life, I would not change my "race." The privilege of being a warrior for my people has given purpose to my life.

I have come to a place where I can look back and tell the story of The Hill from the perspective—not of a rich and famous celebrity—but of an average Black man who lived in Pittsburgh's inner-city community known as The Hill. The story spans the years from 1938 to 1970 and encompasses a time when the community flourished not only in spite of, but also because of, racial discrimination. It also traces the destruction of this community by an ill-conceived Urban "Renewal" project and the cascade of events it precipitated.

As I describe my life and that of my family and friends, White readers may think, "That's pretty much the same way we lived." And that is one point I want to make. Beneath our skin, we are the same. But the color of my skin makes these experiences different in profoundly fundamental and painful ways. That is the other point I want to make. The tensions between same and different play out in themes that weave throughout the book. The theme of inclusion within The Hill community is always in tension with exclusion from White society. Being a valued member within The Hill plays against the tension of "being Other" outside of its boundaries. Safety within The Hill stands in contrast to ever-present danger beyond its boundaries. As I lay out my story, there is a growing tension as I encounter discrimination and lose my innocent belief that all of us are created equal.

I hope to show that residents of The Hill built a vibrant community that could have continued as a source of strength and pride for Blacks in Pittsburgh and across the nation. This creativity is a counterpoint to the destruction wrought through the ignorance, indifference (dare I say racism?) of White urban planners. Finally, there is a tension between acquiescence and resistance, between accommodation as a survival strategy and rebellion against social injustice.

Throughout my life,
Wherever I go in this world,
whenever I'm asked, "Where are you from?"
I stop what I am doing and say,
"I AM FROM THE HILL."

This, then, is a true account about living in The Hill, as seen through the eyes of one of its average residents by the name of Ralph Proctor, Jr.

CHAPTER 1

A Place Called *The Hill*

Early Days

The Hill is a geographic location, a community, and a culture. Although The Hill has its roots in colonial America, it is known nation-wide as a large Black enclave in Pittsburgh, Pennsylvania. Blacks did live—as slaves—at Fort Pitt and the surrounding settlement at the confluence of the Ohio, Monongahela, and Allegheny Rivers. Over the years, these Blacks moved with their White masters toward the slopes east of the growing city. Here the gentry built magnificent mansions and beautiful brownstone homes along wide, tree-lined boulevards with center islands of grass. Soon merchants followed to meet the needs of the rich. Thus *The Hill* came into being.

In the 270+ years since the founding of Pittsburgh, The Hill has undergone a succession of changes. In the late 1800s, the gentry again began to move further from the city, seeking places with cleaner air and more green space. New mansions were built along Millionaires' Row in the East End, Shadyside, and Point Breeze. Other wealthy individuals migrated north across the Allegheny River.

Into the vacant spaces moved newly arriving immigrants lured by the Statue of Liberty and the promise of a better life. Among those new inhabitants were Jewish, Italian, Polish, and other eastern European immigrants. Although The Hill was a good place to live and relatively free of ethnic and racial conflicts, the community was already more than 100 years old. The housing stock was showing signs of wear, but many of the new occupants could not afford to keep their property in good repair.

To accommodate the rapidly growing population, many of the single-family dwellings were sub-divided, creating room for two, three, or more families in housing originally designed for one family or, in some cases, for a wealthy family and their servants. The condition of buildings varied from good to deplorable. Some were so old, tired, and in need of repair, they should have been torn down. Unscrupulous landlords, however, often removed "condemned" signs from their buildings while public officials turned a blind eye to violations of public health laws. Often Blacks bore the brunt of criticism for slum housing, when in fact, they had little choice but to live in uninhabitable buildings owned by Whites.

1.1: Wooden frame buildings including the Church of God in Christ, possibly on Clark Way (c. 1949). Pictures like this were used in the 1950s to justify demolition of The Hill, even though a great deal of this housing had already been replaced.

This crowded situation was exacerbated at the end of the American Civil War when many Black families left the South to escape racism and retribution. Located just across the Mason/Dixon line, Pittsburgh was generally considered to be a "good" northern city. Blacks from the south who had money were treated fairly well as they took up residence and opened businesses in The Hill. Unfortunately, those with few resources did not receive a warm welcome.

The next large increase in the Black population of The Hill occurred during the First World War. In a wave of patriotism, many White men left their jobs to join the military. The steady stream of European immigrants dried up as Europe became embroiled in the war. Blacks, by the thousands, packed their belonging and headed "up North" as the steel mills and other factories recruited them to fill the vacant manufacturing jobs. Although the jobs did not pay well, they required little skill and paid much better than work available to Blacks in the South.

While welcomed as laborers, Blacks were not welcomed as residents in most city neighborhoods. This was a time when Pittsburgh's daily newspapers could run "Whites Only" advertisements for rental homes and apartments. Thus, Black immigrants tended to settle close to people they already knew or who had lived near them "back home" in the southern states. This led to a process called "chain migration," which began when one person, usually a man, came to Pittsburgh, found a job, and made living arrangements. After that person felt secure enough, he sent home for the members of his family; this continued until all immediate family members were reunited. Once the immediate family felt secure, they would send for cousins, uncles, aunts, and other "extended family"—individuals not related by blood but considered family.

Folks back home would be kept informed of the success or failure of those who left for the "Promised Land." Successful folks became famous pioneers who often helped the new arrivals find jobs and homes. As a result, small enclaves formed in which almost all the Black folks shared common geographical and cultural roots. While this fostered a sense of community, it also fostered suspicion of those with different backgrounds. Matters were not helped by the many hills, valleys, rivers, and bridges that separated Pittsburgh into distinct areas. As an example, most of my neighbors in The Hill had come from nearby communities in North Carolina. I dated a girl from the North Side of Pittsburgh whose neighbors had come from Alabama. While her parents were warning her to be careful because all Hill District Black folks were thugs, my parents were warning me about those strange North Side folks.

The Three Hills

Within the area known as The Hill were three distinct sub-areas: the Lower Hill, the Middle Hill, and the Upper Hill. Each area was defined not simply by geographic boundaries but also by the mix of residents, businesses, and cultural traditions shaped by the settlement patterns. By 1950, however, all areas were occupied primarily by Black folks or "Colored" or "Negro" people, as we were called then.

Much of the literature I have read about this community was written by outsiders. Typically these authors focused on the Lower Hill, the oldest, most crowded section and emphasized issues of poverty, crime, and corruption. From my perspective this presented a skewed, incomplete, and inaccurate depiction of a complex community. These inaccuracies became critically important by the mid- to late-1950s when the city fathers began a campaign to remove what was generally thought of as a blighted community. In actuality, while the Lower Hill was in need of upgrading, much in the Middle and Upper Hill could have been preserved. I return to the wholesale destruction of The Hill later in the book. For now, let me present a brief orientation to the three areas comprising The Hill.

Figure 1. The Hill (shaded area) in Relation to City of Pittsburgh

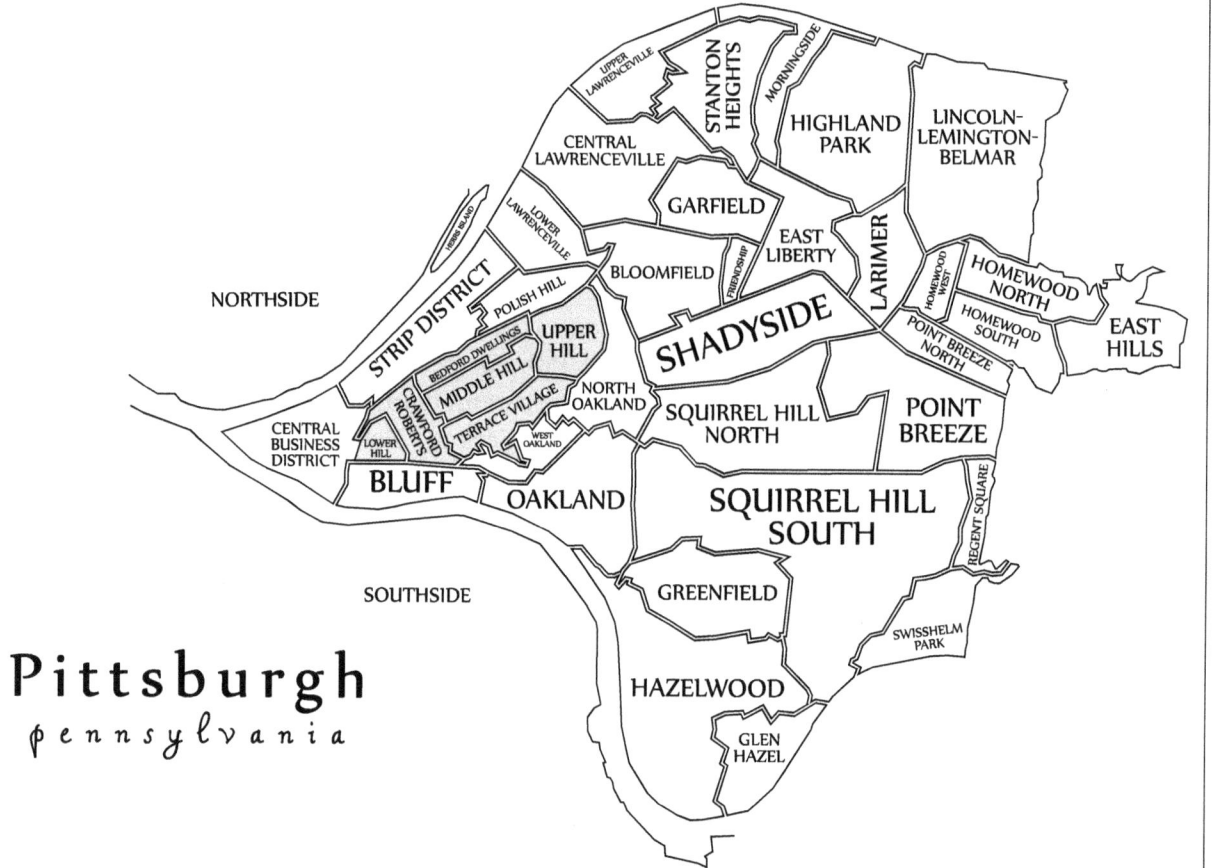

Pittsburgh's central business district included offices and retail shops, but virtually no housing. Politically, all of the surrounding neighborhoods are part of the City, but each has its own distinctive socio-cultural-economic make-up.

The northern edge of The Hill was situated on a high bluff overlooking the Strip District, a railroad terminus and wholesale market area.

The southern edge of The Hill has been debated for as long as I can remember. Some referred to the Bluff as Uptown or Soho and considered it part of the Lower Hill. Others disagreed. However, the Terrace Village Public Housing Project has always been considered to be part of The Hill as were three other projects (Wadsworth Terrace, Aliquippa Terrace, and Bentley Drive) which are not shown on this overview map.

Although the Lower Hill was the smallest in terms of geographic area, it has received the most attention, because it was either the most notorious or the most glamorous.

Figure 2. Orientation to the Three Hills

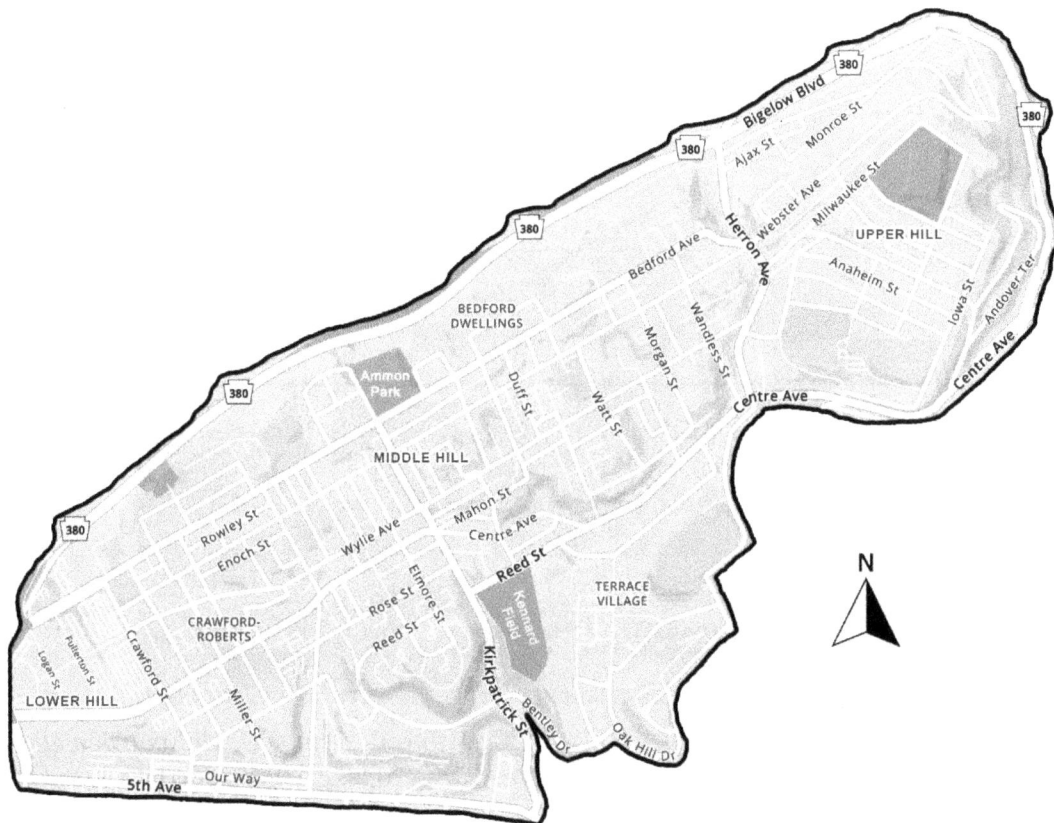

Outer West-East Boundaries of The Hill: Bigelow Blvd (Rt. 380) marks the northern border of all three sections of The Hill. At the Bloomfield Bridge, Bigelow begins to loop around the easternmost edge of The Hill and continues till it intersects with Centre Avenue. Centre, in turn, connects with Robinson Blvd at Herron Avenue. The southern edge of The Hill is marked successively by Robinson, Aliquippa, Bentley, Kirkpatrick, and Fifth.

Interior North-South Boundaries. Herron Avenue marked the division between The Upper and Middle Hills. During the period covered by this book, Fullerton marked the division between the Middle and Lower Hills. Major Throughways: Running from the city center toward the eastern neighborhoods are four major avenues: Bedford, Webster, Wylie, and Centre.

Major Cross Streets: In addition to Herron Avenue and Fullerton Street, a number of other important streets cut through the Hill: Logan, Kirkpatrick, Somers, Chauncey, Junilla, Watt, Duff, Somers, and Francis. These were the streets of my youth, and the memories of this place and its people are woven into my soul.

The Lower Hill was an eclectic mix of housing and small retail shops owned by individuals of many different ethnicities. It was also home to a vibrant, nationally renowned culture of jazz. The nightclubs, bars, and restaurants were frequented by famous musicians, various celebrities, and local residents.

1.2: Wylie Avenue in the Lower Hill with Crampton's Drugs, C. McEvoy Jewelers, Ambassador Restaurant, and Pat's Place (c. 1958-1960)

1.3: Herron Avenue, between Wylie & Centre Avenues, with Hord Printing Company (c. 1955-1965)

1.4: Webster Avenue at Fullerton (c. 1940-1956). Note the divider separating the two sides of the tree-lined street.

1.5: Crawford Grill No. 1 (c. 1945-1949). The Crawford Grill was the most famous of many bars and restaurants that featured performances by local and national musicians.

The Middle Hill comprised a mix of upper and middle class professionals, business owners, and working class people. Housing reflected this socio-economic diversity with many streets lined with modest, but well-maintained homes. In addition, there were many Public Housing Developments including Terrace Village I and II, Bentley Drive, Warrington Court and Bedford Dwellings. When I was a youngster, public housing did not carry the stigma later associated with it. Many of my friends lived in this type of housing, including my best buddy, Arthur Carter, when he and his mother moved from their home across the street from mine on Wylie Avenue.

Serving The Middle Hill were several elementary schools, including the "Colored" school on Miller Street, as well as lounges, restaurants, hotels, social and fraternal clubs, movie theaters, a radio station, recreational facilities, pharmacies, and grocery stores. THIS was MY community, and it nurtured in me a vision of integration that I ached to see spread throughout the country.

1.6: Fullerton Avenue. Frazier's Cleaners with apartment on 2nd floor; located next to Loendi Club (c.1930-1945). This photo illustrates the intermixing of businesses, housing, and social facilities that characterized the Lower and Middle Hills.

1.7: Terrace Village Public Housing Project (c. 1950-1965)

1.8: Corner of Reed and Breckenridge Streets (c. 1959).
Row houses like these were typical of Lower & Middle Hill.

Sugar Top was a middle class White community until about 1950 when the first Black family moved in. Soon Whites started moving out and the area became a Negro or Colored community.[4] The Blacks who first moved into Sugar Top were primarily light-skinned and better educated than folks living in the Middle and Lower Hill. Many were entrepreneurs who owned businesses in The Hill, and later they were joined by Black professionals such as doctors, dentists, lawyers, social workers, and school teachers. Sadly, their clubs, fraternities, and sororities emulated those of White society and refused membership to darker skinned Blacks like me. Many Blacks who lived elsewhere complained that the residents of Sugar Top were "stuck up" and "looked down their noses at other Blacks."

1.9: House fairly typical of many in the Middle & Upper Hill (c. 1938-1950)

1.10: Home in Upper Hill District (c. 1950-1970)

4   One street was an exception to this White flight phenomenon. Andover Terrace had houses comparable to upper-middle class White folks' homes. Even today this quiet street is integrated as families have struggled to maintain its interracial nature.

Schenley High School served this more affluent group of "acceptable" Blacks, and students from these "better families" were treated more favorably than those of us with darker skin and those whose parents had less education and less money. The angry edge in my characterization of Schenley High School is indicative of the tensions that existed among the Black residents of the various areas of The Hill. Some of the resentment toward residents of Sugar Top stemmed from the advantages they had as the Civil Rights Movement made it possible for the lightest skinned Negroes to enter White colleges and be hired by White companies. Ironically even those who gained entrance to the bastions of White America soon learned that superficial acceptance barely masked an underlying racism. Their so-called "friends" still asked, "I know we must treat them as equal, but would you really want your daughter to MARRY one?"

Still, this intra-Black snobbery was insignificant compared to the hostilities in White communities beyond The Hill. For example, Sugar Top abutted Oakland, a highly segregated area in terms of businesses, residencies, and access to higher education at The University of Pittsburgh, Carnegie Institute (later Carnegie Mellon University), and other colleges. These and many other cultural institutions paid little attention to African Americans and offered very few events related to the interests of Pittsburgh's Black community. On the far side of Oakland were homes of poorer families who worked at the institutions in the area. One such institution was Forbes Field, home to the Pittsburgh Pirates baseball team and The Pittsburgh Steelers football team. While there were no explicit Jim Crow laws in Pittsburgh, it was still a highly racist city in which Black access and egress was controlled by an insidious, covert *Jim Crow Culture*. Thus, forced to live within the geographic confines of The Hill, Black residents forged a vibrant community and rich culture.[5]

It is not unusual for individuals to think about their lives in terms of before-and-after. Before I graduated and after. Before I married and after. Before I became a parent and after. For me, a defining divide in my life is before Urban "Renewal" and after. With these brief sketches, I have tried to convey the complex mix of social, economic, and cultural forces of The Hill as I knew it "before."

A Turning Point

In the mid-1950s, government officials, city planners, the Urban Development Authority, and several philanthropic foundations initiated plans to remake the smoky-city image of Pittsburgh. Integral to their vision of "social desirability" was the renewal of blighted areas. In what is now considered one of the most ill-conceived urban planning tragedies undertaken in any U.S. city, these civic leaders (all of whom were White) targeted The Hill.

While improvements in housing were certainly needed, the wholesale destruction of blocks of homes and businesses should not have been the answer. Plans were made without community input. Assumptions about the quality of life on The Hill were grounded in ignorance. Actions were taken with an aura of White privilege and arrogance.

---

5   For a more detailed account of the Black community's struggle against Jim Crow Culture see my book, *Voices from the Firing Line: A Personal Account of the Pittsburgh Civil Rights Movement,* Third Edition (Learning Moments Press, 2022).

It would have been possible to strategically target especially blighted areas and improve conditions for stakeholders in place at that time—residents and businesses—through the use of zoning regulations and building codes. Instead, both the Lower and Upper Hill were targeted for wholesale takeover. Coincidentally, both these areas abutted areas where Pittsburgh's topography afforded no open land for expansion. If Pittsburgh's downtown were to expand, the only place to go was the land upon which the Lower Hill stood. If the University of Pittsburgh's upper campus were to expand, Sugar Top was prime real estate.

Some unscrupulous realtors supported the destruction of The Hill as they eyed potential fortunes that could be made from the huge housing market that would be created by the displacement of Blacks. With a strategy called Block Busting, realtors sowed seeds of fear in White city neighborhoods about living among THOSE PEOPLE. As Whites fled to the suburbs, realtors could acquire properties at below full-market value, subdivide the houses into apartments or re-sell them at inflated prices to Blacks.

While the changes may have satisfied those with the power to impose them, they were devastating to the community and culture that had nurtured me and thousands of other Black residents. Those who know only of the desolation left in the wake of Urban "Renewal" have no understanding of what was lost. While I cannot speak for all of those who lived on The Hill, I do, in the following chapters, share my memories of this special place.[6]

---

6   The world-famous playwright August Wilson and I grew up in the same neighborhood—he on Webster Avenue and I on Wylie Avenue. Although our paths took different directions, he and I had hung out at many of the same places, knew some of the same people, and suffered from the same racial discrimination. Thus, August Wilson introduced many to The Hill through his brilliant plays such as *Jitney* and *Fences*. My goal in this book is to offer a more intimate portrait of the community that shaped the man I have become.

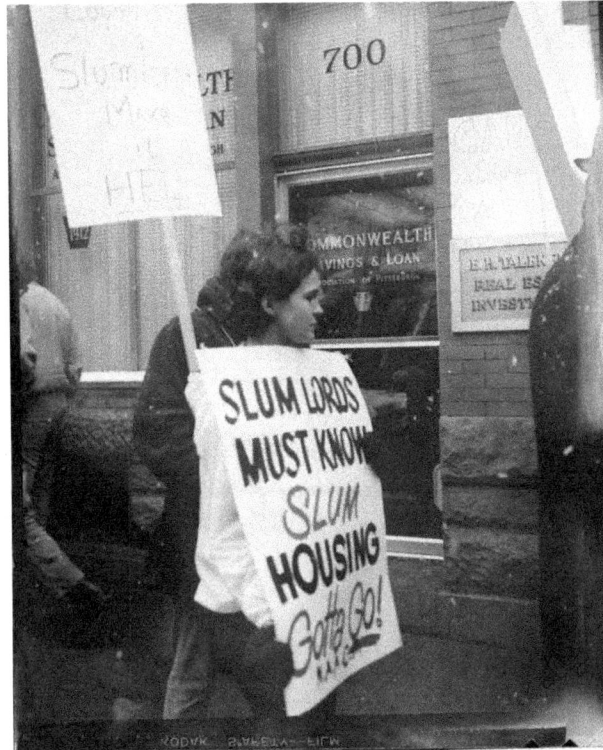

1.11: Protest against Slum Landlords (c. 1950-1970)

1.12: Renewal Not Removal. Those protesting deplorable housing conditions had not anticipated the whole-scale demolition initiated by city government and urban planners. Citizens made an effort to support renewal without displacement.

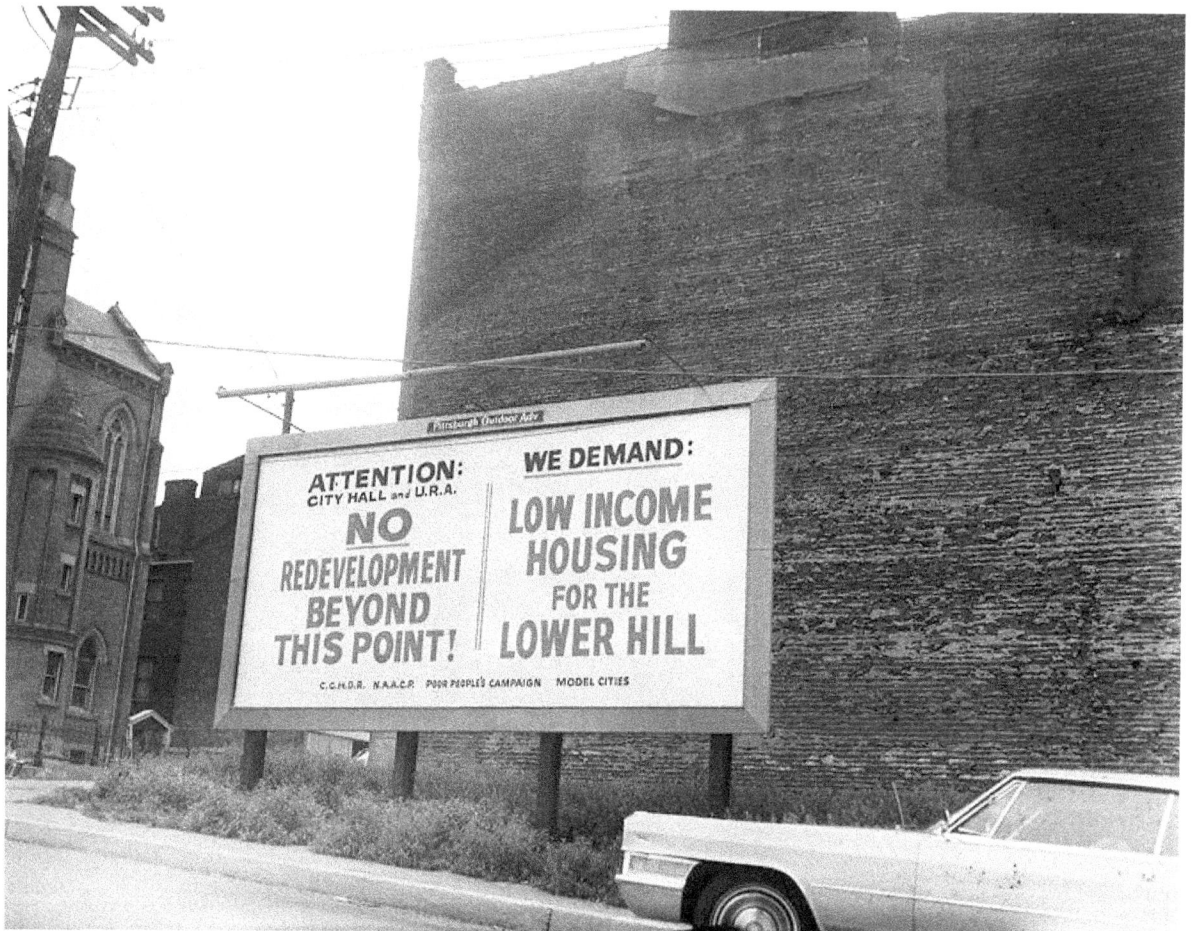

1.13: Community Protests.

CHAPTER 2

A Community of Dreams

I am bound for the Promised Land
Negro Spiritual

I arrived on Wylie Avenue in The Middle Hill on September 22, 1938. Racial harmony was the norm as I grew up among neighbors of all colors, creeds, and nationalities. There were gay and straight folks. There were people with a great deal; others with much less. Despite the obvious differences, I do not recall any ugly, hate-induced incidents—and I would have known, because I was a "neighborhood brat." I belonged to everybody.

As the "neighborhood brat" I spent many hours running errands for older residents and listening to them talk about their dreams and heartbreaks. Sometimes they told me these stories in face-to-face conversations. Sometimes I overheard them talking to neighbors or talking to the television screen as they nodded off to sleep.

They spoke of times when they should have tried something but lacked the courage. They talked about what *would have happened* had they not been too young, too old, too short, or too frightened. They reminisced about actions they *should have taken*. Sometimes as they smiled at by-gone memories, the years melted away; they became young again, and the old arthritic knees started pounding to the rhythm of the music. Sometimes they held back tears as they thought about a love that might have stayed had they just had the courage to say, "Please don't leave. I need you." On occasion they admonished me, "Don't make the same mistake. You listening, Boy?" Yes. I heard you then. I hear you now.

Although I was only a kid with no real understanding of the things they told me, I did hear the underlying message. "Carry this dream for me." I vowed I would. But those were the words of a child who had not tasted life, who had not been slapped down again and again and again. I had yet to take on an important challenge and feel the bitter taste of defeat. But one thing was clear in my young mind. I would not die with regrets. I promised myself that I would try everything in which I had even a remote interest.

I tried my hand at being an artist, but fantasies of my paintings fetching thousands of dollars faded when only my family bought my work. I thought I might be heavyweight boxing champion like Joe Louis. But frankly, I did not like the idea of being punched in the nose. Besides, I stopped growing at 5 feet 9 inches. My dreams of being a famous surgeon were chased away by visions of projectile vomiting induced by the very sight of blood. I wanted to be a famous writer, but had no idea what I should write about.

As I grew up, the grandiose fantasies gave way to real opportunities, and true to my childhood vow, I seized them. I bluffed my way into jobs for which I had no training or skills. I tried every sort of profession about which I was curious. I was driven by the thought that someday I, too, might be telling some young person what I could have, would have, or should have done. So scary was this thought, my resume looks as if I've lived two lifetimes.

I served in the army for three years. I earned a doctorate from a major university and have taught at six top-rated colleges and universities. I held good positions at Fortune 500 companies and human service organizations as well as serving on numerous Boards of Directors. I have worked for newspapers, written articles for major magazines, and hosted and produced several radio and television shows.

As a professional photographer, I have photographed world-famous models and had my photographs included in important publications. From the age of 21, I have been in business for myself. I owned an African Art Gallery and mounted hundreds of exhibitions. I have travelled the world by boat, slow train, high-speed train, airplanes, hot air balloons, ultra-fast cars, horses, and camels. I have crossed both oceans several times; have been to over 15 countries; I have lived in or visited too many cities to count. I have received a myriad of awards including three lifetime achievement awards. I have met hundreds of extraordinary people. But the most extraordinary ones have not been famous.

My point in sharing these accomplishments is not to brag. Rather, they stand as a testament to the promise that took shape as I heard the stories of unfulfilled dreams that haunted my neighbors back on The Hill. This "boy" *was* listening and has worked faithfully to carry their dreams into reality. Whatever I have accomplished was made possible by those beautiful elders who taught me to dream and encouraged me to fly. They are the ones who taught me that no dream comes true unless you have the courage to try.

I was raised by two loving parents who made no demands other than that I treat all people with dignity and respect and that I always do my best. I was part of a huge extended family that nurtured me, loved me, shared their dreams, and allowed me to stand on their shoulders. They taught me to dream. They taught me that little was beyond my reach as long as I was willing to work hard and persevere. They placed their dreams in my hands and asked me to make them come true. They asked me not to forget them. I have not.

I have held you in my heart and on the list you carefully planted in my head. As I carried you with me on my journey, I carefully placed a check mark and said, "This one is for Mom; this one is for Mrs. Russell or Mrs. Bowman; this one is for Fred." To all my old neighbors I say, "You may not hear a bell chime as another dream comes true. Yet, as you look down on my attempts to 'be somebody,' know that I have remained faithful to that long-ago promise. I am near the end of my journey. The time has come to pass your dreams (my dreams, our dreams) on to the next generation." In writing this eulogy for a decimated community, I want to let other young Black men and women know that they, too, have the right to pursue their dreams.

CHAPTER 3

Living Arrangements

Home

As I mentioned, the steady influx of newcomers led to ever more densely packed housing on The Hill. Some of the old Victorian brownstone mansions with huge yards still remained, but they had been sub-divided into apartments. Other housing included single family homes, apartment buildings, boarding homes, and row houses. Row houses typically shared a common wall, or in some cases, were separated by a narrow passageway. In up-and-down duplexes, entry to a first floor apartment was in the front; entry to the second floor apartment was via stairs at the back of the house.

When I was born in 1938 at Magee Women's Hospital in the Oakland section of Pittsburgh, my parents, Ralph and Ruby Proctor, lived in a three-room apartment at 2513 Wylie Avenue. The house had been a kosher bakery, and the owners had grafted a two-story living space to the rear of the original small, three-story, wooden structure. This created a strange 3-story, 2-story building with one apartment on the first floor and another on the second and third floors.

This is my earliest recollection of "home," the place where my older sister Earlyne, my younger sister Carol, and I grew up. Initially, we lived on the first floor. At the front of the house was a spacious, airy living room. A cramped middle room served as the entire family's bedroom. Located off the bedroom was a small bathroom with nothing more than a sink, tub, and commode. At the back was a combination kitchen/dining room with a floor slanting toward the backyard. Mom had to keep an eye on me when I pedaled my red fire engine car around the kitchen so I wouldn't slide right out the door.

We shared this house and backyard with Margie and Elmer Gordon, who rented the two floors above us. Their apartment was a duplicate of ours, except they had two additional bedrooms with a large central closet tucked under the eaves on the third floor. Margie and Elmer were good friends with my parents; I was fascinated by Jackie, their German Sheppard, and by Margie's wooden leg. When Elmer and Margie moved to the house next door, my parents rented the entire house.

Like many houses in the neighborhood, ours did not have central heating or air conditioning. The living room was heated by a big brown coal stove. When I was about eight years old, I became responsible for making sure the fire did not go out during the night. The third floor was heated only by the hot air rising through floor vents. A large gas-fed space heater warmed my parents' bedroom; a smaller gas heater warmed the bathroom; the gas cooking stove warmed the kitchen and dining room. Cooling in the summer consisted of open windows and fans.

I remember this as a comfortable home—except for the roaches, rats, and mice that had been in residence since the days of the bakery. Mom was a fastidious housekeeper who cleaned constantly but fought a losing battle against the roaches. She wrapped food boxes in paper and kept food in airtight containers stored in the refrigerator or a sealed bread box. She washed all the dishes before and after we ate. Every week when we went on our Sunday car ride, Dad set off deadly bombs that killed everything. But a few nights later the roaches were back.

As my mother's diligent cleaning illustrates, roaches were not indicative of Blacks living indifferently in squalor. Roaches have no regard for socio-economic class as illustrated by the following anecdotes. A friend and I were dining in famous restaurant in an upscale Pittsburgh neighborhood. As we were eating our salads, my friend yelped, spat out her morsel of salad, gagged, and pointed to a roach crawling up the wall near our table.

The second incident occurred in the 1990s when I was in Stamford, Connecticut, for a business meeting at a Fortune 500 company. In preparation for my trip, I had spoken several times with the secretary of the executive with whom I was meeting. We became friendly so I accepted her dinner invitation at the end of the meeting. We stopped by her apartment on our way to the restaurant so she could change to a more comfortable outfit. This upscale building was so new that parts of the lobby and landscaping were still under construction. The view of the city from her living room was fantastic and the amenities were as elegant as those featured in the marketing brochure I was perusing as my hostess was fixing a pre-dinner cocktail for herself and for me, my usual Diet soda and two cherries. Suddenly I heard a commotion from the kitchen and hurried to see if my help was needed. Red-faced with embarrassment, my hostess apologized as she eyed the canister of roach-spray in her hand. "I'm so sorry. You weren't supposed to see this. When construction of the building began, a colony of long-dormant roaches was disturbed and invaded all the apartments. Tenants are in litigation to break our leases. But even if we win, many can't afford to move."

The upscale restauranteur and my very elegant acquaintance were learning what my mother knew long ago. Roaches are virtually indestructible no matter how diligently or vigorously you try to combat them. In the end, they always win and the presence of these disgusting creatures is no indication of wealth, profession, location, or race.

Dad fought the rats and mice with traps. When I learned to shoot a BB gun, I sat up at night killing them as they scurried across the kitchen floor. I was such a great marksman, the shoemaker next door hired me to do the same for him. I guess I should be thankful for the opportunity, because by the time I entered the Army I was a very good marksman.

Dad and Mom took great pride in having a beautiful home. Even before they purchased the place, Dad remodeled it. He paneled all the second floor walls with real knotty-pine planks. He built closets, installed real hardwood floors, and acoustic tile ceilings. Mom hung fancy, stiffly-starched curtains and colorful drapes. They were geniuses at finding high-quality, second-hand furniture. Their bedroom furniture was the talk of the neighborhood.

Although we did not have much money, I had no idea we were poor. Mom was a shopper extraordinaire and could do wonders with a few dollars. Dad was a butcher so food was never a problem. He also worked as a handyman for the man who owned our home and a number of other rentals in East Liberty. When tenants moved out, Dad did the repairs and often brought home special finds that had been left behind, even good clean clothes. All in all, I was quite proud to have friends visit my home—except at night when those damned roaches roamed.

Household Amenities

Before we had an electric refrigerator, we had an *icebox*. This looked like a small, old-fashioned, round-edged refrigerator, but the top compartment held a big block of ice to keep food cold. The melting ice dripped into a collection pan, and naturally the ice had to be periodically replaced, a job that fell to Joe, the neighborhood iceman. Each home would place a cardboard sign in the window. As the iceman drove along, he glanced at the brightly colored number—10, 20, 30, or 50—displayed on the sign. He'd stop, grab the appropriately sized block of ice with a pair of huge metal tongs, swing it onto to his massive, tarp-covered shoulder, and carry it into the house (often having to climb one or more flights of stairs). Using an ice pick, which looked like a large screwdriver with a very sharp point, the homeowner broke up the huge chunk and filled buckets to be used in a variety of ways, including making ice cream. When my older sister was pregnant, she would sit around on a summer day, sweating and yelling at me to go chop ice so she could suck on the chips.

Having ice cream was no simple matter of going to the store. We made our own. I'd keep an eye on the ice delivery sign; if Mom displayed the maximum number, she was planning to make ice cream. I quickly volunteered to be the "turner." To make ice cream, Mom dumped a small package of mix into a bowl and stirred in cream, sugar, and sometimes fruit. This concoction was poured into a two-quart, metal cylinder. Then a metal rod with wooden paddles was inserted, waxed paper was put on top, and the lid was attached to the cylinder. This whole contraption was placed into a wooden tub and surrounded to the top by alternating layers of ice and rock salt. All of that was clamped in place by a "yoke" attached to two sides of the wooden tub. A handle was attached to the yoke and that's where I came in. As the "turner," I cranked the handle so the paddles turned at a fairly high speed. As the ice-salt combination melted and ran out of the holes at the bottom, the ice cream formed. It was hard work, but when the cylinder was emptied, the turner got to lick the paddles. When we just had the icebox, we had to eat all that fresh, creamy, home-made ice cream at once. Once we got an electric refrigerator, we had to put some of it away for later. Bah, humbug!

During the summer, the iceman was especially welcomed by neighborhood kids, because he would pass out small chunks of ice to suck on. When Dad bought a new-fangled, electric powered refrigerator, I was a little sad, because Joe disappeared from my life. Buying a refrigerator was an expensive proposition, and many families had no credit at major stores. In order to make sales, merchants offered the refrigerators on a payment plan. A coin-fed box was attached to the refrigerator, and these were connected to electricity. As long as coins were fed into the box, the electricity flowed, and the refrigerator was paid off in small installments. Periodically a White man came by and collected the coins. Making sure the money was deposited on time was crucial, otherwise the electricity was shut off, and all the food would be ruined.

Early one morning, Mom went into a panic when she dropped in a quarter but the coin box shut down. She called Dad who told her to wrap the frozen food in newspapers to prevent thawing. Then he called an icehouse, which still served commercial accounts, and had a block of ice delivered. Upon returning home that evening, Dad disconnected the defective coin device and called the company, uttering a few choice words—many of which I was forbidden to say. A repairman came to install a new device, but I suspect Dad threatened him with bodily harm, judging from how quickly he fled our house. Instead of the coin-operated system, Dad worked out a monthly payment plan until the refrigerator was ours, free and clear.

The coin-operated payment plan was also used for washers and dryers, but not in our house where each Monday was laundry day. Everybody but Dad participated in separating clothes into white, colored, and black piles. One at a time, a pile would be put into the first of two tubs along with soap and bleach for the white clothes. Each tub had wooden "agitators" that moved the clothes back and forth, up and down, and around and around. Once the clothes were thoroughly washed, the excess soapy water was squeezed out by passing them between two hand-cranked, rubberized tubes. The clothes were then transferred to the second tub, where they were again agitated to rinse out the soap. Finally, the damp clothes went into a laundry basket to be hung up to dry. The wringers were dangerous and had no safeguards. Getting an arm, hand, or finger caught was painful. Most of the time, Mom handled that part of our laundry day routine.

During warm weather, we lugged the heavy laundry baskets down to the backyard and used wooden pins to hang each item on lines hoisted as high as possible using a long wooden pole with a notch cut into the end. If it began to rain, everyone who was at home grabbed a basket, ran into the yard, snatched clothes off the lines, ran everything back up the stairs, and rehung them in the kitchen and dining room. I hated wash day, especially when curtains were on the agenda. They had to be washed, starched, and stretched to dry on wooden frames surrounded by hundreds of tiny sharp metal pins. We all should have been awarded Purple Hearts for the number of times we were wounded by these torture devices. We were ecstatic when Dad bought a new-fangled washer and dryer. Now mom had time to watch her soap operas and all the misery they portrayed. Yes, she watched them, even though it was many years before anyone Black ever appeared on one of these ridiculous caricatures of life.

3.1: Laundry Day (c. 1946-1960)

Recently, a television show featured a number of items and asked youngsters to identify their purpose. Particularly perplexing to them was a squarish black, metal box with a round dial on the front and a handheld, double-ended device connected with a coiled black wire. This, of course, was the telephone of my youth. Typically, the phone was hung on the wall and operated as a "party line," meaning that two or more households shared the same line and could listen in on each other's conversations. This was considered rude, but gossips loved it. Sharing a line also prompted verbal and even physical fights over who was using the phone too much. The party line phone system was not just a feature of poor Black neighborhoods, but was the norm throughout the city. Getting a private line for the family was a big deal; I even remember our first phone number; MA (Mayflower) 14780.

Long before Bluetooth and MP3 players, even long before portable transistor radios, radios were large consoles usually located in the living room. Families gathered in the evenings to listen to all sorts of music and nationally-syndicated dramas like *Inner Sanctum*, *The Shadow*, *Suspense Theater*, *Escape*, *Straight Arrow*, and *The Lone Ranger*. The radio was a major source of news and sporting events. We eagerly listened as our hero, heavyweight boxer Joe Louis, beat the crap out of his White opponents. Every punch seemed like a blow to White racist society. Everyone in the neighborhood must have been listening when Joe Louis was declared the greatest boxer of all time. People ran outside or opened their windows to celebrate the news that the Brown Bomber had been victorious once again.

Mrs. Bowman, a rather strange widow who lived with her adult son a couple of doors from us, had the first television I can remember. She liked me, because I didn't charge her anything for running errands. Also, I did not make fun of her pet turtle and was careful not to step on it as it roamed freely through the house. One day she asked my mom to send me to her house. I assumed she wanted me to go to the store for her. Instead she showed me her new acquisition—a television. It had a very small screen housed in a very large cabinet. It was magic. The other kids were afraid of Mrs. Bowman and called her a witch. But when I asked if they could see her TV, she invited all of us over and served homemade cookies and lemonade. Soon Mrs. Bowman's house was full of laughing, giggling kids. She was very happy and no longer lonely. Unfortunately, a short time later, a man up the street got a HUGE television; 17 inches compared to 7 inches was a big deal. The fickle neighborhood kids abandoned Mrs. Bowman. I stayed with her until she died. What else could I do? She was my *friend*.

The man with the bigger TV liked having the kids around, but soon was losing out to someone with a 19-inch screen. He was a gadget freak, so to hold on to his audience, he attached a big, plastic "lens" to the front of the cabinet. This provided a magnified, albeit distorted, image on the screen. Later, when color television was introduced, he purchased a much-touted magic lens for those who could not wait for the new color tubes. It was a big sheet of acetate with three horizontal bands; the top third was blue; the middle third was red or yellow; the bottom was green. Once stuck to the screen, voila, Color TV. It was marginally acceptable for outdoor scenes, because there was an approximation of the blue sky and green grass. In between, however, everything was yellow.

Happily, Dad bought a 25-inch television and for a short time we offered the premier viewing experience in the neighborhood. Of course, we were dethroned by a neighbor's 27-inch monster. Staying on top is such a constant struggle.

When I was a kid, some of the neighborhood houses still had a little wooden house with a slanted roof in the backyard. Inside was a wooden board with a hole cut to fit one's bottom. These were outhouses, the bathroom accommodations where one answered "the call of nature." Some had genuine toilet paper; others had old catalogues. Fortunately, my family had an indoor toilet, and I had to endure the outhouse experience only when we visited my grandmother in North Carolina. By the 1950s, these stinky "amenities" had been replaced by indoor plumbing.

Although many houses had running water for drinking and washing up a bit, bathing was a different story for those without bathrooms. In addition to an outhouse, these bathroom-less homes sported a large, galvanized tin tub, hanging beneath a window at the back of the house. When folks wanted to bathe, they retrieved the tub from the hook, placed it on the floor in the kitchen, and added water heated on the stove. At the end of the bath, the tub was emptied by scooping out buckets of water. This practice helped some of us curious young lads to learn about female anatomy. When we spotted a tub being pulled inside, we would sneak up the back stairs and peer into the kitchens hoping to spy a female taking a bath. If it was a male, our interest wandered to other amusements.

Shared Housing

Next door to our home was a one-story, frame shack that housed a shoe repair shop belonging to Ottaway Davis. The place had no bathroom, so Ottaway used ours. My dad offered to install a commode, but Ottaway declined, saying it cost more than he wanted to spend. Eventually the shack was condemned and torn down. Mom then used the empty lot to extend her garden. She had a green thumb and could grow just about anything. She planted a rose bush when I was a child. It was at least 15 feet high when I left for the Army.

Once my family moved to the two top floors of our house, we rented the first floor to two or three people at a time. Each room had a separate entrance so there was privacy, except for the shared bathroom. One couple, who rented the center and rear rooms, requested exclusive use of the bathroom. Therefore, the person who rented the front room used the bathroom in our part of the home. These accommodations were not without issues, but the apartment was rarely vacant. All the rental units in our home were furnished. As soon as one renter moved out, new mattresses were provided and the whole family pitched in to clean the apartment. As soon as everything was neat and tidy, Dad posted a FOR RENT sign in the front window, and in short order we had a new "roomer." My folks had one of the most desirable spaces available in the area. Tenants soon became part of our extended family, frequently sharing meals with us.

3.2: Row Houses; one with a sign advertising "Furnished Rooms" (c. 1935-1955)

3.3: Notice the tree-lined street and the timeframe for these well-kept row houses (c. 1940-1950). This is quite a difference from the slum housing portrayed in Photo 1.1.

Like my parents, many other families made extra money by renting space in their home, even just a single room. For those who were unable to afford the cost of a house, apartment, or room, there was *The Hot Bed Rental System*. Those with a daytime job rented a single bed or cot in a large dormitory-like room and slept there at night. In the morning, the freshly made bed was then rented to another individual who worked the night shift. The joke was that sometimes the occupants of the beds changed so rapidly that the bed never got a chance to cool down—hence the name Hot Bed Rentals.

I've mentioned the strong sense of community in The Hill. Here are two examples of what I mean in relation to housing. "Rent parties" were common. People held a party to collect money for someone who was temporarily in financial difficulty. I often attended, although as an uninvited guest, because I had no money. My contribution was running around fetching necessary party supplies.

The Satterwhite and the Blanding living arrangement is another example. Both families came to Pittsburgh in the late 1930s or early 1940s from a small town near Hoffman, North Carolina. Ruffin and Eliza Satterwhite had enough money to purchase a very comfortable three-bedroom house at 638 Chauncey Street. They rented part of their home to John and Martha Blanding and their two daughters. Both families had their own private bedrooms but shared the rest of the home, including the kitchen and the living room.[7] This rental arrangement persisted for many years until the death of Mr. Satterwhite. Upon his death, ownership of the home passed to the Blandings. This type of arrangement was quite common and allowed more Black families to become homeowners.

---

7   Interestingly, this form of "co-housing" has become somewhat fashionable these days among senior citizens wanting to save money or desiring company. See, for example, *My House, Our House: Living far Better for Far Less in a Cooperative Household* by Louise S. Machinist, Jean McQuillin, and Karen M. Bush.

Strange Accommodations

I was a friendly kid and was always on the lookout for new playmates. Mom often found me in our living room playing with a stranger. Of course, she'd track down the parents of my new playmates and became acquainted with many new neighbors through my "community outreach." My search for new playmates led to some odd housing discoveries as well.

One day I saw a new recruit standing on some steps about a half-block up the street. With Mom's permission, I was off like a Buck Rodgers' Rocket to greet my potential playmate. "Hey kid" I shouted, "you must be new. I never saw you before. Wanna come home with me and play?"

The "kid" looked at me and spat, "Get the hell away from me! I ain't no damn KID. I'm a damn MAN!"

What! How could he be a MAN, when he was barely taller than me? Just then, a well-dressed woman came out and admonished this strange being, "Don't be pissed at the kid. He probably never saw a midget." Turning to me, she continued, "Come here honey, I ain't gonna bite you. Me and Mike are staying here while we're performing at the Flamingo down the street. Mike is a midget, which means he's a grown man that looks like a kid, because he didn't grow so big. Don't look so shocked. You learned something new today."

Indeed I did! I learned a new word, a new thing about little people, and that a three-story Brownstone right up the street from my house was now a restaurant and hotel called Dearing's. Such conversions were not unusual and provided housing for the growing number of "Colored" musical acts that were appearing at the fancy Flamingo Club.

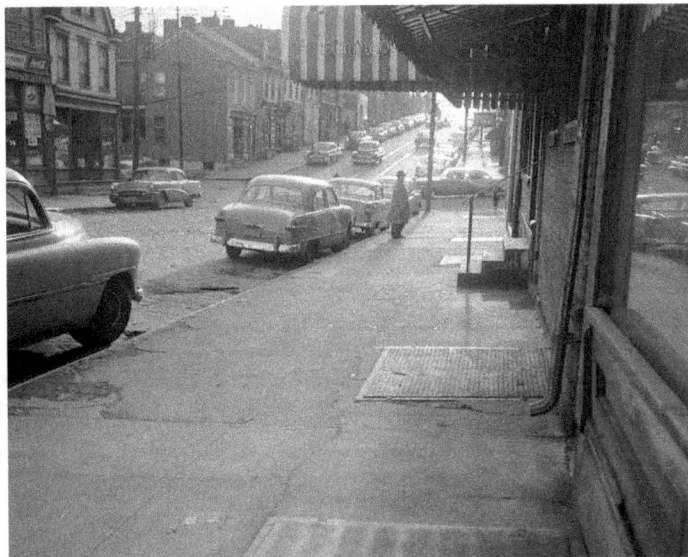

3.4: Flamingo Club (striped awning) near my house on Wylie Avenue (c. 1950-1970). This is where my new "friend" was performing.

3.5: Interior of the Flamingo Club (c.1955)

3.6: Guests at the Flamingo Hotel's night club,
Wylie Avenue, enjoying a performance.

Later that year I got another surprise when I spied another new kid. This time I used my keen powers of observation to verify my intended target was a child. The fact that he was riding a pedal car and calling his companion "Mommy" helped, but his long, curly hair left his gender a bit of a mystery. Running over, I called out, "Hi, my name is Ralph. You want to come to my house to play? Are you a girl or a boy? Where do you live?"

Lester shot back "I'm a boy. Come on. I'll show you where I live." With that, he peddled away, and I trotted alongside. "Here we are. Wanna come in?"

Nope! No thanks! As much as I wanted a new friend, I wasn't about to enter what had once been a live poultry shop. Whenever I had walked past the shop, I'd be assailed by the nauseating smell of dead fowl, blood, and wet feathers mixed with other indistinguishable odors. Then there were the sounds of chickens, geese, and turkeys honking and cackling in distress. Finally there was the sight of butchers wearing their all-season outfits of short-sleeved, white T-shirts and blood-stained aprons.

A few months earlier the place had closed, and I spied men hammering, sawing, and putting in new windows. I could hardly believe it when they told me they were turning it into a home. YUCK! And THIS was where my new-found playmate lived. He finally coaxed me through the front door. Remembering the stench, I held my breath as long as I could. I'm sure Lester thought I was weird when I finally gasped for air. To my surprise, the place did not stink. It was now a small, but tidy, two-bedroom home.

Just as strange was the conversion of the local huckster's stable. Until the 1950s, The Hill, like many other inner-city neighborhoods, had merchants called hucksters. Typically these were White men who drove horse-drawn wagons loaded with fresh fruits, vegetables, and sometimes meat. Moving slowly from stop to stop, the driver announced his arrival with a melodic call. Two hucksters serviced The Middle Hill where I lived. The one I saw most frequently stabled his team of horses in two large barns about 30 yards from our back yard. On my way home from school, I would often stop to feed near-rotten apples to one of the horses. When modernization brought an end to these colorful wagons, the horses were sold or destroyed. I hated that thought given my "friendship" with one of the old nags. One summer day, I visited for the last time. As the horses were being led away, an unkind adult laughed and said I would probably see my old pal in a jar; the horses were going to the glue factory and would turn up in my classroom as a bottle of glue. A few days later, I noticed activity around the former barns. Dashing up the hill, I asked one of the workers what was going on. "We're gonna make these barns into houses." I was skeptical, because these stinky structures were one-story high and rather narrow. But the truth was soon evident—the side-by-side stables were converted into two-bedroom, one-bath homes.

Temporary Arrangements

For many years, Blacks who were visiting Pittsburgh were barred from White-owned hotels. Consequently, when Black visitors needed temporary accommodations, they stayed with relatives, friends, or acquaintances. They could also stay in private homes where people, like my parents, rented out a room. When Black athletes played in Pittsburgh, many of them rented rooms at the Centre Avenue YMCA.

In addition, there were small Black-owned hotels such as The Wylie Hotel, The Haddon Hall Hotel, The Terrace Hall Hotel, and The Ellis Hotel. A number of restaurants and clubs had rooms for rent on a daily or weekly basis. Among these were Dearing's (mentioned above), The Flamingo Night Club and Hotel, Hartzbergers, and the Harris Bar and Grille.

3.7: Perry Hotel and Bar on Perry Street (c. 1938-1970)

3.8: Hub Hotel (c. 1940-1950)

3.9: Palace Hotel on Wylie Avenue (c. 1930-1950)

3.10: Avenue Hotel and Tea Room on Wylie Avenue (c. 1935-1945)

Public Housing Arrangements

In later years, several public housing developments were constructed on The Hill: Bedford Dwellings, Whiteside Road, Terrace Village One and Two, and Aliquippa Terrace. The developments consisted of row after row of apartments arranged in barracks-like fashion. Most were three stories high. Tenants were responsible for keeping their private spaces clean and neat and making sure the entry ways, hallways, and other common areas were clean as well. Their homes were just as nice as ours. Well, maybe not "just as nice," because my father took great pride in making our home special.

When I was growing up, there was no stigma attached to living in these developments. Many of my friends lived there, and I never recall my parents being concerned about my hanging out with them. I won't say there were no problems, but they were minimal. As I recall, the folks who ran these developments screened potential tenants very carefully. Those with a criminal record were not accepted.

The housing developments were meant for both Black and White, low income families. It was assumed their stay would be temporary. The housing authority administration had a direct reporting system with tenants' employers. As salary went up, so did the rent. Once the rent was equal to the market rate for private housing, it made little sense to stay in public housing. This was, indeed, the case for my friends, who sought out their own living spaces after graduating from school.[8]

3.11: Boys playing ball in the field behind Bedford Dwellings Housing Project (c. 1940-1950)

---

8 I later learned that many people wanted to stay in these units even though they were not as nice as market-rate rentals and access to stores and other amenities was becoming more limited. Sadly, the public housing developments eventually became a place to warehouse (and hide) the poverty plaguing lower-income Blacks.

Post-Script

I hope I have conveyed the fact that my home in The Hill provided a nurturing environment. This was not the drug-infested, crime-ridden ghetto so often depicted in the aftermath of Urban "Renewal." I must confess, however, to one scary feature of The Hill. One day as Mom and I passed by the corner of Wylie Avenue and Somers Street, I suddenly noticed smoke rising from the hillside. I had seen this before, but didn't think much about it. Perhaps the smell was stronger than usual, and this caused me to ask about it.

Mom explained, "Under the surface, The Hill is on fire. In the old days, many of the hills around us were mined for coal, and sometimes the abandoned mines catch fire. If the smoke gets too thick, residents complain, and fire trucks come, hook their hose to a fireplug, and pour water down the hole till the smoke dies back."

More than a little scared, I asked if there was a mine under our house. Mom said, "Maybe, because much of the area sits above old coal mines." Then Dad explained that many home owners in the area owned only the surface rights; the mining companies owned the "mineral rights" and could dig under houses to get the coal. Geez, not only did I have to worry about my house burning down, I had to wonder if it might collapse into one of those mines. Scary stuff! I wondered if the White kids in other communities had to worry about these things.

In closing, let me just say, "Thanks Mom and Dad for teaching me that being poor monetarily, did not mean I had to look or act poor; I could hold my head high. After traveling around the world and seeing many people from all walks of life, you are still the best parents anyone could have. I would not trade my time with you for any other life I could have lived. All that I am is because of you. I know readers may be thinking that those words belong in the dedication or "Thank You" page of the book. Naw. They belong right here.

CHAPTER 4

Family, Friends, and Other Characters

On The Hill, the concept of family was rather fluid and included an extended network of blood relatives and "honorary" relatives. Although they had no kinship connection, they were addressed by family titles such as aunt, uncle, nephew, cousin, grandpa and grandma. Often these honorary family members were folks from "back home."

Included in my own extended family were Aunt Martha, Uncle John, Johnnie Mae, Joyce, and Emma. I cannot remember a time when they were not a part of my life. John and Martha often minded us when Mom and Dad had some place they wanted/needed to go. We shared many meals and exchanged gifts on Christmas, birthdays, weddings, and births. Emma was absolutely beautiful, and I had a huge crush on her. However, having been taught it was a mortal sin to "mess" with your cousin, I reined in my sexual fantasies about her. Boy was I pissed when, upon conducting some genealogical family research, I found that Emma was not a blood relative. Wow. Not only had I lost an opportunity to have sex with Emma (as if she really would have wanted that), I had wasted a whole bunch of expensive presents on folks who were just friends. What a bummer! Just kidding. Those gifts, regardless of cost, brought moments of happiness to the recipients.

Of course, I came to realize that the whole extended family phenomenon was a carry-over from a Black southern lifestyle and was of great benefit to Black families in The Hill. As they say, there is strength in numbers and having an extended "family" network was a source of resilience in the face of poverty, racism, and even the stresses of normal daily living. The larger your "family," the more territory—like urban community gardens—you controlled. Extended families had more resources, more money, more clothing to pass down to younger children. In an emergency, there was always someone to help out.

Parents did not have to spend their meager funds to hire a baby sitter, because folks were always ready to pitch in. There was no need for a baby raising a baby when older women could offer young, inexperienced mothers support, a bit of "time off," tips on parenting skills, and guidance on proper breast feeding techniques. If a mom or baby was sick, a midwife or herbalist could nurse them back to health. The extended family was also good for new fathers who could talk with older males about their fears and doubts. There were older men to teach the younger men how to "be a man" and accept responsibility. Even families with an absent father had many adult males to serve as positive role models for boys.

The extended family of uncles—real and honorary—helped young men navigate the challenges of "coming of age." Even when I could not and did not want to fight, they made certain I could defend myself when necessary. It was frightening but comforting to understand that I was from a warrior clan and that certain responsibilities were mine to shoulder.

As children grew up, they typically extended the family network by remaining close to their parents' home. In a longstanding southern tradition, children remained on the family's land, thereby keeping the family intact, increasing its strength, and creating a supportive network. A friend from New Orleans showed me how each time a child "left home" the family simply added on to the original house so that the family home now extended for an entire city block. While I did not see that extreme in The Hill, it was common for children to set up housekeeping near their parents. When my older sister moved, she took an apartment across the street; my younger sister moved a block and a half away. I was a maverick who moved five miles away.

Most of the folks I grew up with were ordinary people. They had jobs, went to work, came home, relaxed, and went back to work the next day. Some had decent jobs; some had low-paying jobs; they came from all but the highest economic level. Except for the color of their skin, they were not much different from the people one would encounter in a White community. The Hill, however, did have its share of characters.

PEANUT MAN was a short fellow who pushed a homemade, two-wheeled cart through the neighborhood. With a stained, "BIG A" cap perched jauntily on his head and a bit of stubble on his dark perspiring face, he called out, "Get your hot peanuts here." Soon he was surrounded by neighborhood kids clamoring to buy a bag of freshly roasted peanuts. He also sold scrumptious, freshly fried pork rinds—doused in Louisiana hot sauce for the brave.

DON, who lived a few houses down from my family, was the first purposefully bald man I ever saw. Very familiar was the sight of men who had gone bald as a cruel trick of Mother Nature. Don stood out, not only because he deliberately shaved his head and face, but also because he wore earrings, something done mostly by gay men in those days. According to the neighborhood grapevine, Don was not gay, but I don't think it would have made a difference if he were. I cannot remember any overt hostility against homosexuals in The Hill. They were just what they were. Don held little gatherings of neighborhood kids in his living room nearly every day. He spun outlandish tales about other lands with magic creatures and fascinating people that he claimed he had met during his travels as a merchant marine. I have no idea whether his stories were real or pure bull, but he was a masterful story teller who kept us transfixed. No parents, even my own, ever seemed to object to time with Don. After all, they knew where we were, and Don was an accepted, albeit weird, member of the neighborhood family.

MR. CHARLIE was a constable for a local Black Magistrate. He wore a gun, clearly visible in its holster. Mr. Charlie had a way of getting free tickets to events like circuses, carnivals, and county fairs. He'd arrive in a big white van, load in as many kids as would fit, and off we'd go on an adventure. He knew all of us by name and would not hesitate to inform a parent that their child had misbehaved on one of his outings. Mr. Charlie was a good and caring man—a saint really—who contributed greatly to the quality of life for the kids on The Hill and served as a male role model to many young boys. Thanks, Mr. Charlie. I hope you had the good life you deserved.

JIMMY SHAW owned a confectionary store right across the street from Vann School on Watt Street. Partially disabled as a result of a college football accident, Jimmy was still strong. His upper body was massive, and no one tried to take advantage of him except for a couple of lowlifes who tried to rob him. He beat them both unconscious with his crutches. We loved hanging out in his store with its soda fountain and large stock of candy.

RUBY, an older daughter of a family up the street, was a wild one. She smoked and drank when she was in her early teens and got into fights with other teenage girls. She left Pittsburgh when she was about 18 or 19 years old, and rumor had it that she had gone to Alaska to be a prostitute. At the time, I was rather naïve and didn't know whether to believe the rumors. On occasion, her brother or her mother showed me pictures where she actually seemed to be in Alaska and really was a prostitute. I was flabbergasted that no one seemed to be particularly disturbed by this commonly-known fact. One Summer, when I heard folks saying that Ruby was returning from Alaska, I wondered if she was going to set up shop as a hooker right in the neighborhood. I got the impression that prostitution was tolerated as a victimless "crime" and was no big deal unless women were forced into it or were abused by their pimps. More about Ruby, later.

EMILY was the neighborhood tomboy who dressed just like all us boys. At 13 she was faster, stronger, and more athletic than any guys of the same age. When picking a team to play football, baseball or cricket, we all tried to make her our first choice. She could also hold her own in a fist-fight.

TOM MOSBY lived just around the corner, but seemed always to be at our home, sucking on a beer bottle (ours) and watching television, especially the fights. Rumor was that he was too cheap to buy a television. He always had the stub of a nasty cigar in his mouth, wore a stained fedora hat, and held up his pants with a rope. Sometimes I resented him and thought he was a bum. But Mom and Dad liked him, and he obviously felt welcome. He had a son about my age, and his family complained about the way he dressed and how cheap he was. I felt sorry for him until I discovered that he was pretty damn smart. This gentleman saved his money throughout the year and used the savings to take his family on a very nice summer vacation. Pretty smart, Tom, pretty smart.

JOHNNY was not much older than I, and the most controlled alcoholic I ever met. He held down a good job at the mill, and his employers said he was a good worker. But he drank non-stop from Friday after work, all day Saturday, and Sunday until noon. From *Sunday* afternoon until Friday evening, Johnny would not touch a drop of alcohol. He told me he had figured out how much he could drink and when he had to stop in order to perform his job well. In all the years I knew him, he never deviated from his plan. On the few occasions when he missed work, his bosses sent someone to check on him. Even though he loved his booze, Johnny was not mean, loud, or obnoxious. Even though he was an alcoholic, I didn't care. He was a good man who harmed no one.

MISS MOMMY, as a notable member of the community, came as a real surprise. I was home on leave during my first year in the Army, when the doorbell rang. Standing on the stoop was a very young girl who said, "I need to speak to Miss Mommy." When I told her nobody by that name lived here, she insisted, "Yes she does; she's Miss Ruby." My mother! After the young girl left, I asked my mother about the Miss Mommy name. With a blush, Mom confessed, "I don't know why they call me that; they just do." Later I asked a few of the young girls about this, and with some degree of surprise at my ignorance, they informed me that all the young kids in the neighborhood viewed her as "mommy." How about THAT! My *mom* was a legendary neighborhood character.

Female Role Models

Just as positive male role models were invisible to outsiders, so too was the important role women played. I am embarrassed to say that I never gave much thought to the issue until I was much older. Looking back, I see how sexism was hidden beneath the veneer of "that's the way things are." In this section, I try to make up in some small way for the sexist notion that women weren't and couldn't be leaders.

As men were often busy holding down one or more jobs, women were the primary caregivers. In addition, many Black women held down good jobs and rose to positions of leadership in the neighborhood. So, there were many positive Black female role models in my community including:

- Billie, who lived across the street, was an excellent artist. She was about five years older, but was kind enough to teach this little thug how to draw;
- Mrs. Russell, the matron saint of the neighborhood who helped everybody;
- Mrs. Bowman, the lady with the pet turtle;
- my Black female teachers from Vann School, and
- Dorothy Cook, our boarder, who was the proud leader of the North Side Elks.

Black women were leaders in many of the churches in The Hill. The women's auxiliary often wielded as much power as the pastor. Many of the teachers I encountered were Black females who had faced extra burdens when it came to being hired by the Pittsburgh Board of Public Education. From the late 1800s until 1936, the Board refused to hire Black teachers. When that barrier was broken, the Board still discriminated against women in general so Black female teachers were still treated unfairly.

During my research on the Pittsburgh Civil Rights Movement, I became concerned that most of the individuals I was interviewing were males. I called my good friend and noted leader of the movement, Alma Speed Fox, and asked for her help. After reciting the names of all the Black women I knew from the movement, I asked, "Who did I forget?"

"You got all of the ones who are still alive," Alma responded. She then went on to explain that at the beginning of the movement, White men were far more comfortable dealing with Black women than Black men. They considered Black men to be too dangerous. For the sake of the movement, many women decided they needed to encourage Black men to step forward. Although Black women may have taken a less visible role, Alma assured me that, "We were still there, at the negotiating sessions and at the planning meetings. We did not abdicate; we simply shared the leadership." That was a time of tension between genders of all races as the women's movement emerged. In a society based on the oppression of women of any color, it's absolutely amazing that Black women ever rose to leadership roles at all, but they did.

Post-Script

As urban "redevelopment" pushed Blacks out of The Hill, extended family and friendship networks were disrupted. When I returned to Pittsburgh after my military service, I moved through a succession of neighborhoods: Homewood for a year or so; Squirrel Hill for a while; Shadyside for two years; Oakland for a year, and North Point Breeze for nearly 20 years. In that entire time, I got to know only a small number of my neighbors. It seemed the world had changed and neighborhoods were just places where you drove your car into the garage, entered your home, turned on your television, went to bed, got up, and repeated the same routine the next day and the day after that. I realized that many of the people I lived near had never experienced the closeness I had experienced in The Hill. I truly missed that.

CHAPTER 5

Food and Meals

Gardens

Gardens were common in The Hill, and I'm not talking about tiny 3 x 3 foot plots. Across the back alley from our house was a large garden tended by a master gardener. He had scarecrows and other devices to ward off critters. Many an unwary squirrel was shot and found its way into a pot of stew. Sure, some of us were poor and some went hungry, but *nobody* in my neighborhood ever starved to death.

Some gardens were as big as a city block and helped to keep residents from going hungry. Folks grew tomatoes, greens, melons, string beans, cabbages, and all manner of fruits for their own consumption or to swap with other gardeners. Extra produce was often sold to Shay's grocery or swapped for merchandise at a few of the smaller grocery stores. Those who were hungry and could not afford to buy fresh vegetables would receive some in exchange for help to be given somewhere down the line. Did the system always work? NO. There were cheaters as there are in any community. But they only pulled a cheat once; then word got around and their free ride ended.

Mom always used fresh ingredients when cooking. Many of the vegetables came from the garden she tended in our yard. Mom and others also preserved fruits and vegetables. This was quite natural for those with roots in the South where gardening and preserving were an integral part of life. In addition to preserving what she grew, Mom preserved fruits and vegetables that Dad brought home from his job. When produce no longer looked fresh, Mr. Fireman gave them by the bushel to my dad.

When I heard Mom and Dad talking about "canning" some peaches I was anxious to see the process. I peered intently as Mom washed, cleaned, sliced, and cooked the fruit. She even let me taste a few. I loved them. Then she got out a box of jars, filled them with the peaches, and added a layer of wax on top. My curiosity grew as she did some sort of ritual that involved putting all the jars in a pot of boiling water. Afterward she pasted on labels, wrote "peaches" and the date, placed the jars back into the empty box, and said Dad would take them down to the cellar when he got home. Now all this was interesting, but I had to ask, "When are you going to put them in cans? THAT'S what I been waiting to see. If you're just putting them in *jars,* why don't you call it jarring some food?" She thought that was hilarious. But hey, what I wanted to know was how they were going to close up the cans, because you always had to open them with a can opener.

Between Mom's green thumb and my Dad's work as a butcher at a grocery store, my family never went hungry. When Dad left the grocery, he worked for a major meat-packing company, made good money, and brought home many things from the plant. In addition, Dad worked another job as a maintenance worker for the man who initially owned our home, so we had enough money to live modestly.

5.1: Marasco's Produce Market on Logan Street. A. Gellman Seafood and butcher shop (c. 1950-1965)

Fish

Not far from my home was a live fish market. I was fascinated by the tanks of brightly colored fish, lobsters crawling over one another, the crabs, and giant green, snake-like fish. There were small and medium sized turtles, and one so huge it seemed big enough to ride. Milling around me was a bustling crowd of Blacks and Whites, pointing to their chosen fish, exchanging money, and carrying away packages with their evening meal. I have to say, I was not fond of fish as a food, but loved watching them. Often we had gold fish swimming in glass globes in our living room, where we also had a very nice aquarium filled with colorful fish.

Fried fish sandwiches were commonplace in restaurants in The Hill. These actually contained a headless fish and came complete with bones you had to pick out. I remember how strange it was when fast food restaurants introduced the so-called "fish sandwich." Those square "fish" were just plain weird.

Not everyone got their fish from the market. My parents and other neighbors were true fishing advocates. Many of them had gone fishing "down home" in the South and used the fish to supplement their diets. My Dad and some of his friends created their own lures. My mother, as did others, had a worm "farm" in the backyard. I thought that was weird until I learned that some commercial fish places actually sold worms. Mom grew big, fat *night crawlers*; they gave me nightmares. In addition to worms and lures, my folks and their friends used fish eggs that looked like little translucent marbles to make "dough balls" for bait. Everyone had their own private "dough ball" recipe that worked like magic, or so they would have you believe.

Fishing seemed like such a big deal to the grownups, some friends and I decided we would try it, too. We set out on the Old Indian Trail—a mini-wilderness of trees and bushes on an undeveloped lot at the end of Junilla Street. The lot lay in a small valley formed by Chauncey and Mahon Streets and in one corner was a "lake," our very own fishing spot. We had hand-made poles to which we attached string and hooks we had swiped from our parents. We had dug up worms, and the bravest among us impaled the worms on the hooks. We sat there for hours, trying unsuccessfully to catch a fish. This was frustrating, because we had seen a man pull a fish out of the water. Many years later we learned that the "fishing pond" was actually just a low place in the road that flooded each time it rained. It vanished when the sewer was finally repaired. We also discovered that the fish "catch" we had witnessed was a neighbor who decided to have some fun at our expense. He had saved a fish from an earlier catch, took it to the pond, then waited until he saw us coming. He threw his fish, with a line already attached, into the water. As we came down the hill, he showed off the fish he had "just caught."

Most folks in the neighborhood fished in one of the rivers, but the "real" fishers travelled to Pymatuning State Park. My folks loved the sport so much, they eventually purchased a small trailer that slept two people. They kept it parked on the property of the White couple from whom they had purchased it. They became good friends and frequently visited one another.

5.2: Fishing was quite popular among residents in The Hill.

Several of our neighbors also indulged in the sport, so Mom and Dad frequently had "fishing buddies." Dad made it a policy to own only station wagons in order to accommodate guests and the growing supply of tackle boxes, poles, cooking stoves, and other equipment. The appeal of fishing was lost upon me. Getting up at 3 a.m., driving for hours to sit by the water, watching for signs that some poor fish got himself impaled on a hook was not my idea of fun. I quit going as soon as I discovered girls and my folks thought I was old enough to stay at home by myself. Thank you, Jesus!

One day, I came home and entered the bathroom. As I stood at the commode, I heard splashing in the tub. Taking a few cautious steps, I jumped a foot off the ground when I saw a huge fish completely filling the tub. Mom had caught one of the biggest carps ever to be landed by hand. Dad took great pride in having "talked" my mother through the long process of landing the giant creature. You would have thought he had just helped Mom deliver another baby. The story spread through the neighborhood and our bathroom became an exhibit space with lines of neighbors coming up to see the "biggest-ass fish ever." Finally Dad put the poor captive out of its misery. Mom baked the giant carp and shared it with neighbors after taking care of her favorite folks.

All the fishers had special recipes for cooking the fish and freely shared them. They also shared the fish with needy neighbors without making a fuss about it. I was proud of my folks for doing that.

Poultry

Although most of our poultry came from The Logan meat market where Dad worked, sometimes he and I went to a live poultry shop to pick out our next meal. Feeling like a murderer, I'd nervously point to the creature that was to be sacrificed. A butcher would then snatch the chosen victim by its neck and carry the squawking bird to the back room where its legs were tied together. The still-live bird was tossed into one of several 55 gallon drums where they thrashed about, making horrible noises until it finally died. The dead bird was retrieved from the drum and quickly transferred to another 55 gallon drum filled with scalding hot water. While still hot and wet, the bird was stripped of all its feathers, then carried to the butcher table where it was cut open; its entrails were removed and packed in a small paper pouch and inserted in the chest cavity. The soon-to-be chicken dinner was then wrapped in brown butcher paper, and handed to Dad

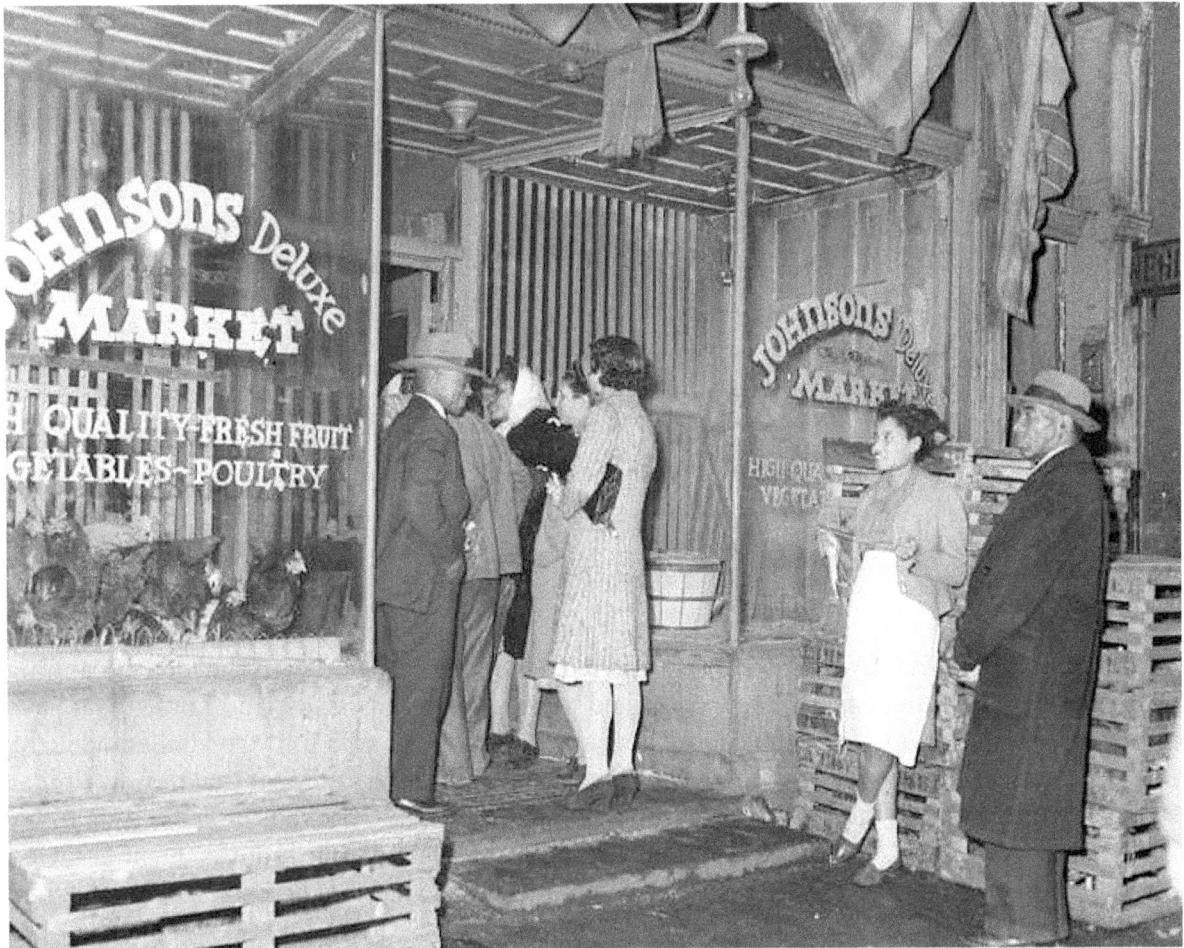

5.3: Live Poultry Market

Wild Game

One seldom thinks about game hunters in so-called poverty neighborhoods, but one of my neighbors, Mrs. Smith, had a boyfriend called "Mr. Joe," who was a hunter. Joe kept a group of noisy hunting dogs in a pen behind Mrs. Smith's home. While dogs in the neighborhood were common, seeing a pack of loud, baying hounds was something new. Joe appeared every so often, loaded the dogs in the back of his truck, and returned much later with a deer or bear draped over the hood. Dad received some money and choice cuts of meat for butchering the critters in our back yard. Mr. Joe with the help of some numbers barons distributed the meat to needy people. I was not fond of venison steaks, because the taste was so strong. But Mom made fantastic hamburgers, meatloaf, roasts and steaks from the deer and bear.

5.4: A Successful Hunting Trip—Bear & Deer Strapped to Cadillac (1941)

Horse Meat?

During World War II when food was rationed, someone came up with the idea of canning horse meat for human consumption. Dad liked to mess with our heads, and horse meat gave him a golden opportunity. He made a big deal about calling all of us into the kitchen while he used the manual can opener on a large can. He scooped out chunks of meat that looked similar to what Mom used to make stew or soup. Saying it was already cooked, he invited us to try it. My sisters and I took a little forkful, but just before we opened our mouths, he announced it was *horse meat*. As we screamed and pretended to puke, Dad laughed so hard tears rolled down his face. Not *funny, Dad*. Horses are for riding, not eating. My dog Red didn't see the humor of it either as he gobbled down this special treat.[9]

I Can Believe It's Not Butter

Mom was a genius in the kitchen, making sure we were well-fed with as much fresh, healthy food as possible. As a butcher, Dad had access to the latest fads in the food industry. So when oleo margarine hit the supermarket shelves as a healthy alternative to butter, he brought some home for Mom to try. Back then margarine didn't come in fancy tubs. The stuff was stark white and came in a plastic bag. In the center was a little packet, which when ruptured, released a bright yellow food dye to be kneaded into the white goop until it looked like real butter. I never touched this vile tasting fake butter after leaving home and felt completely vindicated when many years later studies showed this "healthy alternative" is much worse for the human body than butter.

Meal Time

Weekday breakfasts were a helter-skelter event as Mom orchestrated food (cold cereal in the summer and hot cereal in the winter) and issued orders as we prepared for school.

"NO. You can't wear that shirt; it's filthy."

"Go comb your hair, girl, and wipe off that lipstick; you look like a floozy."

"Didn't I tell you to keep your eyes on the toast?"

"Where's your homework?"

"Don't you be running out that door without kissing me goodbye."

"Tell your teacher I'll send the permission slip tomorrow."

"Close the refrigerator door—NOW!"

"Whose sock is that on the floor?"

"Stop eating like a pig."

At any time there might be two, three, or four kids participating in the melee—my sisters and I as well as a neighborhood kid who had spent the night. Despite all the barked orders, we knew for whom each remark was intended and managed to be off to school on time.

Dad missed the breakfast pandemonium, coming into the kitchen as we were flying down the front steps. His breakfast usually consisted of eggs, bacon, toast and coffee. We children always had to bless our food. I'm not at all sure that Daddy did so.

---

9   During the war, Vann Elementary asked all the children to bring a few pennies to school. When we had accumulated enough money, it was converted to a War Bond with great fanfare. Although I did not really understand what that meant, I knew we were doing our part to help the war effort.

Sunday breakfast was more relaxed as we prepared to spend the whole morning and part of the afternoon learning about Jesus. Everybody but Dad had to get ready for church, but we got up early enough to have eggs, bacon, toast, and milk. Sometimes we had waffles or pancakes.

On weekdays and Sundays, if we were home, attendance at dinner was mandatory. All food was fresh and cooked from scratch by the master chef—Mom. But Dad made it clear that Mom was not a short-order cook. Everybody ate what was served or went hungry. We were expected to finish everything on our plate. I struggled with vegetables. One glass of liquid was permissible and chewing food was a survival technique, because you could not force a mouthful of food down your throat by gulping glass after glass of soda or milk.

When Mom announced, "Dinner's ready," we'd better be at the table; no horsing around allowed. Hands had to be clean and were inspected before we could touch our food. Each of us took turns saying grace, followed by pleasant conversation. Often we had guests for Sunday dinner, and our neighbor, Mr. Mosby, had a keen knack for finding his way to 2513 Wylie Avenue just in time to join us.

Sunday dinner was the best when we had fried chicken. Everyone could have their favorite part, because Dad was a butcher and brought home more than one chicken. Sometimes we had made-from-scratch biscuits. Sunday dinner was also special because Mom always baked our favorite cake for dessert—a double-layer, yellow-batter cake with gobs of chocolate icing. I already knew how it tasted because there was a good chance I, like my sisters, got to lick the batter and icing spoons, followed by a big glass of cold milk. That was heaven. Sometimes we even had homemade ice cream.

After Sunday dinner, we all piled into the family's big green Buick Roadmaster and went for a leisurely drive. For most of the summer, we'd travel in giant loops through familiar and unfamiliar neighborhoods. Later I learned that Dad avoided certain White neighborhoods, because Black folks were not welcome to drive through them. Fortunately, we children were unaware of this sad bias, so the pleasure of our outings was not ruined.

Sometimes we stopped at the Islay's ice cream plant located in a huge building in Oakland. Each of us was treated to our own pointed, skyscraper cone, so sharing was not necessary—except with my dog Red. Red lapping at my cone freaked Mom out; Dad thought it was hilarious. One day Mom and Dad returned to the car with individual ten-cent cones for everyone and a five-cent cone for Red. As I held Red's cone out to him he turned his head away. After a few tries, I said Red must be sick, because he refuses to eat his ice cream. Dad felt Red's nose and said, "Ain't nothing wrong with him. He's fine. Here, give me your cone." When Dad held my cone out to Red, he happily lapped it up, and Dad roared with laughter. "Well, I'll be damned," he bellowed. "That dog is so smart he can tell the difference between a nickel and a dime cone." I ate the small one and beamed with pride that my dog was so smart. Sundays were the best of times. How I miss those days.

Meal-time Manners

On some Sundays our routine changed, and we went to Grandma's house for dinner. As we piled into the family car, Dad lectured us about behaving ourselves: no running through the house; no making noise, AND letting his mom kiss us. (Ugh! She dipped snuff.) As if that wasn't bad enough, Dad watched us like a hawk to make sure we ate every last crumb of Grandma's pound cake. Unlike Mom's luscious cake, Grandma's was so dry I could barely swallow it with a glass of water. Generally we were punished if we lied, but at Grandma's we had to say how good the cake was and then be rewarded with yet another piece of the cake from hell.

For me, Dad had a special lecture on manners—don't be staring Grandma down; don't be talking back to her. Grandma and I had a strange love/hate/admiration thing going on. She liked to pin my arms at my sides in a huge bear-hug while planting kisses all over my face. But she also knew I hated it when she called my daddy "*Black*." I had heard *black* used so often in a negative fashion that I would get very upset when she called my light-skinned dad that dreadful name. Under strict instructions to not "talk back," all I could do was glare at her when she upset me. That was a big NO-NO. In the Black community, one simply did not stare into the eyes of elders. If I violated that order, Grandma would say in a chilling voice, "You trying to stare me down, boy?" I immediately averted my eyes. I also learned, very quickly that staring at *anyone* would elicit a menacing response—"Who you staring at *boy*? You looking for a fight?"

I later learned that these behavioral rules originated in Africa, were drummed into Black slaves' heads, and were carried on long after slavery ended. In the case of African tradition, staring into the eyes of anyone of superior rank and authority was so disrespectful, it could result in punishment. In America, Black slaves were beaten if they dared to stare into the eyes of White men. These ingrained behaviors are problematic in a society where Whites normally look each other in the eye. If a person does not "look you in the eyes," they are lying, lazy, stupid, backward, shifty, etc. Upon learning of these cultural differences, I became angry at the negative attributes ascribed to what I had considered to be respectful behavior. If that's what Whites want, that's what I would give them. I developed the ability to stare into another person's eyes without blinking for several minutes. Instead of being respected for this unique ability, I now found that Whites considered me to be too aggressive and Black men wanted to fight with me.

In addition to receiving lectures on proper behavior at Grandma's, my sisters and I also were instructed on proper etiquette when invited for meals at friends' houses. We were never to ask for anything more than a glass of water. We were never to accept a dinner invitation without calling home for permission and allowing my mother to speak with the mother of the other family. We could never ask to stay for a meal, and we were never to ask for or accept second helpings. This was so we would never be a strain on another family's resources.

A Reluctant Cook

Mom tricked me into learning how to cook. Because I was on the Herron Hill Junior High School soccer team, I had to rise and shine at 6:00 A.M. to be at practice by 7:00. Mom explained that it was too difficult for her to fix one breakfast for me and another for Dad at 9:00. If I wanted toast, bacon and eggs in the morning, I had to cook for myself. Her ruse worked, and soon she convinced me that I should learn to fix other meals, just in case. Fairly soon I could prepare nearly as many meals as my mother, albeit not as tasty. When Mom was bedridden with a broken ankle, she said, "You should fix the family meals."

"Wait a minute," I rebelled. "What about my sisters? They should do the cooking because that's woman's work." (Clearly I had yet to learn lessons about gender equity.)

I expected support from my very masculine father, but he finked out, saying he was not about to eat anything prepared by my sisters because their food was "nasty."

One summer I beat up a kid up who made fun of me when I told him I had to go home and cook dinner for my family. He never called me "sissy" again.

Dining Out

When I was growing up, Blacks were denied service at White-owned restaurants like Stouffers and The Brass Rail as well as restaurants in major department stores and lunch counters at the Five and Dime stores such as Murphy's and Kresges. Ironically, after we sued and won the right to eat in such establishments, I often wondered, "We did all that work for the chance to eat this crap?" Alma Fox, my friend and the mother of Pittsburgh's Civil Rights movement, told me, "I will not be spending a dime in those places. My money was not good enough for them before. Well, it sure ain't good enough now. They can go to Hell."

Fortunately, there were many restaurants serving plenty of delicious food. The Crawford Grille was patronized by Whites as well as Blacks. The Flamingo Hotel/Nightclub a few blocks from my home served a top-shelf menu to its clientele of famous musicians and rich folks. Other restaurants with a reputation for excellent food included Nesbitt's and Dearing's. Ray's Dairy Bar, located near Vann Elementary School, catered primarily to White patrons including most of the teachers who ate breakfast or lunch there.

On Herron Avenue at the beginning of Wylie Avenue were a few mom-and-pop snack bars and restaurants including Proctor's Snack Bar, owned by one of my uncles. They all served very good food at reasonable prices. Scattered throughout the community on Webster, Bedford, Wylie and Centre Avenues were a number of bars that, while they were primarily drinking places, had decent food as well.

5.5: Proctor's Snack Bar on Herron Avenue, owned by an uncle of the author.

5.6: San Antonio Restaurant on Centre Avenue (1945)

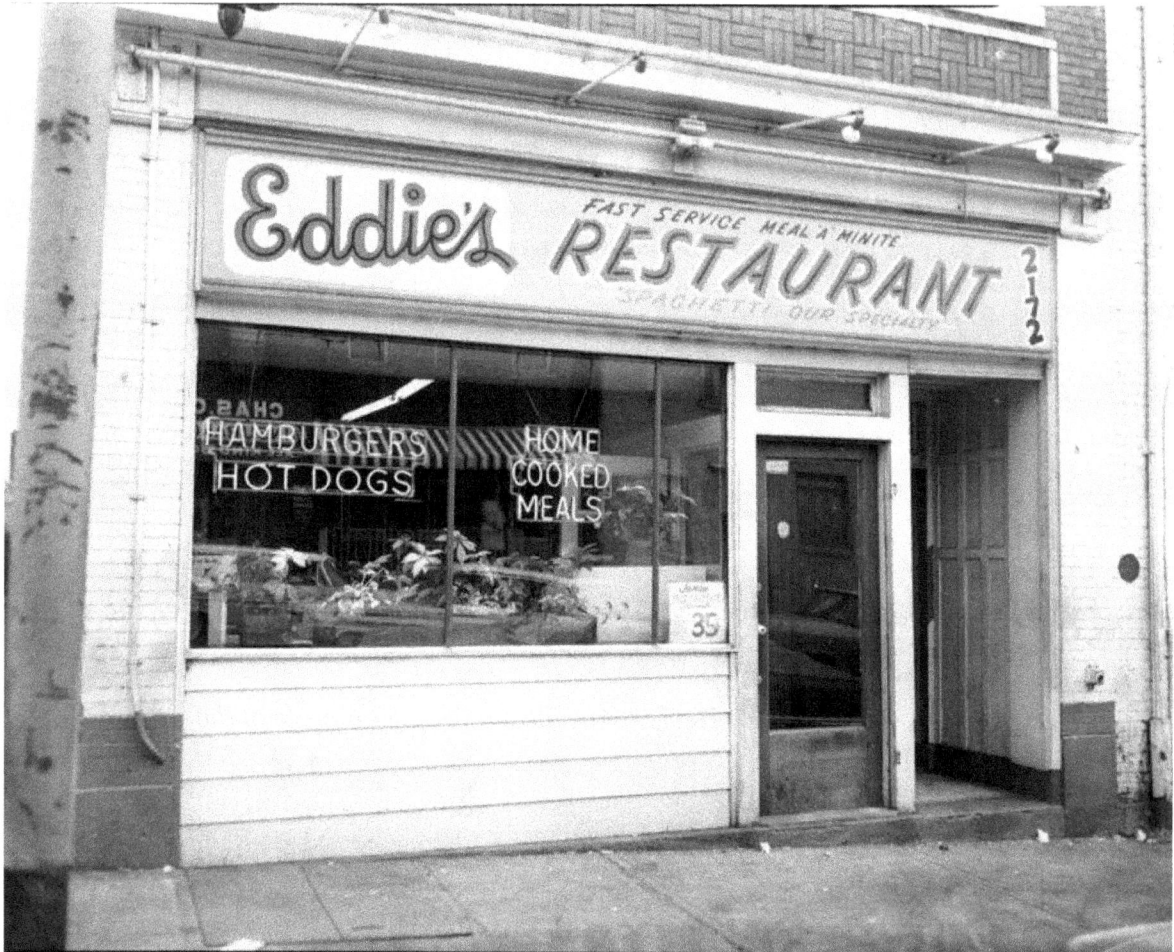

5.7: Eddie's Diner, Centre Avenue, made famous by August Wilson's plays.

Of course, dining in The Hill meant barbeque chicken and ribs served with a variety of sides and delicious pies and cakes. Among the more notable places were Wilson's and Boykin's. Each rib joint had its own secret sauce, allegedly passed down from one generation to another. Townsend's, tucked into a small store on Webster Avenue, boasted two types of sauces—BOY Sauce with a little kick and MAN Sauce designed by the Devil himself. Mr. Townsend considered himself to be a jokester, so if you were a young man trying to impress the young ladies, he would shout out, "What will it be, my man? You want Man Sauce or Boy Sauce?" Of course all the females turned and stared, so we'd order the Man Sauce. When attention turned away, we'd whisper, "Can I have some Boy Sauce to go?" Once home, we'd quickly wipe off as much of the fiery stuff as possible before it had a chance to penetrate into the meat. In its place, a generous layer of the Boy Sauce with its rich and smoky flavor was swabbed on. Timing was everything. If you waited too long, you were in deep trouble.

Post-Script

In recent years, growing attention has been paid to "urban food deserts," impoverished communities with no access to fresh, healthy food. Today, The Hill is often considered such a desert. As you can see, however, The Hill where I grew up was quite different.

CHAPTER 6

Manners and Morals

In addition to table manners, my sisters, friends, and I received instruction on proper behavior. I was shocked, therefore, to learn that many Whites believed The Hill was overrun with immoral heathens headed directly to Hell. Let me tell you, then, about the lessons instilled by family, community, and church. Because these lessons were the norms of many families on The Hill, I say *we* children were taught:

- Do your chores and don't complain;
- Do as you are told;
- Respect your elders;
- Talking back is not tolerated;
- Calling parents and other adults by their first name is unacceptable;
- Lying is wrong;
- Stealing is wrong;
- Violence is a last resort (A fist fight is no big deal, but doing permanent physical harm is wrong);
- Using a knife or a gun on another human being is wrong, unless you had to protect yourself or your family;
- Beating up women is wrong;
- Excessive corporal punishment is wrong;
- Marriage should come before sex;
- Husbands and wives should be faithful to one another, and
- A real man is measured not by the babies he makes but by the babies he takes care of.

These messages about proper behavior came from parents, neighbors, teachers, community members, pastors, police, and even some of the local unsavory characters. Drunks told us that too much drinking was bad. Dope addicts chased us away from areas where they were "shooting up." Men shooting "craps" warned that our fathers would not appreciate our gambling. One pimp told me not to follow in his footsteps even though the money was good. It's no way to live, he said, "always looking over your shoulder, wondering when the cops are going to arrest you." Some barber shops posted signs, ABSOLUTELY NO PROFANITY.

Once, when I tried to join the "mob," the local leader said I was too smart for that. "You should go to school and get a job so your mom will be proud." When I pointed out all the money he and his crew made, he responded, "Yeah, but it's dirty money. My mother would be so ashamed if she knew that we stuck up the paper boy. Besides, I'm going to hell when I die."

When I was very young, Dad would sometimes take me to a pool hall, where much to the chagrin of other patrons, he allowed me to walk on the top of the tables and use the pool cues like a golf club to knock the balls into the pockets. Once I was older, however, pool halls were off-limits for me and other neighborhood kids.

The extended family concept I mentioned in Chapter 4 included an unwritten agreement that every adult was responsible for every child in the neighborhood. Living in The Hill meant you knew your neighbors for miles around, and they knew *you*. Long before today's electronic monitoring devices, parents had a network of "spies" to keep track of their kids' location and behavior. Apparently they had a pact which granted every adult the right to admonish—even punish—each other's children. Everyone shared responsibility for keeping children on the straight and narrow. Even though we children hadn't agreed to this contract, it seems all adults were awarded partial custody of our butts.

One day, I was about ten blocks away from home when I spotted a new grocery store at the crest of one of the many hills. As I stood gazing at the stacks of artistically arranged fruit, especially the rows of different colored apples, I was scared out of my wits by female voice screaming, "You a Proctor. I know who you is, and I knows yo daddy. I'm gonna call him and tell him you was gittin ready to *steal* a apple."

After my heart beat returned to normal, I looked into the eyes of a drunken stranger. She was right in my face and screaming at the top of her lungs. "Why you wanna do that? Yo daddy is a good man, and he and Miss Ruby done raised you children good. Now you gonna mess all that up and steal a *apple*. They put yo ass in jail fo that, boy. You hear me?"

More angry than scared by this point, I shot back, "I wasn't fixin' to steal nuthin'. I was just looking." The lady then reared back and shouted, "Oh, now you gonna sass me, too? You just wait til I tells yo daddy that. Mmm mmm he sho gonna whip yo ass fo *that*. You know better than to sass yo elders boy. I gonna call yo daddy soon as he gits home." With that she staggered down the street, mumbling about "young boys who don't got no respect."

Relieved she was gone and having lost interest in the apples, I returned home to await Dad's arrival. "How could she know when my dad was got home," I wondered. Despite my desire to leave town, I had nowhere to go. So I just sat there miserably contemplating the end of my short life. Sure enough, as soon as he walked through the door, the phone rang. Desperately hoping it was for another family on our phone's party line, I knew I was out of luck as I listened to Dad's side of the conversation. Ending the call, he turned to me, and I immediately began to plead my innocence. "I didn't steal anything. Besides it wouldn't make no sense for me to steal an apple. All I had to do was call Mom and have her ask you to bring some home. Or I could have taken a pop bottle or two to Mr. Shay and traded them for a couple of apples." My self-defense on the charge of premediated theft prevailed, but I still got punished for talking back to that ugly old troll.

This experience was pretty commonplace in The Hill of my youth.

Punishment

Most of the parents I knew seemed to have read the same book on child rearing—the Christian Bible. They took to heart the prescript, "Spare the Rod and Spoil the Child." Breaking the rules meant getting our butts whipped. I know! I know! Physical punishment is bad and should not be condoned. Yet, my sisters and I and most of my friends endured some form of corporal punishment and still turned out to be emotionally unscarred. In those days, spanking was a common practice and never meant my parents didn't love me. I knew the rules and the consequences for breaking them. Mom was the first line of discipline; Dad was the backup. I wish I had a quarter for every time one of my friends told me that their father had said, "Listen, I brought you into the world, and I will take you OUT."

One day, I decided I had had enough beatings. Standing well out of "slapping range," I told Dad I was going to call the cops and have him arrested. To my surprise he said, "Go on and call them."

"What are you going to do when I tell them you been beating me?" I asked.

"That won't be a problem, because you won't be able to tell them anything."

Confused, I persisted. "Why won't I be able to tell them?"

"They won't be able to find you."

Now I was really confused. "I ain't going nowhere, so why won't they find me?"

Dad just smiled and said, "You'll be out in the back yard. Make that IN the backyard and about six feet deep."

Calling in the cops suddenly seemed far less important than I had originally thought.

Typically, most whippings were done with a belt, a brush, or a paddle. Grandma, however, favored the "switch" approach. She ordered the miscreant to go outside and cut a thin branch from a bush or tree. Of course we'd try to find the smallest, skinniest switch, all the time hoping that Grandma would doze off before we returned. Selecting our own instrument of punishment was tricky. If Grandma thought the switch was too thin, she'd send us back to gather one or two more, which she then plaited together. Even so, most kids preferred Grandma's whipping to Dad's.

I was the exception, preferring Dad over Grandma and Mom. With Dad, I could reason (wheedle) my way out of a whipping. My strategy was to convince him that a rule was unclear, or I had really not committed the offense, or I had already been punished so a second whipping would be unfair. Sometimes these even worked.

Demeaning Stereotypes

An area of behavior deserving a bit more attention is that about sexual conduct. It seems that many Whites are either fascinated or repulsed by what they assume to be the sexuality of Black women and men. According to the popular fiction among Whites, Black women are oversexed vixens who know nothing about love but surely enjoy raunchy sex. Plantation owners who routinely raped their Black female slaves blamed the victims for the crime. Had they not exuded such strong sexuality, the master would not have been dragged kicking and screaming down to the slave quarters to satisfy his sick lust. A Catholic nun, who participated in a race-related sensitivity training session I was conducting, expressed the view, "Well you know, all they want to do is have sex and make babies so they can get on welfare and make money. If they have a bunch of babies, they can get a bunch of money and never have to work like normal people." She could not handle information in a report I shared with the class indicating that the vast majority of mothers on welfare are White.

Black men fared no better in the popular notions about sexuality and morality. As one high-ranking federal employees said at a meeting, "All Black men want is loose shoes, tight pussies, and a pot to piss in." He was surprised when he was fired. He claimed he was "just joking." Sadly, all the other White men at the meeting had appreciated his "humor."

I was in the last stage of signing an agreement to purchase a home when the White seller asked, "You know why I am giving up such a nice home?" I told him that his reasons were none of my business, but he felt compelled to continue. "A lot of Black men are moving into the area close to here. Pretty soon they will be moving into this neighborhood and my wife is White." He paused as if he had shared a new reality with me. When I did not respond, he continued. "They will rape my wife." Instead of giving in to my desire to punch him, I suggested he leave as fast as his scrawny legs could move him.

The music industry did not help when it promulgated images of Black men as irresponsible rogues who impregnated every woman they encountered and then moved on. As the 1972 hit song by the Temptations proclaimed, "Pappa was a Rolling Stone and wherever he hung his hat was his home. And when he died all he left me was alone." Many other songs painted the same image of Black men, and unfortunately, many Whites believed that these songs reflected the sexuality and morality of *all* Black men and *only* Black men.

One year during a celebration of Black History Month, I shared a beautiful poem about love with the audience at a government event. When I finished, many people in the audience were weeping. Yet some were surprised when I revealed that the poet was a Black woman. One White woman commented, "I know Black people *lust* for one another, but I didn't know they felt *love*." Even more amazing than her racist assumptions was the freedom with which she expressed them to a Black man. It goes beyond mere rudeness when Whites consider it perfectly acceptable to voice such horribly disrespectful comments and then act shocked that Blacks might be offended.

Morals and THE TALK

Despite these demeaning stereotypes about sexuality, my parents were pretty prudish. They did not talk openly about sex; they certainly did not let us kids know they were engaging in that activity. My friends and I often discussed how little we knew about sex and how our parents clammed up when asked even the most innocuous questions on the subject. All of us had the impression that sex was dirty. I was really confused when I overheard some older women talking about sex. One said, "She is terrible. She put her mouth *down there*." The women suddenly realized that I was within earshot and quickly changed the subject, leaving me totally confused and wondering why someone would suck on somebody's *toes*. UGH!

I was so sure that sex was dirty I beat up a kid who insisted that my mother and father had *done it* or I would not be here. I knew he was lying, because my parents had already told me that babies were brought by the *stork*. The only mystery was why and how the stupid bird put the baby inside the mother. That just did not make sense except for the fact that storks do have very long beaks. Much later, when I learned the truth about the "birds and bees," I wanted to find the victim of my naïve outrage and apologize.

When my father decided it was time for *The Talk*, he came to my room while I was playing with my chemistry set, leaned against the door jam, and gave me the look that usually meant I was in some deep trouble. He stood there for a minute, then uncrossed his arms, pointed one finger and said, "Boy, don't you be bringing home no *babies*." Then he walked away. Huh? Where would I find a baby? I didn't know where storks stored them. And even if I found one, why would I bring it home? After all, it was not like the joy of finding a puppy.

My sisters were no better informed than I. Their sex lesson consisted of "keep your panties up and your skirt down." What the hell was that supposed to mean?

Our parents thought they were being good Christians by lying to us about sex. Because our parents did not, could not, teach us about sex, we were left to learn from our peers. One day my buddies and I were hanging out at the Old Indian Trail, pretending to be tough, streetwise kids. As usual the conversation turned to sex. At that point, one guy stood up, spread his legs apart trying to look tough and announced, "This is important because it will keep us out of trouble with our fathers. I just found out that YOU CAN'T GET A GIRL PREGNANT UNLESS YOU TOUCH THE BONE."

Because I was supposed to be one of the smartest kids in our little gang, I stood up, struck a similar pose, and said, "You think you telling me something I don't know. I know everything about *sex*. I know you can't get a girl pregnant unless you touch the *bone*. I'm going home where folks ain't so dumb." Once our little session broke up, I headed home with my heart pounding. "Damn" I thought. "I'm in real trouble. Daddy just told me 'don't bring home no baby.' Now I find out that you can get a girl pregnant by touching a damn BONE. WHAT BONE? The knee bone? The shoulder bone? The arm bone? I was totally freaked out. Finally I calmed down and came up with a plan that I followed judiciously. *I did not touch a girl for a year.*

By the time I was sixteen years old, I had become far more worldly. One day as I was heading home, I passed the apartment where Ruby's family lived. Ruby, you may recall, was the wild young woman who went to Alaska to ply the world's oldest profession. Just then I heard an unfamiliar voice say, "Ummm, *who* is that fine young hunk?" Paying no attention, I kept walking until I overheard, "Oh that's Ralph Junior."

"My, my, my. That's Ralph junior? Well he has sure grown up to be a good looking young thang! Hey Ralphie, look up. I got something for YOU baby!"

I looked up and hanging out the window in a sheer blouse, with nipples straining against the fabric was *Ruby*! Shocked and scared, I barely managed to stammer, "Oh, hello Ruby. How are you?"

"Baby, I am *fine* and so are *you*! Wanna come up and visit?"

I ran away as fast as my well-honed athletic body would take me, with Ruby's laughter ringing in my ears. I didn't dare imagine what my parents would do if they found out I'd been propositioned by the neighborhood prostitute. It's an understatement to say I was relieved when Ruby left for Texas to "work" with the oil riggers. Yep. This cool, mature dude was *safe*. Thank the good lord I was saved!

The Making of a Gentleman

My mother was determined that I would be a "gentleman" with proper manners. She and other adult women in my life conspired to turn a ragamuffin into a prince. Progress may have been slow, but progress there was. As a student at Herron Hill Junior High School, I received The American Legion Award. During an assembly, I was presented with an embossed certificate suitable for framing, a lapel pin, and a bronze-colored medal with a ribbon hanging from it. All of this was nestled in a shallow, blue cardboard box. Having no idea what this represented, I asked Mrs. Donahue, my homeroom teacher, why I was chosen as the recipient. "It's for the student who displayed the best citizenship for the past year," she explained. Still puzzled, I finally concluded the award was for being a good person.

When I got home, Mom was on the living room couch reading the newspaper. "Hi, Mom," I greeted her along with an obligatory hug. "This is for you." I handed her the box then climbed the stairs to my bedroom, changed my clothes, grabbed my baseball gear, headed for the kitchen to grab a glass of Kool-Aid, and was about to rush past Mom with a hasty "goin out to play ball," when she said, "Wait a minute. This is an award for YOU! Why did you say it was for me?"

"They said it was a good citizenship award for being a good person. It ain't like it's for doing anything special, like being best at math or the fastest runner. It was just for being a good person, and I didn't have anything to do with that. I'm the way I am because that's the way you taught me to be. So the award belongs to you. Bye!"

With tears welling in her eyes, she hugged me close. Nice. But I was off to the ball field so I wouldn't be late for the game.

As a result of Mom's unstinting efforts to turn me into a gentleman, I knew to stand when a lady entered the room; I was to say "yes, ma'am" and "no ma'am" no matter how old a woman was. I knew to open a door, give up my seat on a streetcar, offer to carry loads no matter how small, and not to charge neighborhood women for running errands. Basically Mom conveyed the view that women are angels and men are sort of grown-up bad boys. As signaled by my "good citizenship award," Mom succeeded in instilling a conscience that unrelentingly pointed out any lapses in my "gentlemanly" behavior. It took a lot of growing up, before this "bad" little boy grew into a responsible man.

Unfortunately, Mom and her secret conspirators (aka teachers) turned me into a bit of a misfit—a strong, athletic, macho "gang member" with gentlemanly behaviors. Just how much of a misfit I was hit home when I was the head of a social service agency in which many of the staff came from a blue-collar, White area of the city. One day I was introduced to an older woman. As I shook her hand, I said, "How do you do?" The older woman, however, seemed confused; my staff person howled with laughter. "What *the hell did* you say? What did that mean? I never heard anybody say those words except in funny movies about phony, rich people." Mortified, that was the last time I used my "proper manners" when meeting someone. Another example of my being a misfit occurred when a woman asked if I were gay because I would not have sex with her. Mom had taught me that it wrong to "mess around" with married women. The woman told me I was "weird." Sorry, Mom. I try, but just can't seem to win.

Post-Script—Double Standards

Within any population—Black or White—misbehavior, if not immoral acts, will occur. What bothers me, however, is the assumption that Blacks either don't know or don't care about civil and moral conduct. Let me illustrate.

At one time in my life I directed a youth organization. One day a fight broke out between a Black child and a White child. Ann, a White employee, chastised the White youngster saying, "Billy, you know better than that." I chimed in and told both kids that they were wrong, because violence was never permitted at the facility. Afterward I asked Ann, "Why did you tell Billy that *he* knew better? Weren't they *both* at fault?"

She thought for a moment and replied, "But Billy is from a better neighborhood."

"So" I said, "You think he should have better moral training than Rashid, because Rashid is from a Black neighborhood? That's a very harmful assumption. You expect the White kid to know better, but you don't expect the Black kid to have the same sort of moral training. Be careful with those assumptions because they come out of ignorance. I expect ALL the children to behave in a manner that reflects good manners." My hope that she would take this message to heart was dashed when she accompanied a group of children on a field trip.

I received a call from the manager of the facility that hosted the field trip. He described some absolutely horrible behavior that he attributed to my kids. I apologized and asked him to send me a bill for any damage the youngsters had caused. When the group returned, I called Ann to inquire how the trip went.

"Everything was fine," she assured me.

"Did you see any behaviors that should have been corrected," I probed.

When she said, "no," I described the conversation I had with the facility manager and asked, "You didn't see any of that behavior?"

"I did," she admitted, "But I didn't think it was a big deal, because that's how they behave in their own community."

Containing my anger, I asked, "If they were White kids would you have accepted that behavior?"

"Oh no, if they were from my neighborhood, I would have corrected their behavior, because they know better. But you can't blame these Black kids, because they just behave differently. You can't expect them to live up to the standards of other people."

She was actually proud that she had not judged them by the same standards used to judge White kids. I told her that we had the same moral codes she had and that this was probably not the place for a career for her. I did not want my Black children to be given an excuse for misbehaving, especially since I knew that they understood how they were to conduct themselves.

CHAPTER 7

My Life as a Gang Member

Given what I've said about right and wrong, you may be surprised that I was a gang member. In fact, I was a bit surprised by that turn of events.

There is little official record of the beginnings of Black street gangs in Pittsburgh. They seem to have appeared in the late 1930s or early 1940s and had names like The Black Mask, The Rangers, The Midget Rangers, The Rovers, The Spiders, The Farm Hands, and The Red Aces. At least some of these gangs served as lookouts, runners, and "strong arms" for the numbers barons who operated on The Hill. Others protected moonshiners and speak-easy bars. Protection included keeping out rival White gangs that were trying to horn in on the Black racketeers. Gang members were involved in beatings and robberies. Ordinary folks on The Hill had little respect for the gangs.

By the time I lived on The Hill, there was a new generation of gangs with names like the Bobcats, the Cavaliers, the Comanches, the Cherokees, the Viceroys, the Monarchs, the Amboy Dukes, the Cubs, the Cobras, and the Wildcats. As an 11 year old, I saw no compelling reason to join a gang, because all they did was hang out, drink, smoke weed, and have sex with girl gang members. This changed one night as I inadvertently walked into the middle of a rumble between two rival gangs. Because I did not belong to either gang, I ended up fighting with everybody. At that time, I wasn't a very accomplished fighter, so I joined the Cubs, the gang of my best friend, Allan Goodman. Apparently they had chosen their name so the police would think they were a ball club and not a gang.

Nothing eventful happened while I was a Cub, but I was getting a lot of grief from the Cobras, the gang whose territory was the area in which I lived. The meanest Cobra was Richard who constantly hassled me about being a Cub. I tried to ignore him because, quite frankly, I was afraid of him. If I got beaten up, I'd have to deal with questions like, "Did you win? Did you mark him up?" Despite my efforts to avoid Richard, he attacked me one day in gym class when Mr. Brewer, the teacher, was not around. On that day, I inadvertently became a Cobra.

You see, I had a loose tooth and was trying to coax it out of my mouth before my father used his tried and true dental procedure—tying a string to my tooth and a door knob, then slamming the door shut, while holding me back so I couldn't run toward the door and avert the painful extraction. As I stood in the gym, I was gently pushing on the tooth trying to dislodge it. Suddenly Richard jumped on my back forcing my tongue against the tooth and causing blinding pain to shoot through my head. The next thing I knew, I was sitting on Richard's chest pounding the shit out of him. As a friend later described it, "You was standing there with this strange look on your face like something was hurting you. Richard jumped you from behind, and you let out this awful scream like somebody stuck a stick up your ass. You reached behind you, grabbed poor Richard, held him over your damn head, and still screaming, slammed the dude on the floor. You got on his chest and started pounding the shit out of his face. Man, you was screaming your ass off the whole time. We thought you was gonna kill the sombitch." Mr. Brewer heard the commotion, came running, and pulled me off poor Richard, and that's how the Cobras claimed me as one of their own.

Still, I had to prove I was tough by going through the same initiation as other want-to-be Cobras. In those days, initiations were about personal courage; not about harming other people. Behind Vann School, which was our official hang-out place, there was a retaining wall about the height of a two-story building. To show that you were a "man" you had to jump from the wall to the ground. If you were too afraid to make the jump, you were deemed to be a sissy and the gang members drove you off by punching you about the head and shoulders. Yes, some of us got hurt, but manhood was a personal thing.

I was actually sort of a Junior Cobra, because I was younger than most of the other members. We didn't really do much. We fought to protect our territory, but I was never certain what we were protecting or from whom. I mean, we did not actually *own* anything. We were not involved in protecting bootleggers, speakeasies, or numbers racketeers, as that job went to older thugs with guns. The gangs I knew were not the scourge of the community. We did not harm old people; we saw ourselves as their protectors. We did not sell dope; we did not rape; we did not murder; we did not own guns. We certainly were not fighting to control the dope business; that was for real gangsters. Sure we smoked some pot, but no gang members I knew ever touched coke; crack had not yet been introduced into the Black community.

So why did young men join gangs? Some joined as a way of "being a man" in a society where other avenues to adulthood were closed to Black youth. Gang membership allowed you to "strut your stuff," especially when you wore a brightly colored gang jacket that announced, "Hey. Look at me. I am somebody." If you had a reputation for being a good street fighter, you gained admiration from the young girls and adults. Some joined so they could look "bad," which in the hood meant you looked "good." But for my friends and me, gang life was mostly uneventful. We fought other kids who were not from our neighborhood, but had no encounters with adults. Even though we already belonged to strong families and an extended community network, gangs gave us an extra, special sense of belonging.

Oh yes, there was one other reason. The older gang members were having sex with some girls who called themselves the Cobraettes. In fact, I lost my virginity to one of these auxiliary members when I was 11 years old. I didn't have the faintest idea of what had happened, but knew it was wrong, because she threatened to kick my ass if I told anyone. Hell, who was I going to tell? I didn't really understand what she had just done to me. My second encounter happened a year later when the sister of my initiator said, "Jackie told me what you two did, and you better do the same thing to me, or I'm going to tell everybody." Wow. This sex thing was too damn complicated, and it sure wasn't worth all the fuss. I decided I would rather play baseball.

Don't get me wrong. We were tough kids and had weapons like brass knuckles, home-made blackjacks, car antennae, and bike chains. We fought one another, but no one thought about killing a rival gang member. During the entire time I was in a gang, only one kid died when he was accidently stabbed in a fight. We were stunned; that simply was not supposed to happen.

The knives gang members carried were nothing fancy. Butterfly knives and switch blades were off limits, because the risk of getting arrested was too great. Whether it was true or not, we believed that knife blades, when laid across the palm of our hand, had to be shorter than the width of three fingers. If longer, the violators might be roughed up, thrown in the back of a paddy wagon, and hauled off to jail. Three cops, in particular, were scary. Legend had it that Ollie Mason had interrupted a bank robbery, and when the White robbers opened fire, he retrieved two Thompson submachine guns and dispatched the robbers. Word among the gangs was, "Man, if he shot them *White boys* he sure as hell will kill *us*." The other scary cop was "BIG BLUE," so named because he stood well over six feet tall and was nearly as broad. His hands were so big that he could grab you by the head and crush it like an egg. Finally, there was Fred Clark another tall, scary beat cop who later became one of my mentors. Looking back, I believe these officers instilled fear to keep us out of real trouble.

7.1: Police Officer Prince "Big Blue" Bruce outside Alpern's Clothing Store & LaFrance Beauty Salon, Centre Avenue (c. 1938-1945)

7.2: Police officer Oliver "Ollie" Mason badge no. 287 (c. 1950-1970)

Since we were prohibited from owning switchblades, we experimented with strategies for opening our pocket knives the fastest way possible. I filed the tip of the blade to an angle that allowed me to get a thumb nail under the tip, open it slightly, swipe it quickly across my thigh, and voila, my blade was fully open and pointed toward my opponent. When asked to show this technique to my fellow Cobras, I was proud to do so. Instead of admiration, my friends were staring at me with looks of panic. Suddenly I felt pain and wetness. I had forgotten that I had just sharpened my knife and had just sliced through my jeans and thigh. So much for being the fastest, deadliest blade in the East!

In this era, each gang wore short, baseball-style jackets with their signature "colors." Cobra jackets were Maroon and Grey, with the name emblazoned across the back, the head of a cobra on the front, and our personal nickname stitched underneath. This was the design, but the problem was finding the money to actually buy the jackets. Rejecting options that might land us in jail, we began to brainstorm possibilities.

Someone mentioned that Jimmy Shaw, who owned the confectionary store across the street from Vann School, had a "Help Wanted" sign in the window. A couple of the guys, who were old enough to work, were sent to inquire about the job. Jimmy was selling tiny, plastic, colored figures of cowboys and Indians for $1 apiece. The figures came in 55 gallon barrels and had to be repacked into Cracker Jacks sized boxes.

We agreed to pack the boxes for a low enough wage that Jimmy could make a profit. One gang member's uncle used his open-bed truck to deliver the barrels to his nephew's home. Each gang member would pack enough boxes to equal the price of his jacket; anyone falling short would not get a jacket. We took a vow of secrecy that we were actually *working* to earn money for the jackets. Jimmy put down the deposit needed to have the jackets designed. Then we worked all summer—packing, cussing, and bleeding. We figured that with hard work we could have the jackets before the end of summer. And we did. When we were not packing tiny figures, we were playing baseball.

Let me backtrack for a moment and tell you about efforts to counteract gangs on The Hill. In the "olden days," gangs caused so much trouble that members were arrested, sent to Juvenile Court, and wound up in reform schools like "Morganza." These so-called schools were supposed to provide educational classes, but those in charge often cared little for the incarcerated youth and treated them harshly. It was not unusual for kids to leave reform school worse than they entered.

This system caused untold misery and destruction among poor Black families. Overzealous White social workers were all too ready to send Black kids away, whether or not they truly deserved it. Children could be kept in the system till age 21, although most did not stay that long—if their families could afford a good lawyer. My family, like many I knew, suffered from having someone locked away. My sister was sent to reform school because she was defiant, hard to control, and behaving badly in school. We begged and pleaded with the judge and the social worker, but they would not listen. Consequently, my family spent every weekend visiting the reform school. My sister became very popular, because Mom always baked treats for everyone, and I danced with any girl who wanted to take a spin around the gym floor. That might not sound so bad, but my family and so many others were torn apart because we were Blacks with no power.

Several organizations aimed to curb the incarceration of Black Youth. Two in the lower end of the Middle Hill were the Kay Boys Club and The Hill City Youth Municipality. The Kay Boys Club offered a variety of programs to occupy youth in more productive activities like basketball, boxing, and a marching band.

7.3: Kay Boys' Club, Wylie Avenue (c. 1940-1945)

7.4: Hill City Youth Municipality, Bedford Avenue (c. 1935-1950)

In the 1930s, Pittsburgh Police Detective Howard McKinney started Hill City Youth Municipality, "a city within a city." Black gang members served as a youth mayor and a district attorney. There were two judges, 18 investigators, and 9 council members. The youth policed themselves, held trials, and passed sentences on offenders. They dispensed better justice, because they understood the lives of the young offenders. With the cooperation of the Juvenile Court system the program continued into the early 1960s.

The Irene Kaufmann Settlement House, located on Centre Avenue, originally provided cradle-to-grave social support services for Jewish immigrants, including recreational opportunities for young people. As the Jewish population moved from The Hill, the Settlement House turned to serving Black youth. Eventually, the Irene Kaufmann Settlement House relocated to East Liberty and was replaced by The Anna B. Heldman Center.

7.5: Hill House (formerly the Irene Kauffman Settlement House) on Centre Avenue (c. 1960-1975). This is an example of the magnificent buildings that had been built in The Hill. Clearly it was in need of repairs which may have been quite costly. Yet, other historical preservation projects have been funded by foundations.

Soho House, a Settlement House in the old tradition, was closed by some well-meaning folks, leaving a void of activities for Black Hill youth. Eventually, it was replaced by a new entity called Hill House, named after Jim Hill, an old junior high school buddy of mine. That facility continued to serve the community until 2019.

7.6: Soho Community House Library. Margaret Ludwig seated with book reading to children; Leontine Pullman standing on left (July 1946)

Around 1965, the Ozanam Center was established in the Middle Hill under the auspices of the Catholic Church. It was famous for two excellent programs—the Ozanam Strings Orchestra and its summer basketball program. The first became world-famous by teaching Black children to perform classical music, a feat that seemed to surprise many White folks. The basketball tournaments were of such high caliber that professional and college scouts attended to find new talent.

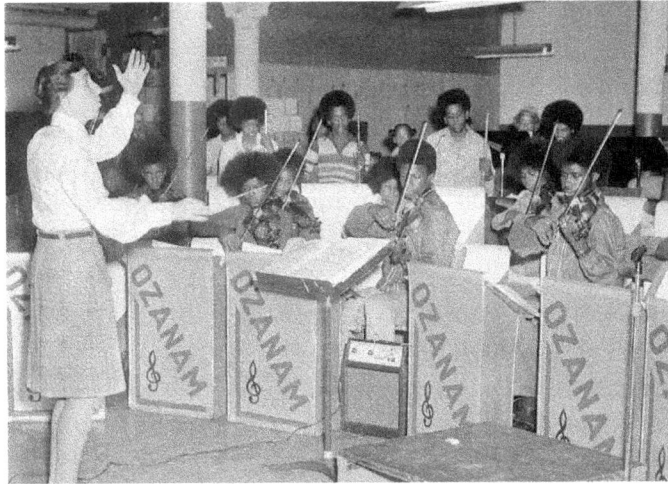

7.7: Ozanam Youth Orchestra

Around 1917, Kingsley House moved from its location in the Strip District into the former Montooth Mansion in the middle Hill. The purpose of the organization was to serve the White, ethnic population in the area. When the population shifted to more Black people as a result of the Great Migration from 1917 to 1925, the owners and supporters of Kingsley House worked with the University of Pittsburgh to identify another White ethnic population they could serve. In 1923, Kingsley House moved to the East End area called "Little Italy" and well into the 1950s no Blacks were welcome there. When Black athletic teams played against the Kingsley House teams, race-related fights frequently broke out. The Montooth facility was sold to a Black missionary society whose purpose was to help Southern Blacks adjust to living in the urban North.

Gangs were a costly problem for the Pittsburgh Board of Education. Apparently gangs "took over" the school playgrounds, using them as a hangout for gambling, drinking, and smoking both tobacco and weed. They used the school windows for target practice, shooting BB guns or throwing rocks until all the windows were broken. One of the casualties was the movie screen in the school auditorium. As the screen was lowered, students hooted, hollered, and laughed at the hole in the middle. In my second year at Herron Hill Junior High, Mr. Mogart, the principal, held a special assembly to reveal a brand new screen and to thank the kids for not breaking out all the windows during the previous summer. That allowed enough budget surplus to purchase a new screen.

In 1941, the Pittsburgh Board of Education decided to address the problem of youth gangs by hiring six Black physical education teachers who had recently graduated from college. John Brewer, the gym teacher who intervened in my pummeling of Richard, was one of those teachers. He began his job at McKelvey School on Bedford Avenue in the Middle Hill. Years after I had grown and left The Hill, I had the opportunity to interview John as part of my doctoral dissertation research. He told me, "Our job was to take over the playgrounds, chase away the gang members, and set up a summer recreation program for neighborhood kids." In addition they were to establish a zero tolerance zone for gang activity.

His first day at McKelvey, Mr. Brewer walked onto the playground and explained to the gang members that they had to take their activities elsewhere. The gang replied they had no intention of giving up their "territory" and one made a move to attack Mr. Brewer. "So, I did what I was hired to do. I kicked his ass, and as he lay on the ground bleeding, I told him, 'Now go get your daddy, and I will kick his ass, too.' The other gang members helped their leader limp off, and they never returned."

Brewer was so successful at McKelvey, the School Board moved him further up the middle Hill to Robert L. Vann School. I had heard fun things were going on at my elementary school and thought I'd check that out. As I entered the school playground, one of my gang buddies suggested that I take off my jacket, because "Mr. Brewer don't allow no gang shit on his playground."

"Who the hell is Mr. Brewer, and why should I listen to him?" I asked. Just then Mr. Brewer walked on the playground and began moving some equipment around. Oh, THAT Mr. Brewer! The same man who, several years earlier, had taught me how "to kick the asses" of boys who teased me about making good grades. Now he looked even more powerful than when I was younger.

He was not a very tall man, but had a wide back and huge shoulders. His arm muscles were as huge as my dad's. I certainly was no match for Dad, so I wasn't crazy enough to challenge Mr. Brewer. I quickly removed my jacket, took it home, and ran back for some fun. I was secretly happy that no gang activities were permitted, because I really was not a hardened kid. Little did I know I had just met a man who would change my life forever.

Mr. Brewer convinced us to form a baseball team; then entered us into league games around the city. To counteract nasty comments about a gang playing sports, we showed our detractors how well we could swing our bats as clubs. We were proud of our athletic ability and by the end of the summer we had won two tournaments, had trophies, and had our hard-earned jackets.

7.8: Leaders & participants in Hill District playground program. Back row from left: Michael Dadasovich, John Brewer Sr., Pomeroyal Fountain, Marion Staunton, John Morton. Front row: Bobby Anderson, J. Morsee, Peggy Carter, Marvin Richter, Lois Roll, Eloise Clark, and Eugene Gelter (July 1941)

Post-Script

My generation did not pass on the mantle of gang lore to the next generation. Organized Black gangs in The Hill slowly died after 1956 and did not reappear until 1993. When they returned, hopes and dreams had been lost. The once vibrant Black community was torn apart by abject poverty, the prevalence of guns, and the introduction of dope with its allure of money. We watched hopelessly and helplessly as Crack was introduced into our communities by White dealers. The city fathers refused to listen to us "Old Head" gang members. We said to the Mayor, "We're former gang members. We know why gangs ended before. We can duplicate those efforts and, at minimum, keep many of the youth out of gangs." The leaders of city government, industry, and the philanthropic foundations said, "We have everything under control. There are no gangs in Pittsburgh; only pretend gangs." I wonder how many of the dead youngsters know that they died from non-existent gangs.

Now, hardly a day passes without headlines of shootings by Blacks in Black neighborhoods. Although most of these shooting do not take place in The Hill, they still reinforce the image of The Hill as an extremely dangerous place teeming with violent gangs. To some extent that image is true. But it is not true that The Hill has always been that way. Nor was the deterioration and violence of this once vibrant, healthy community inevitable. The seeds of drugs infestation and the associated emergence of more virulent gang warfare were sown by those who championed Urban "Renewal" and turned a deaf ear to our warnings.

CHAPTER 8

Law, Order, and Keeping Safe

As mentioned in Chapter 6, residents in The Hill felt a personal responsibility to enforce norms of good behavior. In addition, they took responsibility for keeping the community safe. A neighborhood watch system was in place long before the term was invented. People knew who belonged in the neighborhood and kept an eye on strangers.

Most of the people in my neighborhood did not lock their doors except at bedtime. We did not stay awake at night watching for burglars. Crime was not prevalent, because Black and White police officers lived in the community, walked their beats in the neighborhood, and wanted to live in a good, safe community.

Officer Fred Clark, a family friend, had a custom gun shop in our basement. He was one of my mentors, took pride in my accomplishments, and claimed me as one of his kids. Jimmy Carter, a good-looking plainclothes detective who lived around the corner, always had a smile and a hug for us. Karl Jackson, a Hill resident, was the first Black motorcycle officer in Pittsburgh. Rip, a handsome motorcycle cop, was rumored to be the object of many women's fantasies. These and several other Black police officers were like family. We even exchanged Christmas gifts. They looked out for us, we looked out for them. They kept an eye on us kids and encouraged good behavior, because they wanted us to be good citizens and help our neighbors. If we saw something strange or dangerous going on, we told them without fear of being treated badly. Thieves were not tolerated. On rare occasions when someone's home was burglarized, we had no problem calling the cops. Often the perpetrator was known and turned over to the police officers we trusted.

8.1: Police officers, from left: Prince "Big Blue" Bruce,
Oliver "Ollie" Mason, and Fred Clark (c. 1947)

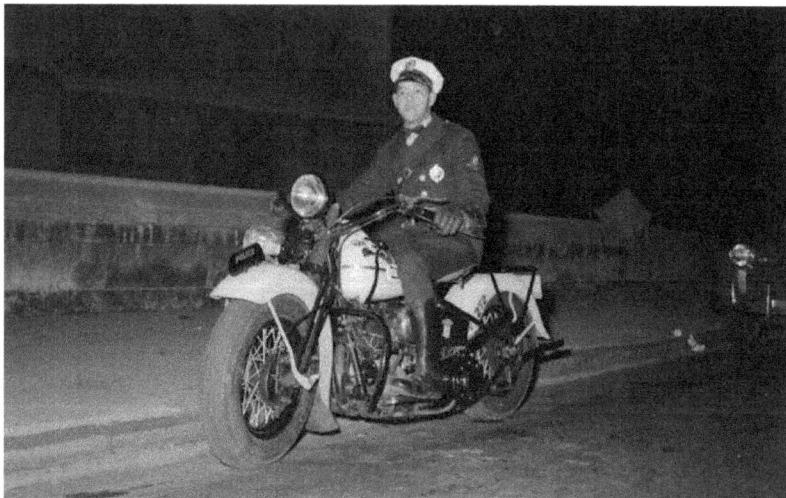

8.2: Police Officer Karl O. Jackson, 1st Black
Motorcycle Police Officer in Pittsburgh (1945)

*8.3: Police Officers in The Hill on Centre Avenue. The New
Grenada Theater is in the background. (c. 1953-1960)*

Crimes did take place in The Hill, but not nearly as many as the media and the Negro-ologists would have you believe. Also, two forms of "crime" served the community. The first was the operation of jitneys—unlicensed taxis—that I discuss in Chapter 14. The second was the numbers racket, which deserves more than a passing mention.

The Numbers Game

The game called "Numbers" or "The Policy Game" is identical to "The Lottery," except the lottery is legal. Regardless of the name, the game involves betting that a specific combination of numbers will be chosen by some process; winnings are proportional to the amount wagered. Many residents of The Hill, including my mother, father, grandmother, other relatives, neighbors, and friends played it.

Publications, like Dream Books, allegedly could help you to pick winning numbers. If you dreamed about a certain thing, you played a corresponding number. Other publications offered "sure-fire" ways of helping you to win. Our house was full of such publications as were the homes of most of my friends.

Mom was pretty good at hitting now and then. She always gave us kids a few dollars of her winnings. As I got older, I'd add a few dollars to what she had given me and buy her a nice gift. If Mom even *thought* she wanted something, the "Gift Fairy" would magically place the item on the dining room table. When I started earning money, I tried to repay my mother for all she had done for us. Of course, no amount of money would do that, but I felt good trying. Dad was too proud to accept money from his son so I tricked him with "loans." These games were more important to me than to Mom and Dad.

Bets could be placed at a local facility such as an alleged "candy" store. I used to piss off the operators of a game located down the street from my home. I would go in and try to buy a candy bar. The operators would say, "Boy, get the hell out of here. You know we ain't selling no damn candy bars."

I would badger them and say, "But you got what I want right there in the case. Sell me one."

Exasperated, the operator would say, "Boy, ain't you got nothing better to do? You know damn well we ain't selling no damn candy bars. If we sell them, we gotta go buy some damn more. Why you wasting my time? Go the hell over to Shay's and buy his damn candy. This ain't funny no more."

Bets could also be placed with "runners" who came to homes or businesses. Each day they made their rounds collecting a dime here, a nickel there, a dollar, five dollars, whatever people were willing to risk.

Numbers were recorded in a little tablet; the bettor got a carbon copy; the runner kept the original. The next day, the runners brought money to the lucky winners. The odds were pretty good. I think one of them paid about 500 to 1, which was good money for a few cents invested. The runners were always armed; not against the cops, but against would-be-stickup men.

Richard, one of my fellow Cobras, became a numbers runner. Had he been White, he probably would have been employed somewhere as a mathematician. He had a photographic memory, which came in handy, because he could keep a whole day's worth of numbers in his head. At the end of the day, he could go to headquarters and "download" the information to one of the bookies. Even if he got busted by the cops, they could not arrest him because he had no numbers "slips" on him. Of course, many of the cops played the numbers, so arrests were not that frequent.

Volumes have been written about the men who controlled the "Numbers" in Pittsburgh—Cumberland Posey, Woogie Harris, Gus Greenlee, and William Robinson. Posey and Harris were the apparent top dogs; Robinson owned the Crawford Grill, the famous Jazz Mecca in Pittsburgh. These "barons" were not shady-looking guys who tried to hide what they were doing. We all knew them. They dressed well, drove the finest cars, vacationed aboard ocean liners, and took big game hunting trips.[10] They were generous with family members. My family doctor and friend, Dr. Charles Greenlee, told me his brother Gus paid cash to send him to medical school. William Robinson left his business to his son Buzzy who continued to make a good living at the Crawford Grill. Woogie bought his brother Charles a very expensive Speed Graphic camera. Charles "Tennie "Harris became one of the most famous Black photographers in the country. Tennie had lots of attention from pretty women and jealousy from Black men. Most people thought he was rich because he drove fancy, fast cars. In truth, the cars were yearly gifts from his brother.

---

10 As a butcher, my father often was the one who carved and packaged the game from these hunting trips.

8.4: Gus Greenlee, Woogie Harris, and Joe Robinson, in Crawford Grill No. 1
(photograph of John Henry Lewis in background). (c. 1942)

Beyond family members, the numbers barons often served as bankers at a time when Blacks could not get a loan or mortgage from White-owned banks. Because of the numbers barons, many Blacks were able to start a small business, build a church, or buy a home. Borrowers may have had to pay a higher interest rate and the penalty for non-payment was a little more severe, but the point is the barons stepped into a breach created by prejudiced White lending institutions.

Long before Jackie Robinson finally broke the color barrier in America's pastime, the numbers barons were instrumental in our being able to watch and play professional baseball. Black players, no matter how good, were not hired by any White team. Blacks were treated badly when we went to watch White-player only games. However, because of the numbers barons, we did get to see absolutely remarkable ball players like Satchel Page and Josh Gibson. Black numbers barons throughout the country used their funds to start the Negro Baseball League. Pittsburgh had two such professional teams—The Pittsburgh Crawfords and The Homestead Grays.

8.5: Pittsburgh Crawfords Baseball Team

8.6: Homestead Grays Baseball Team

So, yes, numbers barons were racketeers. They paid off police and government officials to look the other way as they pursued illegal activities.[11] One of my friends inherited his father's numbers business. Occasionally as we sat and talked into the wee hours of the morning, my friend drank a bit too much. At those times, he would rant about the lack of respect accorded to him and his father by members of the community. "Those people got their nerve to be looking down their damned noses at me and my dad like we were scum. They think they're better than us cause they can drive nice cars, be the head of a fancy church, or have a good business. Well let me tell you, they wasn't acting so high and mighty when my daddy and his friends gave them the damned money to get started. Then they got the nerve to look down their noses at US, like we're some kind of dirt." There's some justification for his outrage. The numbers barons did good things for The Hill. Some even saw themselves as *"Robin Hoods"* of the "hood." Perhaps that is not far from wrong.

Crime did increase in The Hill after Urban "Renewal." A large percentage of Black middle-class residents left The Hill—either because they were displaced or they could move to communities formerly "off-limits" because of housing discrimination. As the economic stability of The Hill decreased, crime increased. Unfortunately, higher crime rates are more prevalent in lower socio-economic areas, regardless of residents' race. At one point I compared crime statistics in The Hill with those in Oakland where the University of Pittsburgh is located. In the years I studied, The Hill was safer than Oakland. Interestingly, when I ventured into this bastion of higher education, I thought I'd escape the negative stigma of being raised on the "crime-ridden Hill."

Sadly I learned such prejudice runs deep, even among those who should know better, when a professor for whom I worked approached me with a problem. His television had died, and he asked if I could help him replace it. I was surprised by his request, because he hardly knew me, but I said a friend of mine sold TVs in his furniture store. I was fairly certain I could arrange for him to buy one at cost. The gentleman hesitated; then said he thought I could arrange for him to get one that was cheaper. I assumed he was talking about a used TV, but that was not what he meant. In total exasperation I asked, "How the hell are you going to get one cheaper than that?" "Oh, I thought you could get me a HOT one." I resisted the urge to punch him in his face. After all, I was a law abiding kid from The Hill.

Another Ph.D.-type told me a neighborhood dog was terrorizing his children as they walked to and from school. He asked if I could help him solve the problem. I suggested talking to the dog's owners, calling the police, or calling animal control. He had tried all those approaches with no results. "I'm sorry," I said, "but I don't know what else to suggest." "Oh" he replied, "I thought you could have the dog 'taken care of' for me." Sorry, asshole, I'm not a canine hit man; nor do I have any among my circle of friends.

---

11 In addition to paying off local law enforcement agents for protection, local Black gangs provided a measure of protection. This is still the case today as the game persists even though there is a legal lottery. "Numbers" offers the advantage of secrecy—nobody knows if you win; no relatives and friends come begging for money; no income tax is filed.

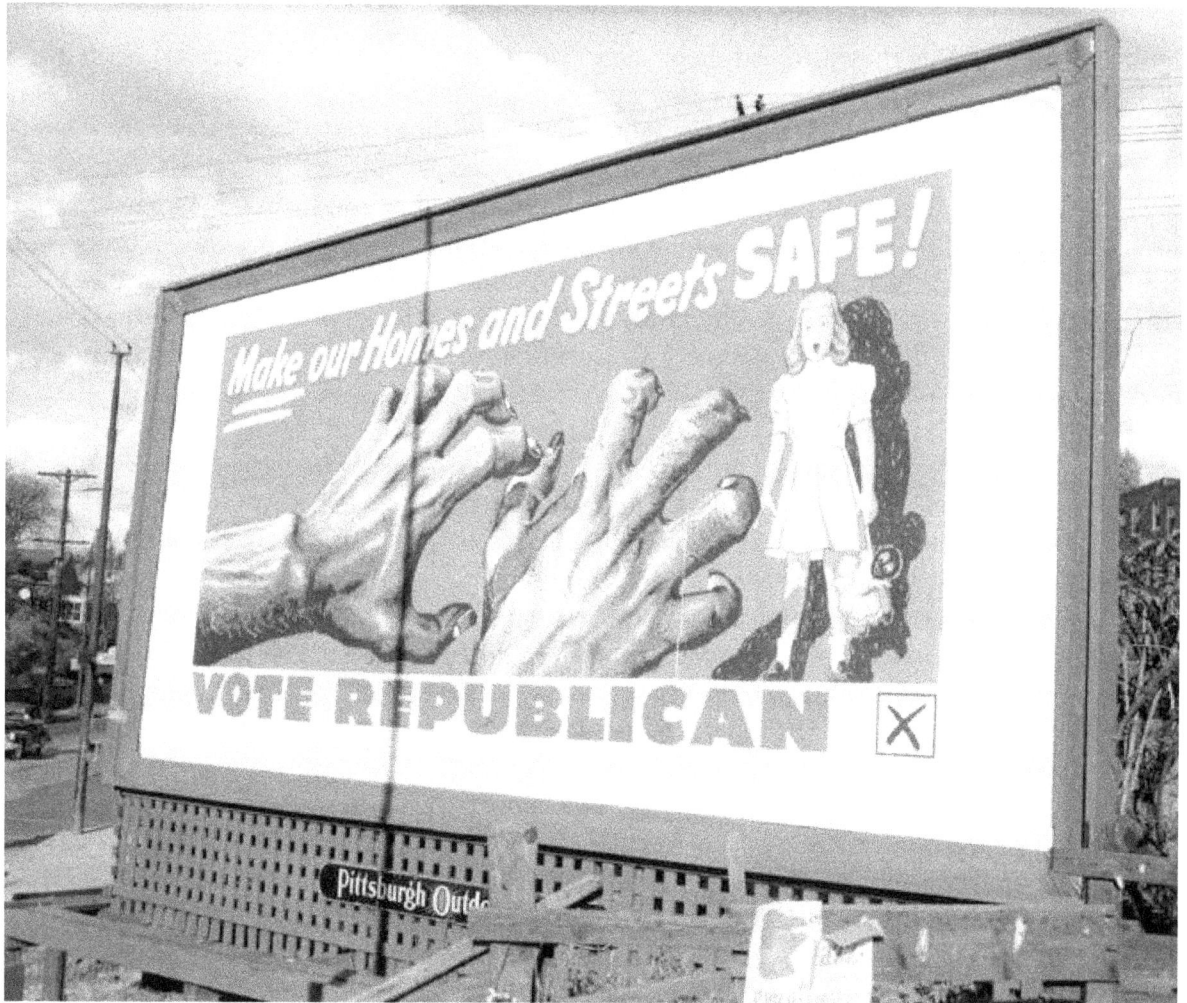

8.7: Safety—The Dividing Line (October 1949). This Republican campaign billboard was located on Bigelow Blvd at the end of The Hill. It was positioned so that the message could be seen by passing drivers, most of whom were White. The back of the sign faced The Hill. The menacing image aimed to engender fear of Blacks by Whites. Yet, when Blacks left the safety of The Hill, it was they who faced danger.

Staying Safe

Within the borders of The Hill, Black youngsters grew up in a safe and caring community. Parents, however, worried about our safety in the racist world that awaited us. They worried about how to let their children know about the ugliness of the world. One day my mother was trying to explain to me why my friend Jimmy was considered White while my sister Carol was considered colored. To me they both were the same color—pink. After several unsuccessful attempts at trying to help me understand something that made no sense to my young, still innocent mind, Mom sent me outside to play. As I ran down the steps, I heard Mom say to a friend, "How do you tell your child that he is going to be hurt every day of his life because he is colored?" The full significance of that question did not hit home until I began traveling beyond the boundaries of The Hill.

Concerned for our safety, parents taught us the survival skill of *scanning*, i.e., recognizing potentially dangerous situations and taking proactive precautions. Actually, this skill was not taught overtly, but rather was assimilated unconsciously as we developed a heightened sense of awareness in unfamiliar settings. Senses are "on target," checking for sounds, smells, and sights that might indicate lurking danger. I listen for strange sounds such as a southern accent. I watch faces to detect negative emotions. Often, I place myself where no one can get close without my noticing them. I am looking for weapons and an escape route. I may be a bit more "*on point*" than most because of my military training. However, I've noticed this scanning behavior in those who have been treated badly—e.g., women, some Jewish people, members of the LGBT community, Muslims, and (now because of COVID's designation as the Chinese virus), Asians.

Here's an example of scanning in action that occurred several years ago during a business trip to Manhattan. I had contacted a former colleague from the University of Pittsburgh who suggested we meet at a local nightclub. Upon arrival, I was a bit uncomfortable because the club was round; no corners in which to place my back. As we chatted, my friend suddenly accused me of not paying attention to her.

"I am paying attention. I know you're a very beautiful woman, wearing a low-cut dress, and a lovely perfume. That's with half my brain; the other half is watching the three White, red-neck, drunken southerners at a table across the room. They're the kind of scum that would lynch me if they had a chance. I'd be foolish to devote all my attention to you and leave us in danger."

"How do you know all that when we've only been here for a few minutes? I didn't even notice them. Besides, this is New York, not the rural south of the 1960s. We do what we damn well please."

"True. But when I walked in, these guys turned to look at me with pure hatred. They're drunker now than when I came in, because their southern drawl is getting more sloppy. After you greeted me with a kiss on the lips and began flirting with me, they became more agitated. We're in danger. With three of them and one of me, I'd be foolish to devote all my attention to you. I have to be ready to do mortal combat should they move in our direction. Because of the narrow space here, they'd have to attack in single file. I'm prepared to take out the first one with such violence he will squeal like a stuck pig and scare the other two. That will give me enough time to take out the second one, maybe the third, and get us out of here before the cops arrive."

Another less volatile example occurred while I was chatting with a friend at the Pittsburgh airport. Having already checked in, we almost simultaneously interrupted our conversation, returned to the check-in counter, and demanded to see the supervisor. Upon the supervisor's arrival, we both charged the person at the counter with racism. We had watched her check people in and realized the only people from whom she requested identification were the two of us—the only Blacks who had checked in. How did we both notice the same action at the same time? We were scanning. Having to use this technique to insure safety is a sad waste of energy that could better be spent on other more positive aspects of life, like enjoying the beauty of a rainbow, the magnificence of a star-filled sky, the gentle touch of a lover's hand, or the sound of children's laughter.

Safety and Police Relations

Among the safety lessons imparted by parents was THE TALK—not about sex, but about what to do *when* stopped by police. The emphasis on "when" reflects the assumption that Black men will inevitably be stopped and harassed by White police officers. A few years ago, the subject of police violence against Black men of all ages came up in a class I was teaching. Some of the White students found it hard to believe until one young Black student said, "My mother gave me The Talk, and SHE is a police officer."

It is interesting to consider how various communities view police officers. When I studied this issue, the differences were startling. When asked about police, many White kids see them as protectors; many Black kids see them as enemies. This is not new. In fact, the mistrust has roots extending back to colonial America.

The role of the police was to enforce laws meant to protect America's founding fathers—rich, White English men. The principle that "All Men Are Created Equal" did not apply to the more than five million Blacks held in *legal* slavery. Police helped to capture and punish runaway slaves. Over the centuries, police and Blacks have continually clashed. From the blatant violence during the civil rights movement to daily insults and assaults, police have failed their duty to serve and protect. When police respond to crimes in Black communities, they often treat all residents like criminals.

Police brutality (euphemistically referred to as "excessive force") occurs in any number of situations. Traffic stops for DWB (Driving While Black) occur when police officers perceive that a Black person who is driving an expensive car must have stolen it, must be selling dope, or must be involved in some other form of illegal activity. My own experiences as well as information from both White and Black police officers confirms the persistence of the racist assumption that Black men who can afford an expensive vehicle must be criminals.

A case that gained notoriety in Pittsburgh occurred in 1995 when police stopped Johnny Gammage, a 39 year-old business man from New Jersey. Gammage, a cousin and business partner of Pittsburgh Steeler Ray Seals, had borrowed Seals' Jaguar sports car. Driving through the Brentwood neighborhood, Gammage was stopped by police even though he had committed no crime or traffic violation. Within minutes, Gammage was dead. In the subsequent trial, none of the police were found guilty.

Miles Davis, a famous Jazz musician, lived in Manhattan. He drove very fancy vehicles such as Lamborghinis and Maseratis. He was pulled over so often, he would call the police station before driving one of his cars and say, "This is Miles, I will be driving a Blue Maserati today. Tell your cops not to fuck with me."

I drive a nice sports car and have been pulled over by police. One day, my eldest son was driving my car and called to say some cops were following him. While he thought it was funny, I thought he was in mortal danger. "Drive straight home," I instructed him and told him the shortest route to my house. "Obey all traffic laws. When you get to the house, use the remote to open the garage, drive in, shut the door, and stay in the car until I tell you to come out. I'll be waiting for you."

As my son turned onto our street, I stood in the driveway in a wide, military stance. A car with two white police officers stopped in front of me and said they had questions about the vehicle they were following. I refused to answer any of them and suggested that they move on unless my son had broken some law. Just then, another police vehicle approached. The Black officer saw me, nodded, and pulled adjacent to the other police car. I "saw" him say (I read lips), "This is a bad stop for you. He is friends with the chief. One wrong word and you will be walking a beat in Homewood tomorrow night." The White officers turned red, glared at me, and left. The Black officer, tipped his hat, smiled, and drove off. Such incidents were common for Black men in Pittsburgh. So, driving a fancy car had its risks. However, it was a risk many were willing to take because a nice car was a status symbol that transcended race and, for the most part, racism.

In addition to bogus traffic stops, untold numbers of Blacks, including me, have been beaten and jailed for the "crime" of registering Black people to vote. My nephew died as a result of police brutality. I have held the hands of a mother as she cried in anguish over the death of her son at the hands of a White police officer who was found "not guilty" of killing her unarmed son. The news is rife with incidents of Black men and women who have been wrongfully killed by White police.

Years ago I did a research project concerning the number of Black men and women beaten or shot by police. Part of my research included a review of all the incidents of police brutality and killings of Blacks reported in *The Pittsburgh Courier*. I then compared the details of the events as reported by Pittsburgh's White-controlled newspapers. I expected to see that the White newspapers took the incidents much less seriously. I was unprepared to find, that in the vast majority of such cases, the White newspapers did not even mention the beatings or deaths.

In a society where racism has persisted since its earliest days, it is not surprising that the police departments have difficulty shifting from their historic role as "Law Keepers" for White America to protectors of all citizens. A complete overhaul of our law enforcement system is needed, but I do not see that happening in my lifetime or the lifetimes of my children. That said, some of my dearest friends have been police officers. I have even been excluded from jury duty by defense attorneys who branded me a "cop lover." I worry about my police friends all the time. I will never forget a conversation with a young Black officer who wanted to protect and help young Black men. With tears in his eyes, he said, "I can't even talk to them; I can't even get close to them, because they see the blue of my uniform. My Black skin no longer matters." I dated a Black police officer and was amazed one evening when I was driving her home. She cautioned me that we should not drive down one street, because it was gang territory and she was afraid we would be shot as we drove by. I have conducted many police/community relations sensitivity sessions and have seen both the good and the worst of police attitudes. I am conflicted.

Legal Representation

During the heyday of The Hill, White firms simply did not hire Black attorneys no matter how brilliant they were. Most White lawyers had no clue what it was like to be assumed guilty by reason of your skin color. Understandably, then, residents in The Hill turned to lawyers who lived and practiced in the community. Even those who lived in the affluent part of The Hill understood what trials and tribulations faced Blacks in the criminal "justice" system. Among the notable Black attorneys were Judge Homer S. Brown and his son Byrd Brown, Everett Utterback, Richard Jones, Robert Vann, Wendell Freeland, Henry Smith, Justin Johnson, and Eric Springer. These legal professionals made certain that we of dark hue had a fighting chance in the court system. Their presence was a beacon of hope for many Black youngsters, offering proof that it was possible to aspire to a professional career. They spent their dollars in The Hill, contributing to a stable middle class. They provided much-needed leadership, especially as the fight against illegal discriminatory practices gained momentum.

*8.8: Judge Homer S. Brown swearing in Atty. Henry Smith Jr.
as Common Pleas Court Judge (January 1970)*

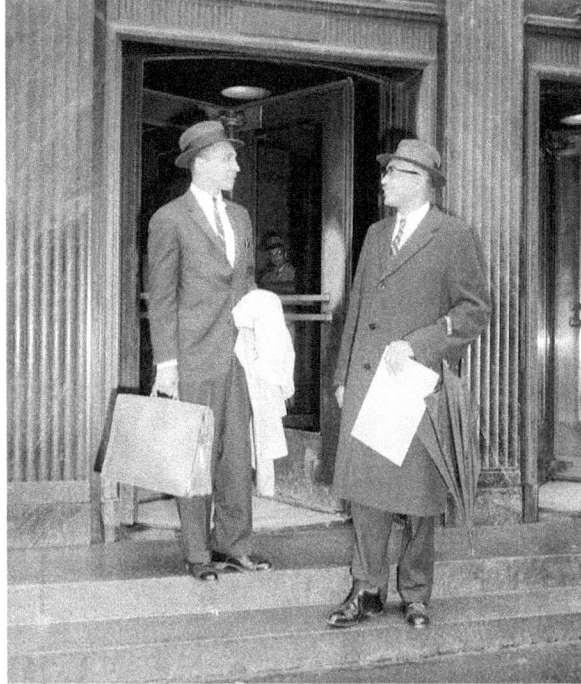

8.9: Attorneys Bryd Brown and Everett Utterback (c. 1956)

8.10: Attorney Richard Jones

8.11: Attorney Eric Springer (c. 1959-1970)

8.12: Attorney Wendell Freeland with William P. Young and Republican gubernatorial candidate William "Bill" Scranton (March 1962)

8.13: Aircraft commander Judge Justin Morris Johnson (c. 1954-1973)

CHAPTER 9

Church and Religion

In addition to the family- and community-based emphasis on good behavior, religion played an important role on The Hill, which was home to congregations of many different faiths including Christianity, Judaism, and Islam. I saw no signs of religious strife. Everyone got along, whether they met in single-room spaces, wooden shacks, converted storefronts, or large, beautiful houses of worship with tall, stately steeples reaching toward Heaven. Faith was not measured by the name by which you called God. A soul has no color, no race, no boundaries. Thank you God, Jehovah, Allah.

Housing the diverse religious denominations were many different church buildings. One golden-brick Christian church was located at the corner of Wylie and Herron Avenues. From that corner, Wylie Avenue wound its way through the heart of The Hill and ended at the county jail in downtown Pittsburgh. As the story goes, Wylie Avenue is the only street in the world that begins with a church and ends with a jail.

9.1: Church that anchored one end of Wylie Avenue; the jail anchored the other end. Intersection of Wylie and Herron Avenue.

In terms of Black churches, several were truly stunning. Wesley Center AME Zion Church in the Middle Hill was an impressive building, as was Warren Methodist Church, and the Triumph Church in the Lower Hill. Ebenezer Baptist Church's steeples rose high as it beaconed to worshipers and civil rights activists. Central Baptist Church and Monumental Baptist Church were also civil rights churches. We kids used to make fun of the Macedonia Baptist Church, because we heard that only "uppity" folks went there. Regardless of our childish snobbery, in warm weather, church doors were thrown open and music floated into the streets. We were serenaded by music that was soft and sweet or so loud you couldn't help tapping your toes to the beat.

The church my family attended was Carters Chapel AMEZ, originally located in a small, red brick building on Bedford Avenue at Somers Street. Even though it lacked air-conditioning and central heating, it was not rundown or dirty. Later our congregation moved to a large, black-domed, former Jewish Synagogue at Webster Avenue and Erin Street. We had a first and second floor, a two-level balcony, a full basement, and church office. It was splendid, and we were so proud on the day, during Sunday services, we said goodbye to the old church and proudly marched right down the hill to our new place.

I'm sure I haven't mentioned all of the churches on The Hill, but my point is that we were a God-loving people, who spent many hours singing praises and getting ready to go home to Glory. The music coming from the churches was enough to make a rock cry. If you were not moved by the fiery sermons of the ministers, you had a hole in your soul.

9.2: Wesley Center AME Zion Church on Centre Avenue

9.3: Warren Methodist Church, Centre Avenue

9.4: Triumph Church in Lower Hill (c. 1968-1972)

9.5: Ebenezer Baptist Church on Wylie Avenue (c. 1940-1960)

9.6: Central Baptist Church under construction at the corner of
Wylie Avenue and Kirkpatrick Street (c. 1942-1949)

9.7: Monumental Baptist Church on Wylie Avenue (c. 1940-1947)

9.8: Macedonia Baptist Church on Bedford Avenue (c. 1938-1970)

9.9: Bethel AME Church on Elm Street (c. 1950-1957). Bethel AME Church the oldest and most beautiful church, was located in The Hill. As can be seen in the top photograph, it was a solid and imposing building. Where Bethel AME members saw a family, a home, and a social and spiritual center, city officials saw a slum to clear. Then-city council member George E. Evans wrote in an editorial in the 1940s that most of the buildings in the Lower Hill had "outlived their usefulness," so "there would be <u>no social loss</u> if they were all destroyed."

9.10: Bethel AME Church in ruins (July 1957). It serves as an example of the callous disregard for the condition of buildings that stood in the way of the "renewal" juggernaut. Interestingly, a Catholic church with a White congregation was left standing even though it was in the same vicinity as Bethel AME.[12]

---

12 Today, a group has come together to seek reparations for the destruction of the church. According to the group, Bethel was the first "colored" church in The Hill and certainly had been worthy of preservation. Other store front congregations led by un-ordained ministers did exist, but Bethel became a key center of worship, community life and social activism.

9.11: Kether Torah Synagogue. This is the synagogue to which my congregation moved. (c. 1940-1950)

9.12: Beth Hamedrish Hagodol Synagogue on right (c. 1955)

Churches as Meeting Spaces

Before addressing the nature of worship in Black churches, I want to mention their role as meeting houses for many important events held by Black non-religious organizations. Well into the 1960s, White-owned hotels, convention sites, and meeting halls would not rent their facilities to Black organizations, no matter how well-regarded the Black groups may have been. That meant we had to find a place to host our events. Some venues were spacious enough to accommodate large groups, but they were usually associated with dance and liquor. That meant that many people would not frequent those places on supposed moral grounds. The only places left were often the banquet halls or basements of churches. As a former photographer, I photographed many awards being handed out in the basements of churches. Thank God they were available. They allowed us to hold our important events without begging to rent White-owned facilities. In the face of adversity, the Black church allowed us to meet in dignity. Can I get an AMEN?

Worship

One year, a White friend of mine who was the pastor for a small, non-integrated church was invited to preach at a Black church. He called for my advice about what he should do and what he should talk about. I told him that I could not and would not choose the topic of his sermon, but he should, above all, speak from his heart.

When we had dinner together after his experience, he exclaimed, "I think I'm in love."

"Oh? Does your wife know?"

Laughing, he said, "It's not a person. I'm in love with the Black church where I spoke. I did what you suggested. I spoke from my heart about love and Jesus and salvation. I was scared to death, so I closed my eyes to steady myself and continued to speak. Suddenly I heard someone say, 'Uh huh. PREACH, brother.' I opened my eyes and saw a woman repeat the same statement. She was talking to ME. I was stunned. Nobody in my church has ever uttered a word when I was preaching. I looked at the preacher who had invited me; he just smiled and said, 'Uh Huh. Go on now.' I said another few words, and someone shouted, 'AMEN.' Then someone said, 'Go on, Brother. Tell it like it is.' They were talking to me. I felt so *good*. I just kept on saying the truth of what I was feeling. I had never felt anything like that in my life. I'm afraid I spoke too long. I kept preaching for more than fifteen minutes. Was that too long?"

"No," I assured him. "They probably were surprised that you quit that soon. Most Black preachers speak a lot longer than that."

Then he said, "After I spoke, their choir sang. First a slow song, and I cried like a baby. It was so beautiful. I have never heard anything so moving. Then they did a fast song. Oh my *God* I was up dancing and shouting just like everybody else. I have never been so moved by a religious ceremony in my life. Is it always that way?"

When I replied in the affirmative, my friend looked a little sad. "Wow. I am in love. Next week I will be back at my old church in South Hills, and it is my turn to give the sermon. I'm only the assistant pastor, but I think I'll follow your advice as I prepare my sermon. Thank you."

When I talked to my friend a few weeks later, I asked, "How was the return to your own church?"

"Disappointing. I prepared a powerful sermon, borrowing from the one I had delivered at the Black church. I made a profound statement and waited for a response. They all just sat and looked at me. I tried again; same results. I thought I could get them started, because of that 'call and response' thing you told me about. I thought if I primed the pump, so to speak, I would get a response; so I said something I had heard in the Black church. I said, 'Can I get a witness?' Now instead of just staring at me, they were staring at one another. I felt naked and embarrassed. As I sat down, the music part of the service started. I was struck by how unanimated the congregation was; how the choir director really wasn't doing much more than swinging his arms. The folks in the choir seemed rather bored. I think that was because the music was very dry. Only the choir sang. At the Black church, everybody including the ushers and the preacher was singing. What a difference. I was so disappointed."[13]

"I'm so sorry that happened to you."

He shook his head and replied, "Oh, no need to feel sorry for me. I'm okay. I called my friend at the Black church and asked if I could come back. I'm now the assistant pastor at a *Black* church. How about that!"

Post-Script

When Africans were brought as slaves to America, they were forced to abandon their own religions and accept a distorted form of Christianity; one designed to serve the interests of slave owners. Slaves were told their ascent into Heaven was in direct proportion to the extent of their suffering on Earth. Thus, the pain and anguish of slavery should be gratefully accepted, because the master, in inflicting suffering, was really helping slaves attain salvation. White preachers spoke eloquently about living a good and sin-free life, while having no shame or guilt about enslaving Blacks.

Even as Blacks were taught about Heaven, salvation, and a forgiving God, we were forbidden to sit next to Whites in their magnificent cathedrals with fancy pipe organs. We could not taste sacramental wine or eat consecrated bread. Then, oblivious to the hypocrisy, Whites pitied Blacks for their small, often impoverished churches. Yet there was no need for pity. Under these inhuman conditions, we forged our own ways to lift our voices and our spirits toward heaven. And, we taught our children the difference between right and wrong. And, we were fully capable of living moral and ethical lives.

---

13 My friend's experience captures so well a cultural difference in speech patterns that I have observed on many occasions. I return to this point again in a discussion of cultural norms that continue to create tensions between Whites and Blacks.

9.13: Wedding party in front of altar of Church of God in Christ (c. 1930-1950)

9.14: Wedding Reception (February 1945)

9.15: Church Service (c. 1960)

9.16: Funeral at Wesley Center A.M.E. Zion Church, (c. 1945-1950).

CHAPTER 10

Education

Background—The Fight for Education

The Pennsylvania State Temporary Commission on Urban Colored Population, charged with the task of studying the status of Pennsylvania Negros in 1943 stated: "The Continental Congress considered it useless to educate Negroes and for a long time it was a felony for a Negro "to be caught with a book in his hands." The Acts of 1802 and 1804, which provided free education for poor children, did not mention the Negro.

When free public education finally came to Pennsylvania, Blacks were excluded. It was up to Pittsburgh Blacks to educate their own children.

Initially, Pittsburgh Blacks did not ask that their children be allowed to attend school with White children. Certain that such a request would be refused, they asked that Black children throughout Pittsburgh be allowed to attend a school operated by Blacks and paid for by the Central Board of Education. The request was ignored. Prominent members of Pittsburgh's Black community mounted a sustained campaign for the education of Black children and finally succeeded in 1837 when the Board opened a school for Negro children. Records about the first "colored" schools are sketchy and contradictory, but Bethel AME claims that it had the first such school; a second opened in 1838 in Litenberger Alley. These schools moved to different locations over the next few years.

In 1854, Act 610, Section 24 directed Pennsylvania districts to set up schools for "Negro and Mulatto children."[14] Therefore, in 1855 the Pittsburgh Board of Education directed that a "colored school" be opened by April 1st. The school was established in the Wesleyan Methodist Church on Wiley Street. In 1867, the Board erected a new elementary school building on Miller Street in The Hill and dubbed it the "Pittsburgh Colored School." Apparently the school employed both Black and White teachers to instruct the Negro children. By 1881, as a result of a petition by The Pittsburgh Central Board of Education, the Miller School was closed, and the

---

14 I find the distinction made between "Negro" and "Mulatto" children to be interesting. The term referred to Blacks who had one Black and one White parent. Whites considered the term *Mulatto* to be more complementary, because it indicated that a person was "almost White" and had more acceptable features. Blacks did not use that term on any regular basis. For Blacks, the acceptable words were Negro and Colored.

Black children were then "integrated" into neighborhood schools. Of course, Black children were still in segregated schools, because all of Pittsburgh's neighborhoods were racially segregated.[15] With the closure of the Miller School, the hiring of Black teachers stopped until 1936.

Despite attempts to deny a quality education to Black youngsters, and despite the fact that Black teachers could not find employment in Pittsburgh Public schools from 1881 to 1936, the Black community did manage to make certain that Black youngsters got as good an education as White youngsters. At least that was the case prior to 1958. Elsewhere I have given a detailed account of the Pittsburgh Board of Education's racist policies.[16] What follows is my recollected experience of education as a Black child and young adult.

Education Denied—My Parents' Generation

There seems to be a misconception that by growing up in The Hill I was surrounded by people of little intelligence or ability. Lack of schooling, however, does not equate to inability. In the early years of Black migration to The Hill, many residents came from southern states where it was legal to limit the education of Blacks and poor Whites.

My parents were forced to stop their education at the 6th grade, which was considered normal and adequate for Black youngsters. I want to state very clearly that had my parents and many of their generation in The Hill been given the opportunity, they would have excelled at high school and college.

My father was scary at math. When he worked behind the counter at various grocery stores, including the two he owned, he tallied the cost of customers' purchases using the stub of a pencil he kept behind his ear. He could write down a huge column of numbers and without hesitation add the entire column in a few seconds. I tried to do that and was so slow Dad laughed. Of course, I had to show him up, so the next day I brought one of those huge paper-fed adding machines to the store.

"Dad, I'm afraid you may be making mistakes using the manual method of adding up people's purchases. You should use an adding machine."

"I don't need an adding machine. Been doing this all my life, and it works just fine."

Determined to show off the value of my high school education, I said, "Tell you what. Let's have a contest. You pull some canned items from the shelf; I'll say go, and we'll both add up the items. If I do it faster, you promise to at least try the adding machine. Okay?"

Dad agreed and the contest began. I proudly finished before Dad. "See I was faster."

Dad smiled and said, "But your total is wrong." Damn! In my haste, I had entered one price incorrectly.

Agreeing to a rematch, we started again with a new group of items. This time I was more cautious. As my fingers flew across the keys, I made no mistakes. I finished and looked up at my father who was standing with his arms crossed and his pencil behind his ear. We had the

---

15 This residential segregation was contradictory, because Pittsburgh was one of the first United States cities to pass fair housing laws. Despite the law, illegal discriminatory practices were openly carried out. The city passed Fair Housing laws in 1955.

16 Ralph Proctor, *Racial Discrimination against Black Teachers and Professionals in the Pittsburgh Public School System: 1834-1973* (Learning Moments Press, 2021.)

same total, but he was faster. Obviously taking high school math had not made me better at arithmetic than his 6th grade education. Dad enjoyed math and used to teach my sons shortcuts that my teachers had never even mentioned.

My mother had a different kind of intelligence. Had she been given the opportunity, she would have made an excellent school teacher or psychologist. I was an active, inquisitive youngster who would always have been underfoot as Mom tended to household tasks. In the interest of self-preservation, Mom would sit me down with a book and challenge me to reproduce the letters. I finished that so fast, she started teaching me the alphabet; then how to spell simple words; then how to print them on paper. I thought this was great fun. Because of Mom, I could read and print before I entered kindergarten. My teachers were pretty freaked out at my leaving "I love you" notes on their desks.

As I got older and pestered Mom with "why" questions, she drew upon her instincts to appeal to my logical mind. At one time, I asked why my older sister was being spoiled by having special privileges. Mom explained, "Earlyne is a girl and girls require special attention." That made sense; so I went away but paid close attention to Earlyne's development. When I decided she was old enough for the spoiling to end, I announced, "Mom, now it's my turn for special privileges."

"Well, you're right. But now we have a new baby girl and baby girls need even more care. So, when she is old enough to take care of herself, it will be your turn." Once again I was satisfied with her logic and went off to play.

Before I knew it, I was leaving for the Army. "Hey, Mom, what happened to my turn for being spoiled? How could you placate me for so long?"

"Well, you could be such a pest. But I realized by giving you an explanation that made sense to you, I'd get some peace and quiet—at least for a while."

"Nice trick, Mom."

She just gave me a "whatever-it-takes" smile.

Mom had an innate ability to relate to children, to engage them in learning, to make them feel okay. As mentioned in Chapter 4, her kindness and wisdom earned her the title of Miss Mommy among the neighborhood children.

As you might imagine, my parents, along with most others on The Hill, valued education and wanted their children to have opportunities denied to them.

Education—A Community Value

Education was an important community norm. There were several very good public schools in the area. The teachers were excellent and made certain that students learned and learned well. Our parents helped with homework and made sure it was done before we were permitted to play. Each summer a team of teachers fanned out through the neighborhood searching for youngsters who were old enough to be in kindergarten but who were not yet enrolled. Each level of education prepared us for the next.

The pressure on my generation to excel was tremendous. People in the community put an extra burden on kids who appeared to have some talent. Adults who had not been successful themselves, or whose children had not measured up, expected us to prove that Black kids could be as smart as White children. In Elementary and Middle school, children were expected to study hard and "be somebody." We fearfully carried the hopes of the community on our young shoulders. My mom told me the same story that other parents told their children. "Honey, if you want to get a good job, you have to be twice as good as White kids; otherwise the White people won't hire you. If you're twice as good, they might take a chance on you." That sucks!

I was expected to behave in school. Dad told me that everyone in the family had a job. His job was to go to work and earn money for the family. My mother's job was to use the money he made to take care of the family. My sisters and I had a job, too. That job was to go to school, keep our mouths shut unless the teacher asked us to speak, be a good student, and bring home good grades. I took my job seriously, because not doing my job did not mean getting fired; it meant getting my ass whipped.

At Vann Elementary school, corporal punishment was the norm. If you misbehaved you got spanked by the teachers. In fact, if one kid misbehaved, it was likely that the entire class got an ass-whipping. (Trouble makers were often victims of playground vengeance.) Yes, some kids misbehaved, but most of us did not. We were taught that education was vital to our survival.[17]

Elementary School

I attended Van Elementary School where we had excellent Black and White teachers.[18] I loved most of my teachers and appreciated their dedication. Thanks Florine Robinson. Thanks Gladys Stallings, my music teacher. When my voice changed in the fifth grade, she cried like a baby. Hearing my new, deep, croaking voice, she kept saying, "My beautiful first soprano; my beautiful first soprano. Now he's an alto." I felt bad, but what could I do? Adolescence brought an end to my voice lessons.

---

17 Corporal punishment in Pennsylvania public schools was not officially banned until 2005. As of today, it has not been banned in private schools.

18 Vann was one of only a few schools in the city that hired Blacks. So they were the best academically prepared and the best in their commitment to their students' education.

10.1: Vann Elementary School (c. 1940-1960)

Special thanks go to John Brewer, my mentor in more ways than one. You see, although I was getting very positive feedback from my teachers, and my parents were proud of my getting good grades, the neighborhood boys had a different view of being "book smart." I was constantly pushed, shoved, and taunted with names like "*sissy,*" "*four eyes,*" and "*bookworm.*" Heeding my parents' orders to behave in school, I did not fight back. Besides, to tell the truth, I was afraid to fight back.

Tony was my constant tormentor, chasing me home after school. Somehow, John Brewer, my gym teacher, found out what was going on. One day as I entered the gym, he stopped me. "I hear you make good grades; all 'A's'. Is that right?" I told him I did.

"Do the other boys mess with you; do they call you names?"

When I admitted that they teased me and pushed me around, he asked, "How does that make you feel?"

"Bad and sad. It makes me want to quit making 'A's' so they'll leave me alone; so Tony will stop chasing me home, and my daddy will stop being ashamed of me," I blurted out.

"No, no," Mister Brewer replied. "It's important that you keep making good grades. All the teachers think you're special; that you can be somebody; you got to keep making good grades. Instead of making bad grades, I have a better idea about stopping them from bothering you. I want you to kick one of their asses so they'll leave you alone. Can you fight?"

I was stunned. A *teacher* telling me to beat somebody up? I stammered, "I can't do that. I can't fight. I'll get in trouble."

Brewer smiled. "Don't you worry about the trouble; I'll take care of that. I bet your dad will be happy when Tony stops chasing you home. Come to the gym every day after school. I'll teach you how to handle yourself."

I spent the next several weeks doing pushups, pull-ups, running, and building my strength. Then Mr. Brewer taught me how to wrestle and punch. When my training was over, he put one hand on my shoulder, looked me in the eyes, and said, "Now, the next time somebody calls you a name, I want you to KICK HIS ASS."

As fate would have it, the day came sooner than I thought as I entered Brewer's gym. "There he is. SISSY. BOOKWORM," shouted one of my tormentors. Mr. Brewer heard the words, grabbed the kid by the arm, and said, "Oh, you think Ralph is a sissy huh? Well, *on the mats.*" My mentor kept a few gym mats on the floor in the corner where kids had to wrestle one another. "Ralph, you on the mat, too. Best man wins."

As I stepped on the mat, Mr. Brewer took my arm and whispered, "Now *kick his ass.*" I was surprised how easy it was to toss the kid around. Soon I had him on his back and was pounding his face while screaming like a maniac, releasing the pain from all the years of torment. Mr. Brewer had to pull me off the kid who was now scared to death and covered with bright red blood from his nose. I looked around and saw all the boys staring in quiet disbelief. Brewer made us shake hands and said, "Okay, now you gonna call Ralph any other names?"

"I ain't gonna call him nothing. He's *CRAZY.*"

Brewer winked at me and said, "Now go on and make as many 'A's' as you want. Ain't anybody in THIS school going to bother you."

The next afternoon I waited for Tony and kicked his ass, too. Many years later I thanked Mr. Brewer for teaching me to fight and for being my mentor. He said I had already paid the debt, in full. I hope that is true.

One other memory from Vann Elementary doesn't quite fit the stereotype that all poor Black kids went to school hungry. While that may have been true for some kids back then and is certainly true for many children now, my classmates and I walked home for lunch and were generally well fed. We did have a free milk program, so all of us got milk and some sort of a snack in the morning. By the 5th or 6th grade, I was fortunate to be among those who got chocolate milk. Several of us were chosen to help count the milk when it arrived, assign it to classrooms, and push the milk carts to each room. We chosen few felt very special. I think it was the chocolate milk.

10.2: Children and teens gathered at Madison Elementary School playground across from Herron Hill Park (c. Fall of 1955)

10.3: First graders on 1st day of class at Crescent Elementary School

10.4: Art Class at Herron Hill Junior High

10.5: Music class (c. 1946-1949)

Junior High School

I attended Herron Hill Junior High for 7ᵗʰ through 9ᵗʰ grade.[19] As was the case at Vann, most of the students were Black, but it was a rough school that brought together kids from neighborhoods that did not get along. Most of the teachers were White. Among the Black teachers were Elmo Calloway, Jody Harris, Herb Parrish, and Florence Williams. Regardless of race, the teachers pushed us to do our best. Consequently, we received a very good education.

One example of teacher dedication was Gladys Donahue who had been teaching at Herron Hill long before I arrived. She was a matronly-looking White woman with a heart of gold. I was still a shy kid, and even though I was a gang member, Mrs. Donahue took an interest in me. One day she surprised me by saying she did not understand what I had just said. I was stunned; no one had ever said that to me; I spoke like most of the folks in my community. Most certainly I did not have a southern accent, because Mom and Dad believed that a southern (and Pittsburgh) accent marked you as stupid or backwards. So, what the hell was Mrs. Donahue talking about? Nevertheless, at her request, I repeated myself.

"Oh, did you know there is another way to say that?" She then taught me a new way of saying what I had just said. That began a series of lessons that changed my slight "Ghetto Drawl," my "swallowing" word-endings, some slight mispronunciations, and grammar mistakes. Next came impromptu lessons that entailed layering another way of speaking over my natural language. I was being taught another version of English without being made to feel that the way I already spoke was inferior. It was, as far as I was concerned, just a funny-sounding way of speaking that "proper" (White) people used. That did not change my way of communicating outside of school. I hardly ever used the new words I had learned, or so I thought. By the time I got to High school I scored very high on Standard English tests even though I did not know the "rules." I was speaking Standard English "by ear" in the same way I played the piano and the bass. Mrs. Donahue's lessons came in handy as I continued my life's journey.

Years later, when I was studying at The University of Pittsburgh, an anthropology professor accompanied me on a visit to my parents. On our way back to Oakland, the professor asked, "Do you do that on purpose?"

Huh??

"I noticed that as soon as we entered your parents' home your speech pattern changed, including word usage. Now that we're back in the car you're speaking the way I'm used to hearing you. I was wondering if you do that on purpose and why."

"When I'm with my parents and my friends I speak the language I grew up with. When I'm with you academic types, I speak your language. If I did otherwise you would make negative inferences about my intellectual capacity. You use jargon that is specific to academia and words that are far bigger than necessary, as if you are trying to show off your language acuity. That kind of speaking is totally out of place in my parents' home. Why would I show them disrespect

19 Herron Hill Junior High was in the Middle Hill as was Madison Elementary school. Although Madison was situated in the middle of a Black community, it had no Black teachers until about 20 years after the Board of Education began to hire Black teachers. It seems that many of the well-to-do Black residents did not want Blacks teaching their youngsters. Or so the story goes.

by using academic language? Language is just a tool. Would you be surprised if my parents' native tongue was Spanish, and I spoke that language with them? In fact, it's an automatic process. I have no need to think about it." While he pondered that, I continued, "Let me give you a couple of illustrations.

> I have a friend who is one of the best Scrabble® players I've ever met. She absolutely trounces me every time we play. Sometimes she makes a long-assed word while I am trying to get enough letters to spell CAT. When I scream, she says, 'Are you challenging my word?' Hell, no. I know it's a damn word, but who the hell but *you* would ever even *think* about that word?"

> Another example comes from when I first started co-hosting a radio show. My college-educated, very articulate wife would be waiting when I got home. She held a yellow legal pad on which she had written every big word I had used during the broadcast. She'd say, "Honey, you don't need those big words when you're just talking to people. You're not giving a lecture at Pitt. You're talking to the people you grew up with."

> I knew what she meant. I did not want to be one of those Black folks who go off to college and forget their roots. I am still from The Hill, and my people are just as intelligent, just as capable as the folks from academia.

> One day I was visiting with some old friends who still live on The Hill. They said, "You know what? You ain't like some of those other ones who went off to college and got an education and now think they better than us. You just like you was when you was a kid living on Wylie Avenue." I wear that compliment with more pride than any introduction to any award I ever received.

After I received my Ph.D., I called Mrs. Donahue. She already knew about my doctorate. She had kept a scrapbook in which she preserved the accomplishments of all "her kids." When I asked why she had done so, she said, "I saw something different about your generation of Black youngsters. You were more aware." She knew we would face the same racial barriers our parents had, but believed we would not accept the same treatment. She decided to prepare us for leadership roles and that is exactly what she did. She groomed us, made sure we were ready, and then created situations that forced us to use the skills she helped us develop.

I became proficient in Standard American English; English of the Hood, and Academic English. Depending on the social context, I shift between these versions of English and may mix them when I'm around people with whom I feel comfortable. At times, I may inadvertently slip into my "birth language," as was the case when I turned down a promotion to an administrative position in higher education. Realizing what I had done, I called the official who had offered the position and apologized for not using the "appropriate" language in turning down the position. I then offered a more formally worded rejection of the offer, but explained my first response came from my cultural heritage and was the way I would turn down a friend's offer. The administrator replied, "Actually, I liked your "turn down" better than your apologized version. I'm honored that you responded to me as though I'm a friend."

Like the administrator, White folks can understand the language I speak around friends and family. Unlike the administrator, many judge that way of speaking as a sign of inferior intelligence or lack of education. I find this frustrating and always challenge such prejudice as I did when I heard a White man complaining about the way a Black, inner-city woman spoke. I asked if he had difficulty understanding what the woman was trying to communicate. When he said he understood her, I retorted, "Well, if you understood her, what the hell was so wrong with the way she spoke?"

The years I spent in public education in The Hill were relatively free of negative encounters with White teachers. Elementary school staff seemed to be comfortable with Black kids. The same was true in junior high, except for one White student-teacher. Although I had written a one-page paper while sitting right in front of her, she claimed it was plagiarized and gave me an "F." Of course, I argued and as we were yelling at each another, my regular teacher heard the commotion and intervened. After telling both of us to shut up, he looked at my paper and said, "Give him his damn 'A.' That's the way he writes all the time. He's a bright student. Before you challenge one of my students, you check with me first." Later I heard that she said no eighth grader could write that well. One of the Black teachers said, "What she was really saying is that no eighth grade Black kid can write like that."

Not all White teachers at Herron Hill were as gifted as Mrs. Donahue, but they taught us in a way that did not turn us off to education. Thank God for the best teachers—both Black and White—at Herron Hill Junior High School. Without them, we would have been ill-prepared to survive the virulent racism we would face in the hellhole called Schenley High School.

High School

At Schenley, I began to hate school, because of the blatant racism exhibited by Whites who inhabited this "excellent" school. Many of the White students were our "friends" in school, but would not say "hello" when we passed on the streets after the school bell rang dismissal. The only Black person on staff was the janitor. The teachers favored the White kids. The athletic coaches gave all the best opportunities to the White kids. My friends and I began to mount protests and, as a result, I was the second Black student elected as class president. My Black predecessor came from *Sugar Top*; he was very light complexioned, had light-colored hair, and dressed quite nicely. The administration was surprised and disconcerted by the election of an "ordinary" rather than "model" Negro. The battle was on. We protested everything from not being called on to answer questions in class, to not being chosen for the best spots on athletic teams, to not having Black teachers or staff people. The principal was happy to see us graduate and leave.

10.6: Knott Manor Apartments on Centre Avenue (c. 1950-1970). Black students had to hold their prom here because other venues, where White students held their separate prom, were not open to Black students.

10.7: Schenley High (c. 1940-1955)

The guidance counselors thought it was their job to prepare Black girls to be housewives, secretaries, or maybe nurses. In the rare event that a girl went on to college, it was assumed she did so to find a "good catch" to marry. Black boys were counselled to work with their hands.

My dad, who could build a house from the ground up, refused to teach me those skills. He wanted me to work with my mind, not my hands. As an adult, I had to pay folks to do the types of repairs he did. Thanks a lot, Dad. I finally hired myself out as a common laborer for a few bucks a day so I could learn how to use tools. But having been denied the opportunity for advanced education, my parents were determined I would finish high school and go to college.

One day, I was called into my so-called Guidance counselor's office where she began the conversation with, "Well Mr. Proctor, what are you going to do after high school?"

"Go to college."

Removing her glasses, she asked, "Why would you do that? No one is going to hire you to use your brain. You know they don't hire Negros for those positions. Why don't you just go the Connelly Trade School? Then you could always get a job. Besides, your grades aren't good enough to get you into college. You have to be realistic about your future."

"What are you talking about? I'm a straight 'A' student. Why wouldn't I be able to get into college? Do you even know who I am?"

She looked at me with a condescending smile and said, "Of course I know who you are, Kenneth. I have all your records right here in front of me."

I grabbed the folder, took a look, and said, "My name is RALPH Proctor, the folder you have in front of you is for KENNETH Proctor, maybe you should talk to HIM. I AM GOING TO COLLEGE."

The dreams of many Black youngsters ended in the office of this ignorant guidance counselor. As a result of such treatment we Black kids decided we could not depend on the "system." We knew we had only ourselves, our parents, some friends, and neighbors to help us. Perhaps this was good because we were certainly more self-reliant than many of our White friends. We had no other choice.

Thanks to our truly dedicated teachers, my friends and I had been better prepared for the rigors of high school than many of our peers at Schenley High. Because of segregation in Pittsburgh, excellent Black teachers taught at Black Schools. At Herron Hill Junior High these dedicated teachers knew what we would face in White schools. So they made sure we were better prepared than students coming from other schools. Thus, in spite of the prejudice we encountered at Schenley, my friends and I could continue to prepare for college. In addition, many professionals lived in The Hill, so we had chances to talk with people who were already employed in our fields of interest. We could talk about our dream career and knew we didn't have to settle for trade school if that wasn't our goal.

Somewhere along the line, John Brewer and other Black school teachers began to compare notes about those of us who were gang members, athletes, and semi-thug leaders. They began to talk to us about giving up the gang stuff and going on to college.

It is one thing to talk to a group of gang members about college; it was another thing to translate that talk into action. Many of us had already surpassed our parent's educational achievements just by entering high school. Except for Jim Tyler, we would be the first of our families to go to college. So the Cobras morphed into a college exploratory group. Aware of the pervasive racism in White colleges, we decided to focus on Black colleges where we would actually be welcomed, have Black instructors, and feel at home on campus. One of the Cobras belonged to the Centre Avenue YMCA and convinced a staff member to arrange for college recruiters to come with films and printed materials to help us understand what was involved. Eventually, as five of us neared the end of high school, we decided to give college a try. Receiving little help from White teachers and guidance counselors, most of us pursued college scholarships on our own.

Our lives were about to change dramatically as we prepared for college. All around The Hill, hopes of a new life began to overshadow the attraction of gangs. The Cobras slowly died away. The Bobcats morphed into a community service group. Other gangs lost their leadership. A new day was dawning. We did not know what the future held, but it looked much brighter than even a new gang jacket.[20]

---

20 I have written about high school from my experiences. I do not mean to suggest, however, that Black girls did not receive similar encouragement to believe in themselves and what they could accomplish.

10.8: The author (far right) with Schenley High School students "Ed" Lucenti, Elaine Luick, Frances LeDonne receiving an award (c. February - March 1956)

College—The First Time

My buddies and I applied to two Black universities—Howard and Lincoln. Lincoln University accepted all of us, but I was the only one to be accepted at Howard, which offered me a full scholarship and a campus job. My only cost would be traveling to the school.

I decided to forgo the Howard offer in order to stay with my friends. On our bus ride to Lincoln, I read over my enrollment papers and noticed a check from a finance company made out to the university. Suddenly it hit me—my parents had once again sacrificed their financial future for me. DAMN! If I had accepted the Howard offer, they wouldn't have had to pay anything for my college education. Worse yet, by the time they paid off the present loan, it would be time to get another. Feeling like crap, I decided to call Howard and ask if I could still accept their offer.

After taking care of some paper work at Lincoln, I found a pay phone and called Howard. The response was devastating. My scholarship had been awarded to someone else. It was Lincoln or nothing.

To make matters worse, I started having a recurring nightmare. I was climbing a ladder that seemed to go on forever. Disembodied voices would be calling, "Come On. You can do it!" I would get exhausted and, barely hanging on to the rungs, I'd try to go back down. As I'd begin to descend, I'd see the faces of Doc Bridges, Officer Clark, Mrs. Bowman, Mr. Charlie, and some of my teachers. They were yelling, "Don't quit. Keep climbing. Remember the dreams you promised to keep!" With a pounding heart and spinning head, I'd start climbing with no idea of where I'd end up. Then I would wake up, soaked in sweat.

I had to do something. Lincoln's business office told me if I dropped out right then, I could get a refund of my parents' money. I promised myself that I would return when I could do so without my parents going into debt for my education.

I had been home about a week when there was a knock on my parents' front door. A group of neighborhood youngsters had heard that I dropped out of college and came to tell me that I had to go back. If I couldn't make it, neither could they. DAMN! Talk about pressure. I made up a story about being drafted by the Army. They bought my lie, because they knew many of our neighbors had been drafted. Actually, an "UNCLE SAM WANTS YOU" letter was not far away. I had been reading that the GI bill would pay my way to college and that seemed like the answer to my problems. In exchange for three years of my life, I would have a chance to grow up, see some of the world, take some classes, and have enough money to attend college. Less than six months later, I had cast my lot with Uncle Sam.

College—The Second Time

In September 1961, with a mix of excitement and apprehension, I enrolled in the University of Pittsburgh as a second term freshman. Having completed my military duty, I was ready to fulfill my promise to return to college when I could pay my own way. With money from the G.I. Bill, my savings, some scholarship money, and a loan from an angel named Goldia Dargan at the Urban League of Pittsburgh, I once again entered academia—but not the supportive environment of a Black college.

I walked into the office of my assigned advisor, a young White woman and handed her my carefully planned schedule. Smiling, she looked at the papers for so long I felt compelled to ask, "Is anything wrong?"

Looking up, she said, "Well, I need to get some more information from you. You plan on taking 15 credits this term, right?"

"Yes. I had planned on taking more but decided not to, at least not the first term. I need to take more than 12 credits per term to make up for lost time."

"I see," she said. "I also see that you have a job here at Pitt and will be working about 32 hours per week."

"Yes, I have to work. While my GI Bill will pay for my tuition, it does not pay for my daily living expenses, including my car payment."

After studying the papers some more, she said, "Well, as your advisor I have to be concerned about your success. Working almost full-time and taking more than a full-time load of courses is going to be very hard."

"I have given this some thought. Since I was at the top of my high school class I thought I could handle the load. Besides, I took—"

"Well, I don't see how you could possibly be successful with such a heavy work and school load," she interrupted. "After all, you are the product of a *Negro* education." Clearly she meant an inferior Black school, so naturally an inferior education.

I was livid. I had fought racists in the Army and in the streets of southern towns. I had thought more educated people would be less prejudiced. Obviously I was wrong. Equally obvious, was a need to fight racism here and now.

"You don't know a damn thing about me. You have no idea about the quality of the education I received in those *Negro* schools. Well let me tell you, the education I received at those *Negro* schools and delivered by *Negro* teachers was as good as and in many cases better than what you White folks received in your allegedly superior schools. I met and challenged many people like you when I was in the army and bested them. I attended college classes with White officers who were pissed that a Black PFC beat them in school. What the hell is it with you White folks who need to feel superior to us? Well guess what? You ain't! So from now on, when I come in here, I will say, 'Hello, here are the classes I am taking.' You will say, 'Hello,' and sign the papers. I will say "goodbye"; you will say "goodbye." I will leave. There is no reason for us to ever exchange any other words."

When I returned for the next semester, I had a White, male adviser. I calmly explained what had happened with the previous adviser. He assured me that he had no preconceived ideas about intelligence based on race. We had no difficulties.

I persevered at college and, after completing my Bachelor's degree, entered an advanced placement program. By passing a "Master's Equivalency Exam," I was admitted directly into doctoral candidacy and earned a Ph.D. in history.

Throughout my studies, I have pursued a deeper understanding of racism and its effects on education. Throughout my life I have sought opportunities to pass on both what I have learned academically, but also the important lessons I learned from my parents and other members of the community on The Hill.

10.9: Students in front of University of Pittsburgh's Cathedral of Learning. Notice that these students are light-skinned Blacks who were considered more "acceptable" than darker-skinned Blacks and therefore admitted to colleges.

Paying It Forward

One year, a White teacher in Pittsburgh asked for my help with resistance she was encountering to a lesson on Africa. I empathized, saying it's not unusual for White parents to resist having their children learn anything about Africa. "That's not it," she said. "The opposition is coming from Black parents and children. Maybe you can convince the students their African ancestry is nothing to be ashamed of."

When I agree to speak with the class, she warned me that one young man might be disruptive. "He denies he is African American. We're working on an art project that requires each student to make a mask reflecting a specific culture. He is working on an "Indian" mask because he says he is an *Indian Prince*. He refuses to participate in any discussions about Africa. He'll participate when we start talking about *his* people."

When I arrived at the class, a young Black boy walked in. "That's him," the teacher said. The youngster took a seat in the front row and immediately turned his back to me. The teacher reached out to turn him around and chastise him. I asked her to let him remain as he was and began my presentation. Soon the young man turned and was listening over his shoulder. I talked a bit more; he turned a bit more. I continued to speak; he turned completely around and began listening intently. When I finished my talk he raised his hand. "Mister, can I ask you a question?"

"Sure, ask away."

Staring into my eyes, he said, "From what you've been saying, Africans did a lot of things, and White people took the credit for them. Right?"

I told him he was correct and gave him a small booklet on Africa. A week later I heard from the teacher. "I just had to call you. You have made such a difference in that young man. He changed his mask from Indian to African. Now he is telling everybody that he is an African King."

This young boy's denial of his African heritage was not uncommon. Indeed, as a child I was oblivious to the ways in which the dominant culture creates images that demean subjugated groups in order to justify inhumane treatment. Unknowingly, my friends and I had been brainwashed by the official fiction perpetuated through our education system's teaching of Euro-centric history. Blacks and Native Americans were painted by the same brush as evil, stupid, uneducated, inferior savages who should consider themselves fortunate to be tolerated by the "educated, more highly evolved Europeans." Belatedly, I came to see the irony of watching movies and cheering for the cowboys instead of the Indians whose culture was obliterated as wantonly as African culture. Hidden by the sanitized narrative of the European's conquest of the new land was the history of victimization shared by Blacks and Native Americans—a history of enslavement, exploitation, the stealing and adoption of children, rape, torture, murder, and genocide.

In our youthful naiveté, we shamefully cheered for the cowboys instead of the Indians in the movies and never wanted to take on the role of Indians when we played cowboys and Indians. Even when we were being entertained or entertaining ourselves, we were victimized. That victimization led us to believe horrible things about "Indians" while they were taught to believe the same kinds of negative things about Blacks. We did not know enough to challenge these notions. Playtime is not just a time of idle, meaningless amusements. Play is a crucial way in which children learn and express their learning. Included in such learning is the assimilation of societally-sanctions norms—who are the good guys and who are the bad. Play was used in the Hitler Youth Camps, cultivating a generation of Germans to hate and fear the "non-Ayrian other." Such brainwashing paved the way to the death camps for 12 million "sub-human" others; 6 million of whom were Jewish.

When history is told from the conqueror's point of view, other cultures can be demeaned, the contributions by people of color can be omitted, and the injustices rationalized. The catalogue of racist bias in our White-washed history is long and painful.

The decimation of Native Americans....

Failure to acknowledge that 41 of the 56 signers of the Declaration of Independence were slave owners...

The exploitation of Chinese immigrants in the building of railroads in the western United States...

The omission of Latino and Latina contributions to the building of this country...

The hypocrisy of a Constitution that declares all men are created equal, while denying the humanity of Black slaves...

The disenfranchisement of Blacks and women from the fundamental right to vote...

Silence about George Washington as a slave owner, about Thomas Jefferson fathering children with his slave mistress, about Abraham Lincoln wanting to send all Blacks to Africa after emancipation...

No mention of the Greeks borrowing from Egyptian civilization and upon discovering this, portraying Egyptians as *White*...

No mention that Hippocrates learned about medicine from an Egyptian by the name of *Imhotep*...

No mention that two Egyptians (Abul Feda and Ali Omari) wrote that the world was round about 100 years before 1492 and that mariners from the West African kingdom of Mali had already sailed to the so-called *New World*...

No acknowledgement that many famous European "Master" painters were inspired by African Art...

No mention that one of the first universities in the world was established in Timbuktu in the African country of Mali...[21]

The list is virtually endless, beginning perhaps with the most egregious omission that the very earliest roots of human civilization took hold in Africa.

As a result of the civil rights movement, African American studies became integrated into colleges and universities. As multi-cultural education filtered into the public schools, Blacks began to comprehend how dis-information permeates U.S. culture. This, in turn, led to distrust of educational systems, government, and other institutions. As I've heard it expressed so many

---

21 It is worth noting that although my focus here is on racial discrimination, a comparable list of discrimination on the basis of gender could be compiled.

time by members of oppressed groups in this country and around the world, "If they lied to us about THAT, what other lies have they told?"

I have spent some time on this issue, because I have found that many folks do not understand the degree to which such duplicity is discussed among members of "minority "groups. The impact of these feelings cannot be minimized. Such are the feelings that create revolution. For this reason, the current backlash to the teaching of critical race theory[22] is dangerous. It sets the stage for suppressing accurate information about race in our country and allowing hateful dis-information to be promulgated.

I have spent most of my adult life combatting the omissions and distortions of White history that robbed Blacks of their heritage and instilled an unwarranted sense of racial shame. My historical research and teaching is my way of paying forward the sacrifices of my parents and the faith so many teachers placed in me.

Post-Script

When I was studying for my Ph.D., I had an opportunity to interview all my former elementary school teachers for my dissertation. I was deeply saddened as I heard how they had been rejected for teaching positions because the Pittsburgh Board of Education did not hire Blacks. Still they persisted and when they were finally hired, they were permitted to teach only in schools with predominantly Black student populations. That meant they were confined to The Hill. They never spoke of their struggles to our parents or us students. Even as they suffered the insults of racism, they never flagged in their commitment to give us an excellent educational foundation. To them, and the countless other dedicated teachers who have taught Black students, I say, "Thank you."

---

22 It should be noted that critical race theory is not taught in public schools. It is an academic discipline. Unfortunately, the term has been used as a code for eliminating information about slavery and other forms of discrimination from teaching of United States history. Students in my college courses on African American history, culture, and art often asked, "Why weren't we told about this earlier?" Given the current socio-political climate, it is likely that a new generation of students will learn a White-washed version of our country's past.

CHAPTER 11

Fun, Recreation, and Celebrations

Free-Range Play

In the olden days, before adults organized their children's leisure activities, we were left to entertain ourselves. Summer was the best time. We played outside—in our backyards, the open areas behind our houses, streets, and alleyways. These were carefree days, limited only by our imaginations and two rules.

Rule 1: "You better bring your butt home as soon as the street lights come on." Of course, we pushed this to the last possible moment. As twilight fell, a horde of kids made a mad dash for home, racing against the illumination of the streetlights.

Rule 2: "Make sure you have clean underwear on before you go outside." One day I asked, "Mommy, why you always worrying about my having on clean underwear that don't have no holes."

"Cause you might have an accident and have to go to the hospital."

"Huh?" What kind of accident?"

"You might get hit by a car."

"If I get hit by a car, it don't matter if I don't have no underwear. I ain't gonna be worried bout that."

Mom smiled and said, "But I would be embarrassed, because when the doctors treated you they would see that you have on dirty, holey underwear, and they'd think I don't take good care of my children."

"Okay. So I get hit by a car; they rush me to the hospital; you come to see me, and the man says, 'Mrs. Proctor, your son is totally messed up, but his underwear sure is CLEAN'."

Mom popped me upside the head.

Concerns about clean underwear aside, parents didn't worry much about our safety, nor did we kids. All adults in the neighborhood knew each child by name and family. They kept an eye on us, and the eyes, ears, and mouths were *everywhere*. Although we kids hated this, it kept us safe as we roamed blocks from home. There was no "stranger danger," because children were under the watchful eyes of the neighborhood women. It takes a whole village to raise a child, and our folks took that seriously.

We had plenty of things to do after completing our chores. Many of our toys were hand-made. We made stilts out of discarded lumber and menaced the neighborhood as evil giants.

We stomped on tin cans until they clung to our shoes. Then we clomped around making noise until our parents came out and smacked us for ruining our shoes. We found old worn-out brooms and cut off the handle for a game called Cricket. This involved cutting the broom stick into two pieces; one was about six to eight inches long, leaving the rest as a "bat." We stuck the shorter piece into the ground with one end sticking up. Using the longer stick, we'd strike the smaller one so it popped into the air, where you could then hit it again like a baseball to see how far it would go. When you got good you bounced the small stick as many times as you could before swinging at it. The distance the stick went was then multiplied by the number of times you bounced it. Mom was very good at this game.

We also used a knife to play a dumb game called "mumbly peg." Girls played Jacks or with baby dolls. Many of those dolls were *black* as White dolls did not appear in my neighborhood until well into the 1950s. We all played hopscotch. There were rag-tag baseball games played in empty lots; I think at least the catcher had a mitt. We played tackle football with absolutely no equipment except for a beat-up football. We made wooden guns that shot huge rubber bands that we had cut from old inner tubes. We flew kites; some home-made; others purchased for a few cents from a drug store or Shays' grocery.

We also had commercial toys much like those that White kids had, except cheaper because they came from the Five and Dime stores. We had scooters, wagons, and bikes. Most of the bikes were second hand or assembled by one ingenious young man who salvaged discarded bikes and used the parts to build new ones.

During the evenings and in the winter, we played endless hours of Monopoly and card games like Old Maid, Fish, and Double Solitaire. Of course we read and traded comic books. Between homework, chores, and fun, we were rarely bored.

A Bit of Mischievous Fun

During summer months, when my friends and I spent much time outside, we were frequently visited by White social workers. Speaking in hushed tones, they asked strange, leading questions about our lives and our parents. Liking the attention, we soon discovered that the social workers would give us money when their inquisitions were over. The sadder our stories were, the better the money. Our fathers would have killed us had they known about our outlandish tales. Dad worked full-time as a butcher and part-time as a handyman. Most of my friends also had fathers at home, but the social workers seemed to like hearing about absentee fathers. So we told them our dads were not home most of the time or that they visited only on weekends to drop off some food. As soon as the social workers left, we divided up the loot and headed to Shay's grocery store to fill our mouths and pockets with goodies. We wolfed them down before going home so there was no evidence of our misdeeds.[23]

---

23 As an adult, I realize our lies may have contributed to the negative stereotypes about absentee, deadbeat fathers. But the far-too-eager, prying social workers should have known better. For years, "native" informants lied to anthropologists and other experts. So, if you are inclined to condemn our dishonesty perhaps the greater offense was committed by professionals who offered their "findings" without verification. I have read several books written by White "experts" about Black lives and culture. Yet, most of them never lived among us, so how would they know about us?

Organized Play

In addition to our free-ranging activities, van loads of kids were often ferried to special events like the circus or a ball game. Two blocks from my home was a bowling alley.

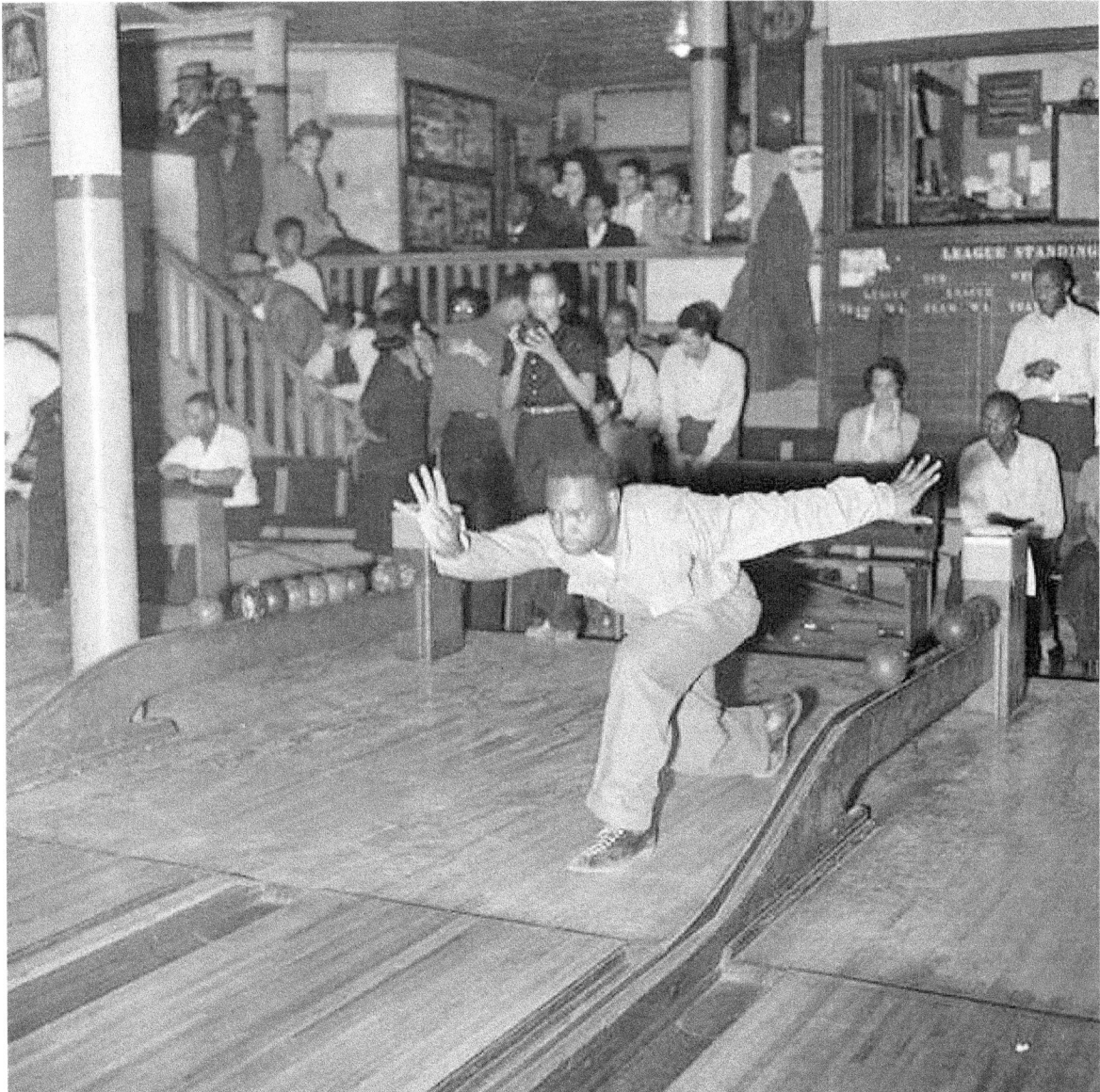

11.1: Hillvue Bowling Alley (c. 1935-1950)

Although Black basketball teams were not permitted to play against White teams, we had facilities like the Centre Avenue YMCA where Black teams could play one another. The discrimination we experienced then is ironic given that now most professional basketball players are Black.

Swimming was a mandatory gym class activity at Herron Hill Junior High and Schenley Senior High. Both schools had very large pools, and there were even some Black students on the Schenley swim team.

Not far from my home was the Ammon recreation center, a part of the Bedford Dwellings Public Housing Development. We all spent much time at the facility's swimming pool as well as at the Kennard Field and Recreation Center located in the Terrace Village housing development.

11.2: Ammon Recreation Center Swimming Pool (c. 1946)

Sadly—outrageously really—Blacks were prohibited from swimming in public pools like the one in Highland Park. I say "outrageously," because our tax dollars supported these pools. It took 30 years to break this discrimination, and even then, many Whites did not want to swim with us.[24]

11.3: The gentleman in the middle often brought his horses into The Hill for show and to allow youngsters a chance to ride.

---

24 I provide a more detailed account of efforts to integrate the Highland Park and other public pools in *Voices from the Firing Line: A Personal Account of the Pittsburgh Civil Rights Movement* (Learning Moments Press, 2022).

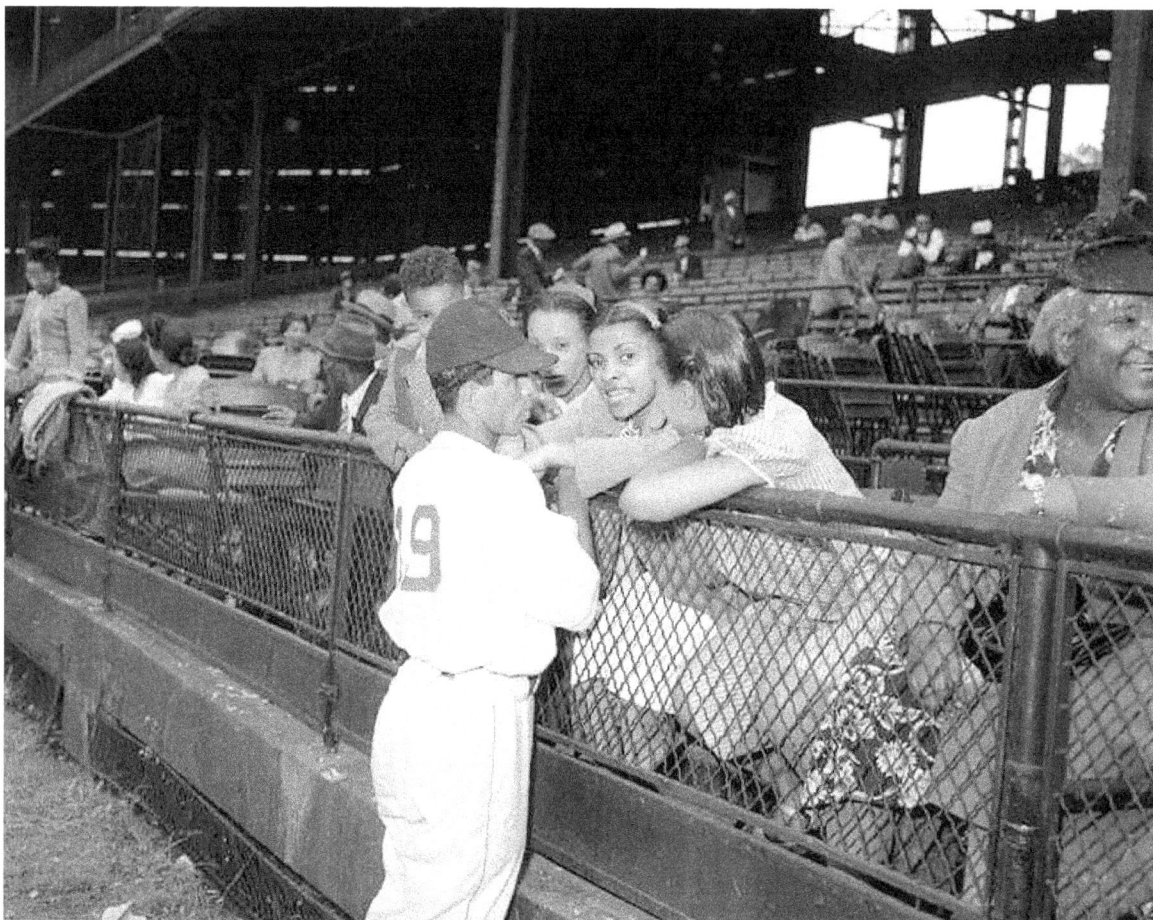

11.4: Take Me Out to the Ball Game. Fans talking to baseball player (possibly Pittsburgh Crawfords No. 19 in Forbes Field (c. 1945)

Amusement Parks in Pittsburgh

In the 1950s, Pittsburgh had three amusement parks. Swan Lake was a small, roadside park on the way to the Pittsburgh Airport. The other two were West View and Kennywood. Only Kennywood survives today. Neither Kennywood nor West View welcomed Blacks.

Kennywood hired no Blacks to work as ticket sellers, ride operators, or in any other capacity. Blacks were not allowed in the swimming pool. The NAACP sued the owners and won the right for Blacks to use the swimming pool. The members of the NAACP Young Adult Chapter were going to be dispatched to see how Blacks would be treated. Before that happened, the owners razed the bathhouses, demolished the swimming pool, and turned the space into a parking lot.[25]

Blacks were not barred from Kennywood, but Black schools were not permitted to hold official gatherings at the park, including annual school picnics. Although "ethnic" events designed to attract Europeans to the park were held, the owners ignored requests from Black groups to use the park for similar events. When Blacks arrived in small groups, they were carefully watched as if they were criminals. We were treated so badly we should not have spent a dime there. Unfortunately we did go, and we did spend money so there was no incentive for the park owners to treat Blacks fairly.

West View Park was nearly as bad. No blacks were employed in any capacity at the park and the Danceland facility was closed to Blacks. When the NAACP won the right to go there, we were sorely disappointed to learn they primarily played Polka music. They did allow Black schools to hold their annual picnics at the park. My point is that despite the rampant discrimination, we did manage to have a good time, because we were not barred from rides or concession stands at West View.

Movie Theaters

The Hill had several movie theaters including The Rhumba, the New Granada, the Roosevelt, and The Grant. The Rhumba was nice when it first opened, but then deteriorated into a ratty place that we avoided because of the filth and rats. The New Granada and Roosevelt, however, were glitzy, clean, and air-conditioned movie houses. Both were more appealing options than going to the larger theaters in downtown Pittsburgh where we would have to sit in the second balcony and be poorly treated by the Whites who ran them. For less hassle and less money, we could see all the good movies, even if we had to wait awhile for the films to play in The Hill theaters.

---

25 In a classic case of cutting off one's nose to spite one's face, a number of municipalities closed their pools so Blacks could not swim there. Of course, that meant that Whites also did not have the benefit of this public amenity.

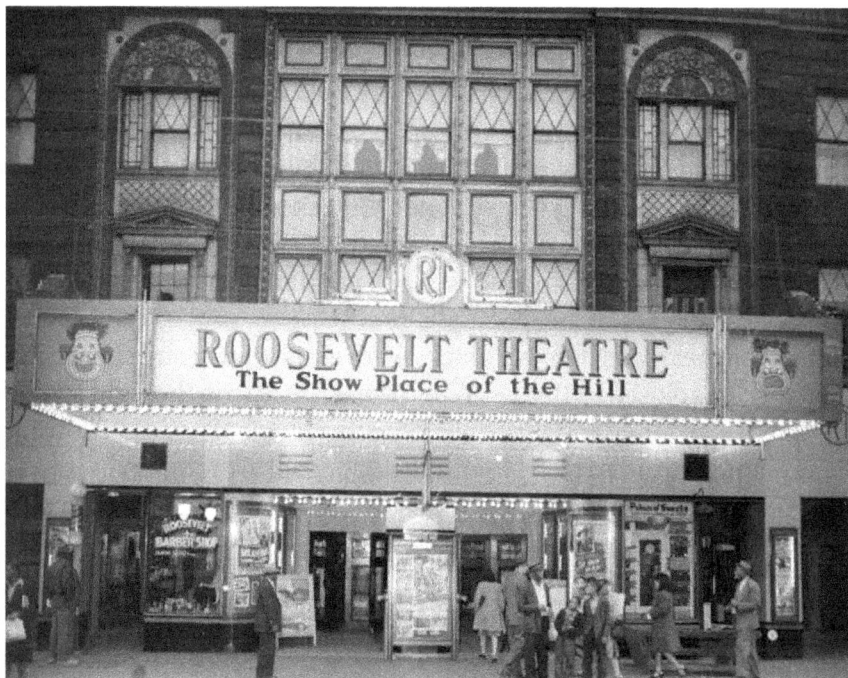

11.5: Roosevelt Theatre, Centre Avenue

11.6: New Granada Theater & Savoy Dance Club, Centre Avenue

11.7: Rhumba Theatre, Centre Avenue

11.8: Grant Theater on Herron Hill advertising "Phantom of the Rue Morgue" and "Three Violent People" (c. 1957-1960).

At the theaters, we could see two movies, 17-21 cartoons, and one or two serials. Before TV, serials were corny, 10-15 minute movies that ended just before the hero would meet an untimely death. We would hoot, holler, and stamp our feet, knowing that in next week's episode he would miraculously escape from his dire circumstances, only to be trapped again by the end of the new segment.

If our parents could not afford to finance our movie ventures every weekend, we kids worked all week on a group plan. Our goal was to raise about 50 cents for each of us. For that amount we could buy a ticket for 17 cents, popcorn for 10 cents, a drink for 10 cents, and a candy bar for 5 cents. If we had the good fortune to raise one dollar for each of us, we could go to *both* movie houses in the same day. That would mean *four* movies, anywhere from 34 to 42 cartoons, and *four* serials in the same day. That was *Heaven*.

To gather the necessary funds, we would go to all the neighbor houses and beg for pop bottles that we could turn in to the grocery store for 2 to 5 cents per bottle. Then we would scour the neighborhood for old newspapers and chunks of scrap metal that we could sell to the scrapyard man for a few cents. Occasionally, a kind-hearted neighbor would just give us a penny or two. None of us minded working for the money. We young entrepreneurs even had a business strategy. We decided who would knock on which door, because some folks liked some of us better than the others.

The Centre Avenue YMCA

The YMCA had a swimming pool, a multipurpose gym, weight training equipment, and ping pong tables. The gym was built primarily for the basketball players, but once or twice a week it was turned into a roller skating rink. While the basketball players were not thrilled with this arrangement, the skaters loved it, because they were not permitted in the White-owned skating rinks.

11.9: Girls Roller Skating at YMCA

11.10: School children in Centre Avenue YMCA for exhibition and lecture by artist John W. Gore (December 1945)

While the Y eventually became a mainstay of the Black community, it had not always been welcoming. Originally the Y was started for White, non-Jewish immigrant children whose families lived and toiled in the area. Eventually, the Y began to accept the "right type" of Blacks, even asking some of them to serve on the Board of Directors. To qualify for this honor, the person had to be from one of the "better" Negro families, hold a professional position, be light skinned, and have money. Attorney Byrd R. Brown, arguably the most famous Black leader in Pittsburgh during the 1960s and 1970s, told me the following story:

> My father fit the criteria for appointment to the Y's board and, as a result, I was able to work one summer as a counselor-in-training for the Y-operated camp. Although I wasn't too fond of the outdoors, I worked my butt off. I didn't want to embarrass my father. Besides, I didn't want the leaders saying that Negros couldn't do the job.

> The next summer all the trainees were invited back. When I got there, all the White trainees had been promoted to full counselors. When I asked why I wasn't, I was told, "Now Byrd, I'm not saying you're not as good as the others. I would promote you, too, if you were White. The White parents just won't accept a Negro leading their children."

> Mind you, Ralph, some of the campers were Negro as well. I quit, and when I told Dad, he resigned from the Board.

Those who came along later saw the Y as a boon to the community. One of its best known services was renting rooms to Black men on a nightly or long-term basis. They were not fancy, but they were clean. There was also a cafeteria where residents and others could get decent, inexpensive food.

Reverend Jimmy Joe Robinson, an important civil rights leader, also recalled the Y with mixed emotions. He was a star football player for the University of Pittsburgh and lived at the Y:

> At first I saw nothing wrong with that. I thought I was hot stuff. I was a big time star for Pitt. Then one day I realized that when the football team played away games, the players, coach, and other team employees stayed at a hotel, while I had to stay with a colored family. I got really angry when I realized I was living at the Y, because I was not permitted to stay in Pitt's dorms like the White players.

Reverend Robinson also recalled one away game where the White people of the opposing team hung a Black football player in effigy to show their anger that a "Nigger" was going to be playing ball on their field. Reverend Robinson's experience was not uncommon during the 1950s and 1960s. Any Black athlete coming to play against Pittsburgh college teams stayed at the Centre Avenue YMCA. So, too, did Black entertainers and other Black visitors.

Parades

Parades were an important part of our lives. They gave us a reason to celebrate. We'd all line up in front of our homes to watch the marchers strut their stuff. Don't all neighborhoods have a parade just about every week? At least that's what I thought as a child, because I was treated so often to the spectacle of parades winding their way along Wylie Avenue to downtown.

I think most of the parades were sponsored by The North Side Elks which had its headquarters, banquet hall, and bar a few blocks from my home on Wylie Avenue. Joining in at times was the marching band from The Carney Post, a Black American Legion Post named after a Black Revolutionary War hero. Often high school marching bands joined in as did men in military uniforms and police officers.

I didn't care who was marching as long as they had drums. I was absolutely fascinated by the drums. Interestingly, the Black bands varied their style depending upon where they were marching. In mixed or White neighborhoods, the beat and marching steps were somewhat subdued. In Black neighborhoods, the beat was far more complicated, a bit more jazzy; the steps more intricate and sexy. These parades were for *us*, not the rest of the world. The marchers were performing for HOME. Sometimes kids and adults were so moved by the intricate, poly-rhythmic beat, they marched alongside the bands. Nobody discouraged this impromptu participation; they just laughed and shouted words of encouragement. Parades were supposed to be fun, and in The Hill they were.

Neighborhood parades were the best, because we were likely to spot someone we knew in the line-up. One of the parade leaders was Dorothy Cook, who looked regal in her white and gold uniform. Dorothy and her husband rented the first floor apartment in our house, and we always felt special when Dorothy paused, turned, and waved to us. On occasion, she would turn to the right and point to the roof of our home. Damn! She was letting my parents know that I was up on the roof—again. I had discovered I could have the best seat in town by crawling out of the window in my third-floor bedroom, creeping up the backside of our gabled roof, then inching down the front side so I could stand on a small gable. I had no thoughts about falling off the roof; I was just having a good time.

Neighborhood parades also meant we did not have to go to White communities and worry about parents pushing us aside to give their kids a better view. Several of my friends have bitter memories of White folks stepping in front of them as if they and their parents didn't exist. This happened to me as an adult when I had lifted my son onto my shoulders so he would have a better view. A White man pushed from the back of the crowd, placing himself and his kid in front of us. When I said we had been there first, he just shrugged and said, "My son can't see from back there." I told him, in a very calm voice, that very shortly his son was going to have a very difficult time seeing anything at all. With a sense of entitlement, he replied, "Yeah? Why is that?"

"Well," I told him, "if you do not move your ass out of our way, I'm going to knock you unconscious. Then your son will be busy trying to wake you up." He moved. Using intimidation and fear to gain some modicum of respect and courtesy is painful to me. I wonder if this interloper would have felt the same entitlement had I been White. Would he have so blatantly shoved in front of another White man and responded so rudely? He, like so many others, would never see my gentle side—the side I prefer to have as the basis of my interactions with others.

On The Hill, we never had to deal with that kind of bullshit—what has come to be called micro-aggression. We respected one another. No person would think of stepping in front of someone else or taking one of the many chairs folks set out in front of their homes.

This was, however, a catch-22. If we stayed in The Hill, we did not have to deal with this kind of disrespect. At the same time, we were angered that such casual racism kept us from enjoying so many things taking place in White communities. Quite frankly, this fueled our determination not to be controlled because we were Black.

11.11: Annual Elks Parade, with members of Washington D. C. Elks club marching near Northside Elks Lodge No. 124, Wylie Avenue (August 31, 1943)

11.12: Parade on Webster Avenue

Holidays

The most important holiday was Christmas, complete with far more food than we could eat. Friends who visited were loaded down with goodies as they left for home. Of course Christmas was a religious holiday, and Mom took us to church at some point. But for us kids, the magic of Christmas had less to do with the birth of Jesus than the gifts appearing under the tree between Christmas Eve and Christmas morning. Santa, a sled, flying reindeer, a decorated tree, and presents—every child's dream holiday. Let me say, we didn't have an issue with White Santa, because we were told he was from Norway or the North Pole where no Black folks lived. We played the whole silly game including writing dumb letters to Santa and going to downtown department stores to sit on Santa's lap and tell him our wish list. Our parents explained discrepancies between what we asked for and what we got by saying Santa had run out of those things by the time he got to our house. My only sad memories came after I found out that my parents were "Santa," and they saved all year long so they could afford to buy all the magical gifts. Had I known the truth, I would have asked for less.

Thanksgiving was another big holiday. Dad was a butcher so we had plenty of food. Mom cooked for days; making pies and cakes, and all manner of side dishes to complement the turkey. No arguments erupted over who got the light or dark meat; Dad made sure there were enough drumsticks for everyone who wanted one. Neighbors and relatives came and went all day long. All of them left with a plate of food. Even the roomers who lived in our first floor apartment came for dinner. We were not rich, just lucky that Dad was a butcher.

My only problem with Thanksgiving was the endless meals of turkey leftovers. Friday's meal was the same as Thursday; the next day was turkey sandwiches; then turkey croquettes; followed by turkey soup. There was even creamed, chipped turkey on toast, which in my army days I learned had the appealing name of "crap on a shingle." In desperation, I began inviting all my friends over so they could help polish off whatever was left of that damn bird.

11.13: A Turkey Headed toward the Thanksgiving Table

One day, I reached my limit and just sat staring at the miserable lumps of meat, dressing, and gravy. Mom said I had to eat, because millions of children in China were starving. No sooner had I said, "Send all this crap to them," than I was flat on the kitchen floor, counting the holes in the acoustic ceiling tile. Two broken rules. Disrespecting Mom; not eating everything on my plate. As I grew older, I vowed to never eat another mouthful of turkey. I have kept that promise.

Easter was a weird holiday. We started celebrating a few days before by dying hard-boiled eggs. No matter how frequently I asked, no one could tell me what this had to do with the resurrection of Jesus. Since this made Mom happy, I went along with it, even though I hated eating hard-boiled eggs; except in potato salad. Egg-dying was followed by creating an Easter basket for each of us, another ritual I couldn't comprehend. But at least these had jelly beans and chocolate eggs.

Easter also meant going to church. In my neighborhood we had our own impromptu Easter Parade as kids were shooed outside in their new outfits while the parents finished getting ready for church. There was a sense of urgency, because parking spaces around the church filled up more rapidly on Easter Sunday than on any other day of the year, including Christmas. All the family had to have a new spring outfit to wear even if the clothes cost more than the family should spend. I did not mind the suit so much, but I hated the damn fedora that I had to wear. That is probably why I do not wear hats today. But the new outfits came in handy, because we had to put on fancy clothes even if we were just going window shopping in Downtown Pittsburgh. I kept saying we didn't need any more windows. Mom made me go anyhow.

The 4th of July was celebrated by all. Of course food played a big part in the day's celebration. Mom fried chicken, made potato salad, and baked a cake. Dad set up the grill for barbeque ribs. Sometimes we packed up the food and went to Highland Park for a picnic. This was definitely not my favorite holiday tradition. Why eat in the grass and dirt while fighting bugs when we could dine in comfort at home?

The culmination of the day was a big dance usually held at Kennard Field and at A. Leo Weil School playground. Thousands of people gathered, danced, and listened to Walt Harper and his band play. All the beer gardens and food places had special 4th of July menus. As night fell, the crowd moved up the hills toward the Terrace Village public housing development. We found good seats on the grassy slopes overlooking Kennard Field and waited for the fantastic fireworks. They were visible from almost any place in The Hill, but there was something magic about being right next to them, hearing the loud BOOMS, feeling the concussions, seeing the fire trails in the sky, and gasping in delight as miraculous arrays of color exploded.

My childhood was a more naïve time, when I did not understand that independence day had nothing to do with my people. When the Declaration of Independence was signed and proclaimed "All Men Are Created Equal," this country held five million black souls in slavery. Many years later, the incongruity of celebrating a holiday that had nothing to do with the independence of Blacks led me to write the following poem.

SING A SONG
Sing a song of this holiday
Celebrate the 4th of July.
Sing a song of this holiday
As American as apple pie.
Sing a song of women
Without the right to vote.
Sing a song of "INDIANS"
Robbed of their land and hope.
Sing a song of White freedom won
While Blacks in slavery lay.
Whose FREEDOM do we celebrate
On INDEPENDENCE DAY?

Post-Script

Looking back on these times, I feel a mix of pride and anger. Denied equal access to recreational facilities, the Black community created its own. Even now, I wouldn't trade a moment of our spontaneous, imaginative playtime for all the highest quality toys in the downtown department stores. I have nothing but pride for how we kids and The Hill community at large nurtured a deeply genuine joy. At the same time, I am outraged at the indignities to which we were subjected. My anger grows exponentially when I think of the ways in which Urban "Renewal" destroyed what we had accomplished in spite of discrimination.

CHAPTER 12

Culture

During the time of my transition from junior to senior high school, I learned I was *culturally deprived*. A teacher was explaining that my friends and I came from an "underprivileged neighborhood," where we had not been exposed to the *finer things in life,* and by implication, were inferior. This didn't sit well with me, so I asked, "What do you mean by culturally deprived?"

"I'm talking about the symphony, ballet, theatre, opera, Phipps Conservatory, the Carnegie Museum, and so forth," she responded.

"Miss," I said with barely contained anger, "you are new to this school and us students, so let me tell you something about our lives. Every Saturday morning, mothers in my neighborhood send us kids out of the house so we won't be underfoot as they clean. When we don't have money to hang out at a movie theater, we walk to Oakland where there's free stuff for us to do. We hang out at the library and listen to people read stories. Sometimes we go to the museum and conduct "pretend tours" until the guards kick us out. Or we go to Phipps Conservatory and hide in the fake houses in the gardens until those guards kick us out. We go to the grottos to hear live concerts or to Flagstaff Hill or to Carnegie Tech where something artsy is always going on. How *dare* you call us *culturally deprived* when you know nothing about *my* life and *my* people?" Of course, I was reported to the principal.

Had this culturally naïve teacher done her homework, she might have learned that for many years The Hill was a cultural Mecca for both Blacks and Whites. She would have understood that music—both religious and secular—was a life force in the culture of The Hill.

12.1: National Negro Opera Company (c. 1940-1946)

12.2: Members of Pittsburgh Chorus gathered for the National Negro Opera Company performance of "La Traviata" (1944)

Music

Throughout The Hill, voices were lifting up joyous music to the Lord. From the sweet refrains of *Steal Away* to rousing choruses of *Onward Christian Soldiers*, religious music flowed from the churches. Music so beautiful it could bring tears to your eyes or joy to your soul was pounded out from well-worn pianos or squeezed from organs. Gospel music filled the air, accompanied by the refrains, "Yes Lord. Take me home. Uh Huh. That boy can Sing." You could hear the preacher exhorting the choirs to keep lifting the words to Heaven, let the Lord hear us lift our voices in prayer.

12.3: Ebenezer Church Junior Choir led by choir director Naomi O'Neal (c. 1945).

12.4: Women's Choir

12.5: Men and Women's Choir

Some music sounded like church music, but it wasn't. Ray Charles borrowed from church music and transformed it into Rhythm and Blues. Church folks did not like that one bit and told us Ray Charles was going straight to Hell for stealing the Lord's words for worldly enjoyment instead of salvation. Even so, Rhythm and Blues wafted through the air from jukeboxes in local bars and from live performances at nightclubs like The Flamingo Club, The Savoy Ballroom, the Epiphany Hall, The Roosevelt Theater, and The Hurricane Club run by Birdie Dunlap.

Birdie's Hurricane Club was a very successful stop on what was called the "Chitlin Circuit." This was a series of performance venues in the eastern, southern, and mid-western United States where Black musicians and comedians could perform safely. On the circuit Blacks and Whites mixed freely without fear or controversy. Performances varied from Rhythm and Blues, to Jazz, to Boogie-Woogie.

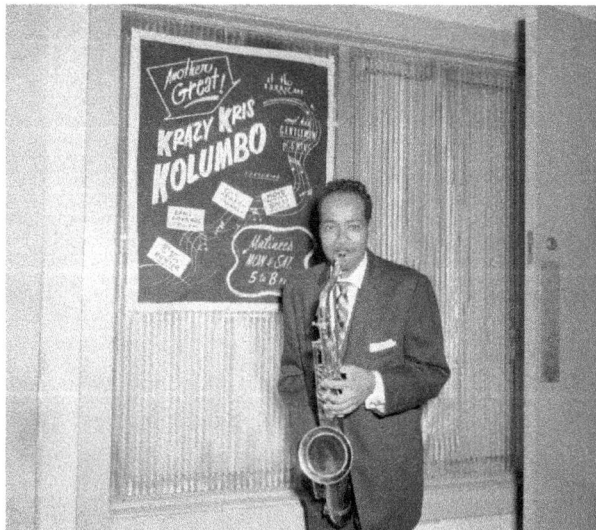

12.6: Danny Turner playing saxophone in front of the Hurricane Club (c. 1953-1970)

The Hurricane Club was one of my favorite stops, because Birdie always kept things jumping. There was no such thing as being overcrowded. If you had money, you got a seat. Many a night I would be sitting with a date, trying to be suave and debonair, only to hear, "C'mon, Ralph. You know I love you, but move over a bit so I can fit these folks in." Then Birdie would move my drinks and slide in a couple of strangers to share "my romantic night out." Black, White, Blue or Green—everyone was welcome at The Hurricane Club as long as they had money. I asked Birdie about that once, and she said, "Ralphie, honey, if them White folks had any problem sitting next to Black folks, they would not have brought their asses in here. All I'm doing is making certain they have a good time, and they sho' nuff do." I loved the lady and the fantastic music she supported. The Hurricane Club was to Rhythm & Blues what the Crawford Grill was to Jazz.

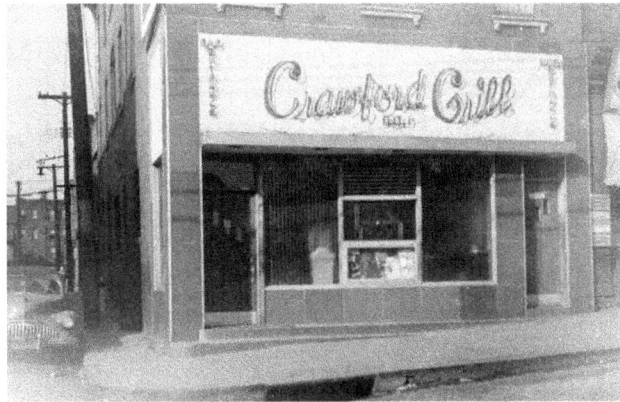

12.7: Crawford Grill No. 1, 1401 Wylie Avenue (c. 1945-1949)

12.8. William "Woogie" Harris at piano in Continental Bar at Crawford Grill No.1 (c. 1945-1950)

On any given weekend, both young and old, Black and White, Jazz and R&B musicians came to The Hill to test their mettle against the world's best. One night I was hanging out at a club owned by famous jazz musician Walt Harper. In the club was a well-dressed, young White man who had come to Pittsburgh for one of Nathan Davis' Jazz seminars. At Walt's invitation, the young man mounted the stage, holding a bright, shiny trumpet in his hand. He played with Walt and his house band for a bit; then performed a solo. His technique was superb, his notes clear and strong. Just as I was wondering what else he had to learn, an older Black man with a weathered face and wrinkled clothes arose, walked on the stage, smiled, shook the young man's hand and said, "That was good, very good." As the young man beamed, the old Black man placed the trumpet to his lips, and the place grew quiet. The notes that came out of that horn were magic. They soared; they glided; they wrapped around your brain; they warmed your heart; they brought a smile to your lips; they were mesmerizing. The young White man's eyes widened as if to say, "Where the fuck did THAT note come from?" The old man finished his solo. The audience rose whistling, shouting, and clapping. The old musician looked up, wiped the sweat from his forehead, wiped the mouth piece of his magic horn, waved, and sauntered off the stage. Such was the opportunity to learn during the heyday of The Hill.

The music scene in Pittsburgh produced and hosted many world-famous Black entertainers including Nat King Cole, Count Basie, Duke Ellington, Cab Calloway, Jimmy Smith, Slide Hampton, Errol Garner, Stanley Turrentine, Ahmad Jamaal, Billy Ekstein, George Benson, Mary Lou Smith, Pearl Bailey, and Lena Horne. It was no big deal to see Nat "King" Cole getting into an Owl cab, or Cab Calloway standing on the steps of Dearing's Restaurant/Hotel, or other famous performers walking through the neighborhood. Because Black entertainers were not permitted to stay in Downtown hotels, they stayed in rooming/boarding houses, small Black-owned hotels, The Centre Avenue YMCA, private homes, and rooms above some of the larger bars.

12.9: Walt Harper at piano

12.10: Lena Horne

12.11: Nat King Cole entering an Owl Cab

12.12: Cab Calloway

12.13: Lionel Hampton

12.14: Jazz Ensemble featuring Walt Harper

The iconic Crawford Grill was a numbers joint, a meeting place, a fine restaurant, and a nightclub to hear some of the best jazz bands in the country. It was THE place to be seen. Taking a date to The Grille was sure to impress. A photographer friend of mine made a great deal of money taking commemorative photos of couples sitting in the booths and at the bar of The Grille; so too, did the famous photojournalist Charles "Teenie" Harris. Both indicated that they made more money from those who did NOT want their pictures taken. As one of the top numbers places in The Hill, it could be a bit shady, but still a lot of fun. The Grill was also a meeting place for Black leaders and politicians. I heard folks say many times, "I'll see you at the Grill."

The Grill served an excellent mix of top-plate food and soul food, including ribs and fried chicken, biscuits, cornbread, sweet potato pie, and frog legs. Even wild game was occasionally on the menu. But it was fried chicken wings that were internationally famous. One time I was doing a consulting job for a Canadian company. When they came to town, they asked with some embarrassment if I could arrange for a chicken wing dinner at The Grill. The wings were so good that the group took a supply of them back across the border.

In addition to The Hurricane Club and The Crawford Grill, a number of large and small establishments served as cultural hubs in The Hill. The New Granada and Roosevelt Theatres on Centre Avenue had live entertainment. The Musicians Club on Centre Avenue housed the headquarters of the Black Musicians Union, but also provided space for cabarets and live shows. The Aurora, which started as a literary club, later added a bar and grill and was considered to be a "snobby" place. So, too, was The Loendi Club, which was originally intended for "upper level" Blacks. Many of the early members were light-skinned, professional Blacks. Ordinary, middle-income Blacks did not feel welcome until the later years, when integration gave wealthier Blacks the option of frequenting White-owned clubs.

The bar at The Terrace Hall hotel featured very potent Zombie drinks. A sign behind the bar stated that anyone who could drink three Zombies, turn around three times on the bar stool, go out the door, come back in, and sit on the stool again, would drink free for the rest of the night. I'm not sure how many tipplers won the challenge, but I am sure many enjoyed trying.

12.15: Loendi Club on Fullerton Street (c. 1940)

12.16: A relaxing night out at a Local Night Club (c. 1930-1950)

Dancing

Dancing was an important social activity, and every weekend there was some sort of "dance" in The Hill. Nearly every night club and bar had a dance floor and live music. In addition to this casual, social dancing, several big events called "Cabarets" were held in very large venues such as the Musicians Club and The Savoy Ballroom that was part of the New Granada theater complex. Depending upon the venue, the music was performed either by a famous large band or a local group. The expressed purpose of these events was to get together, drink, and have a good time. The music did not have to be great, but it did have to be *loud*. Folks would come in, buy a ticket, and stake out a table that held anywhere from 6 to 12 people. If you wanted to "party" with more folks, you'd just pull a couple of tables together.

12.17: Savoy Dance Club, Centre Avenue

12.18: Dance Band performing at Union Hall, with Edgar "Chandu" Thomas on bass, Horace Turner on piano, Hosea Taylor (Jose Gonzales) on saxophone, and Paula "Pola" Roberts on drums (c. 1945-1955)

In most cases, each table ordered a *"Set Up"* consisting of soft-drinks, glasses, an ice bucket, and various utensils for mixing drinks. Sometimes potato chips and pretzels could be purchased. The alcohol was purchased separately from the bar, or in some places you could bring your own. Partying lasted until the wee hours of the morning. It was hard for a non-drinker like me to fit in, but you were expected to go to these events, especially if you wanted a social life. For many, these gatherings were an excellent outlet for relieving life's pressures.

12.19: Formal Adult Dance (c. 1956)

12.20: Teenage Dance (c.1966)

For those who wanted to polish their dancing style, there was a dance school located in the Terrace Hall Hotel in the Middle Hill. Keep in mind that Blacks were not welcome in the White-owned studios in Pittsburgh. Renee Young, a beautiful Black woman, owned Renee's Dance School which offered lessons in ballet, modern Jazz, tap, and ballroom dancing. Believe it or not, I was a ballroom dance instructor and specialized in Latin-American dances. I obtained this position through a strange set of circumstances.

I had been dating a young lady who found me inadequate as a dance partner. Her critique went something like, "I never knew a Negro who could not dance. What do you mean, you can't dance? Every time we go out I have to dance with some guy I don't even know. That is embarrassing."

One day *The Pittsburgh Courier* carried an ad stating—Dance Instructors Wanted: Free Training. All right! Sign Me Up! Several of us reported to the Musician's Club where a White guy told us he worked for a major White-owned dance studio located downtown. The studio did not welcome Black folks, nor did it have Black instructors. This enterprising gentleman planned to make a fortune by opening a studio on The Hill and teaching Black folks to dance. I cared less about his vision than stopping my girlfriend's harassment. I made the cut and was told to report back the next day to begin the lessons.

12.21: Dance instructors Ralph Proctor, Betty Dunson, Alberta Thompson, Sara Burney, and Rudolph Moses posed in Terrace Room of Terrace Hall Hotel for opening of Renee's Dance Studio (c. 1958)

We practiced six hours a day, five days a week. I devoured the Cha Cha like a man who had not eaten in years. We danced and sweated and cursed, until we finally took our practical exams and received diplomas. Unfortunately for the instructor, his White employer fired him, and his plans for a dance studio in The Hill never materialized. But now I was prepared to surprise my girlfriend.

My big day finally arrived when the biggest cabaret of the year was scheduled. Despite my girlfriend's misgivings, I convinced her that we should go. Playing it cool, I waited till the band struck up a Cha Cha, then said, "Come on. Let's dance." With a look of sheer derision, she snapped, "YOU? Why would I get on the floor with you and have everyone staring at us because you can't dance?"

"Come on, give me chance. I've been practicing."

Glaring, she took my hand. "Okay. Try not to make too big of a fool of yourself."

Once on the dance floor, I broke into the professional routine I had been practicing. As is appropriate in the Cha Cha, I made her the focus of the dance. Other folks stopped dancing to watch. "Damn, look at that. Man, that Cat is *good*." "Go on Brother man, *dance*." People were clapping their hands, and I responded by doing even fancier steps. Not being able to follow my intricate moves, my date got pissed and stomped back to our table. Now I had other women asking me to dance. My girlfriend was not amused by my "surprise" performance. Revenge was sweet, and I am not at all ashamed.

Another dance-related cultural event was a "cotillion," modeled after the White custom in which wealthy families presented their daughters to society. To me, these seemed like opportunities for conspicuous consumption and flaunting social status. I'm embarrassed to say that a number of Black organizations felt a need to sponsor cotillions, as if to say, "We can do this, too." Of course, this assessment came later. As a teenager, I paid little attention to this custom and had no interest in participating. Consequently, I lived in a state of "cotillion-deprivation" until a young lady caught me by surprise and asked me to be her date. Walking home, I shook my head, wondering why on earth I had agreed to do such a dumb thing.

When I arrived home, I casually told Mom about the invitation, to which she replied, "That's nice honey. You look so good in a tuxedo." YIKES, a tuxedo! I hated wearing those things. You see, when I was much younger, Mom was enamored of "Thom Thumb Weddings," where little kids dressed up in tuxedoes and fancy dresses as though they were "little people" getting married. Mom thought I looked so cute, she signed me up for these ridiculous events as often as possible. I still vividly recall walking past my friend Art Carter's home, and seeing him literally rolling on the ground in laughter as I was led to the church kicking and screaming about looking like a penguin.

Totally bummed out, I went to watch TV. Soon the phone rang, and I could hear Mom talking—softly, pleasantly, and politely at first. Then her tone became more strident as she spoke in short staccato sentences. "Yes, Mrs. Jones. I see Mrs. Jones. Is that *right,* Mrs. Jones? Well I certainly will tell my son, Mrs. Jones. You have a nice day, too, Mrs. Jones." Mom slammed down the phone with a final word, "BITCH." Now I was all ears, because my mother did not use profanity. "Honey, I'm sorry but that was Sarah's mother. You can't take her daughter to the dance." My casual "okay" did not reveal the sense of relief seeping through me. Looking surprised, Mom said, "You don't seem upset. I thought you wanted to go."

"Mom, I don't know why I even agreed to go, I hate wearing those damn tuxedoes and have hated them ever since you made me go to those silly Thom Thumb Weddings. I'm *glad* I don't have to go. But why are you upset?"

"That nasty woman had the nerve to say you could not possibly escort her daughter to the cotillion because you are *too dark*." Mom was pissed, but I did not care. Over the years, I was invited to a number of formal dances including high school proms. I'm not sure why I became so popular, even though my skin was "so dark." Ironically, I eventually attended so many functions that it was cheaper to buy my own "penguin suit." How embarrassing.

Radio

In addition to live music, we listened to music on the radio. In my younger years, most of the White-owned radio stations did not play Black music and had no Black deejays. The first Black disc jockey I recall hearing was Mary Dee Goode who broadcast on WHOD, a small station in Homestead, Pennsylvania. Initially, the station catered to the Jewish, Italian, Polish, Croatian, Slavic, and German populations. In 1950, Mary Dee Goode convinced the station that it needed a Black presence, so they agreed to give her a 15-minute show if she could find a sponsor. Luckily her uncle, who owned a couple of pharmacies, sponsored the show which was so successful it eventually expanded to four hours. Mary Dee brought in her brother Mal to do a *Courier* News segment. He later became the first Black TV correspondent, covering stories for the ABC Television Network. In 1951 she began broadcasting from a glass-fronted studio at the back of one of the Goode pharmacies. As I watched her in that studio, little did I know that about 10 years later I would be broadcasting from the same station that this iconic lady made famous. Thank you, Mary Dee.

12.22: Disc Jockey Mary Dee Goode, the first Black/woman dee jay in Pittsburgh

Mary Dee was indeed a Black media pioneer. Because of her success, competition soon sprang up. In 1956, WILY began to broadcast a Black-oriented format. The stars of the new station were Bill Powell and John Christian. They were broadcasting so many hours a day, they soon overshadowed WHOD. Powell was more than a disc jockey and became very popular as he immersed himself in the lives of Blacks in Pittsburgh. John Christian became wildly popular, in part because of his proper British accent. His radio persona was "Sir Walter," and he was shown all over Pittsburgh wearing a derby and a monocle. When I first heard him, I thought it was just a weird gimmick. But when I started my radio career in 1963, I met him and learned that his accent was real. He had been born in a New England town where everybody spoke with a British accent. John and I became good buddies. Later, we both made a successful transition from radio to television.

In 1958 WHOD morphed into WAMO, the call letters represented the three Pittsburgh rivers—the Allegheny, Monongahela and Ohio. As WILY began to fail, WAMO hired both Bill Powell and John Christian. WAMO became a dominant force in the entertainment life of many Pittsburgh Blacks and spawned dozens of very popular entertainment and news personalities. The one troubling aspect of WAMO was its White owner, Leonard Walk. Although the station provided employment and entertainment for Blacks, the profits of this lucrative station were not going to them. Finally in 1973, a group of investors headed by Ronald Davenport, then the dean of the Duquesne University Law School, purchased WAMO. For the first time in its history, Pittsburgh had a radio station featuring Black music and controlled by Black people. Unfortunately, as of this writing WAMO is no longer a Black owned station. Its rise and fall, however, could be the subject for another book.

Before Black music was broadcast on the radio, records and record players were an essential part of a family entertainment center. The record player sat on a stand with shelves to hold the family's collection of fragile "78" and "45" discus-shaped wax records. The numbers referred to the speed at which the records "spun" on the turntable. The record player had an arm with a "needle" at the end. Before record players had a mechanism for automatically swinging the arm into place, we would carefully move the arm into position so that the needle rode in the grooves of the records and released the magical sound through built-in speakers. Initially, the 78s and the 45s held only one song on each side. Later someone invented record albums with up to ten songs per side. We listened to Rhythm and Blues, Gospel, Boogie-Woogie, and Jazz. We supported many businesses that sold the records we played. Dorsey's was one of the big music stores. Pace's on Centre Avenue specialized in religious music. There were even Black-owned repair shops to keep the turntables in good working order.

Television

As was the case with broadcast radio, television was slow to move beyond caricatures of Blacks. Most Blacks who appeared on TV were either athletes, real and fictional criminals, or "primitive" African tribes. Early pioneers on television were news reporters, and among the earliest were Vic Miles and Kathy Milton. The first Black to be featured regularly was William R. Robinson who worked for the Urban League of Pittsburgh. His program, *Job Call*, was sponsored by the H.J. Heinz Company and aired on KDKA TV. The year was 1967 and Robinson announced job openings for which all Pittsburghers could apply. A year later, I was given the job of host/producer of *Black Horizons* on WQED television. This was the second such show in the history of American television; the first being *Say Brother* broadcast from Boston. Finally the Black community had a voice on television. Later, the commercial stations got into the act. WTAE hired Kathy Milton and Dee Thompson to co-host *Black Chronicle*; KDKA hired Joe

Freeman and Yvonne Forston to do *Together*; WIIC hired John Christian to host *Black Impact*. At long last Black folks could see people who looked like them doing important work in our community. Even so, there were few Black folks in this vast land of television.

The Pittsburgh Courier

When I was a young man, three main newspapers—*The Pittsburgh Press, The Pittsburgh Sun Telegraph, The Pittsburgh Post-Gazette*—reported events in Pittsburgh. Let's just say that the lack of Black reporters and editors lent a white cast to the news. Black birth announcements and wedding events were not included in the society pages; no prominent Blacks were featured in the "seen around the town" column. Black obituaries were not published. Sport pages did include some accounts of Black ball players, and Black performers might be mentioned in the entertainment section. Far more likely to be reported were accounts of Black criminals. None of these papers accepted announcements about Black social and cultural events or advertisements. Real estate ads could blatantly state, "Whites Only" for home sales and apartment rentals. The only newspaper position Blacks were deemed fit for was that of janitor; few of the delivery boys and none of the truck drivers were Black.

Thankfully, a fourth paper—*The Pittsburgh Courier*—served as the voice, eyes, ears, and soul of Blacks. *The Courier* published a weekly edition for Pittsburgh as well as specific editions for other US cities. It grew to be the largest Black-owned newspaper in the world, even though White trucking companies refused to deliver its papers. In the face of this discrimination, the owner, Robert L. Vann, reached an agreement with the Black Pullman Porter's Union. These brave Black men carried the papers with them on the nation's railroad system, dropping the newspapers off at designated cities around the country.

The Courier covered wars, civil rights or wrongs, and important events that impacted Black folks, including births, deaths, and marriages. It even helped raise money to fight World War II with its DOUBLE V US Bonds promotion. *The Courier* provided good jobs for Black reporters, writers, photographers, equipment operators, and delivery people. Some of the most famous Black intellectuals wrote for *The Pittsburgh Courier*. Charles "Teenie" Harris, whose photographs are featured throughout this book, became the most famous *Courier* photographer of all time.[26] Even I did some freelance photography work for *The Courier* and came know Teenie.

When I was growing up, a myth seemed to circulate that residents of The Hill could barely read and had little interest in doing so. This certainly wasn't true among the families I knew. We not only read *The Pittsburgh Courier*, we also read White-owned newspapers to understand what was going on in the White community.

---

26 Charles "Teenie" Harris was an acclaimed photojournalist whose work provides a stunning visual documentation of life on The Hill. Many of his photographs have been compiled into books—e.g., *Teenie Harris, Photographer: Image, Memory, History* by Cherly Finley & Laurence A. Glasso; *Spirit of a Community: The Photographs of "Charles "Teenie" Harris* by Charles H. Harris; *One Shot Harris: The Photographs of Charles "Teenie" Harris* by Stanly Crouch. The photographs in this book have been provided courtesy of The Carnegie Library of Pittsburgh which houses an extensive, searchable archive of Harris' work. (https://cmoa.org/art/teenie-harris-archive)

The Courier, in its heyday, did a magnificent job. Unfortunately, Urban "Renewal" killed many of the Black businesses that once advertised in its pages. In addition, integration took its toll as White-owned papers began to hire Black reporters and photographers. Sadly, under integration, the best writers left and became token employees of White newspapers. When it became illegal to run racist ads for jobs and dwellings, Blacks could obtain information from White papers. The financially-starved *Courier* finally closed. It was eventually reborn as *The New Pittsburgh Courier*, now owned by one of the old *Courier's* competitors. While a welcome addition to the Pittsburgh newspaper scene, *The New Pittsburgh Courier* is a mere shadow of the original.

Magazines

As was the case with White-owned newspapers, magazines also catered to an exclusively White readership. *Life, Look, People, The TV Guide*, and other national magazines included little or no information about Black lives or interests. If aliens from Mars had visited Earth in the 1950s and read our magazines, they would probably have concluded that the planet was inhabited only by White people. No Black faces appeared in the housekeeping, automotive, hunting and fishing, firearms, or other magazines so often found in physician's and dentist's waiting rooms. Again, most material about Blacks related either to athletes, entertainers, or criminals.

Fortunately, Luther Sewell published *Talk*, a magazine featuring the local Black political, entertainment, and social scene in Pittsburgh. From time to time Sewell published other periodicals including *Shooting Star Review*, which focused on literary articles.

To keep up with national human interest stories and the events impacting the Black community, we turned to *Jet* and *Ebony*. *Jet* was a smallish, pocket-sized magazine, designed to be carried and read on the go. Most of the content was fun and light-hearted. *Ebony*, on the other hand, was our answer to the more popular, full-sized, general circulation magazines. It covered a wide variety of events, including the National Civil Rights Movement and updates on the lives of Black celebrities like Nat King Cole and Sarah Vaughn. I confess I was not fully aware of the scope of these publications until the late 1960s when *Ebony* did a key story on my show, *Black Horizons*, and several acquaintances living outside of Pittsburgh let me know they'd seen the piece. This is just a small illustration of how these publications disseminated information about Black culture throughout the country.

So, in a White-dominated media industry, residents of The Hill turned to these Black-owned publications. *These* were the publications we read at the barbershops, beauty parlors, Black doctors' and dentists' offices. *They* told us what was going on around the world, what products Black folks were buying, and what White companies thought was important enough to advertise in a Black-owned publication.

We also read books written by Blacks about Blacks. There are too many of these to mention. Suffice it to say, these authors wrote about our feelings, our hopes, and our dreams. White writers ignored us; perhaps that was best, because they did not understand our lives. How could they?

Post-Script

Perhaps my young teacher's ignorance of Black culture can be excused. What is not excusable—or forgivable—is the cultural ignorance and callous disregard for Black culture among those who championed Urban "Renewal." As the wrecking balls began to smash the homes, businesses, and nightspots, the glorious music of The Hill was silenced. Many churches were shuttered as Blacks were pushed out of the community. The Crawford Grill went through two incarnations. The original was torn down during Urban "Renewal," but reopened further up Wylie Avenue. Unfortunately, as a result of the riots of 1968, Whites no longer felt comfortable coming to The Hill for entertainment. Gone were the small clubs where Blacks and Whites came together in harmony; where the threads of understanding and friendship were woven into a vibrant culture. As the bulldozers ripped apart those threads, the music seeped away leaving my beloved Hill in ruins.

12.23: *Crawford Grill No. 1 with fence being erected for demolition (1956)*

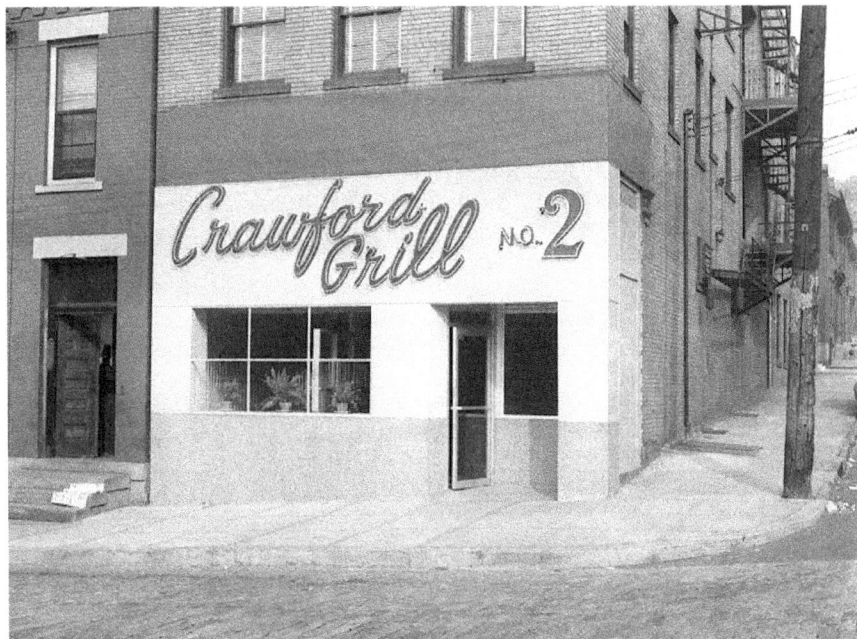

12.24: *Crawford Grill No. 2*

12.25: William "Woogie" Harris' house in Homewood. The house later became the headquarters of Mary Cardwell Dawson's National Negro Opera Company. It is included here because the house was very similar in design to a house near the author's on Wylie Avenue.

CHAPTER 13

Goods and Services

When I was growing up, the Lower Hill was a thriving community teeming with bars, nightclubs, and small businesses. Many retail establishments were still owned by Jewish and Italian merchants, even though the majority of clients were Black. Usually, store owners employed workers from their own ethnic community. Still, some did employ Blacks, and they provided goods and services needed by the Black community. In the face of discrimination, however, Blacks began to create their own businesses, including bars, Tyson's Bakery (my favorite), grocery stores, drug stores, a hardware store, a radio station, a movie theatre, and a couple of small restaurants. My father owned two small grocery stores, my uncle Guy owned a sandwich shop, and another relative owned Proctor's Doll Hospital.

13.1: Tyson's Bakery on Centre Avenue (c. 1940-1970)

My family did a lot of shopping in The Lower Hill. I loved visiting Logan's Meat Market where my dad worked. There were always so many sights to take in, languages to hear, and things to do in the area. We bought our Christmas tree from Dom, an Italian man, who played Christmas songs for us on an old beat-up guitar. One year Dad tried to shop for a tree closer to home and faced a revolt. We all refused to let Dad buy a tree unless it was from Dom. All us kids cried mournfully when we were told that the gentleman had passed away.

Mr. and Mrs. Shay sold just about everything in their grocery store, including fresh eggs and live chickens that came from a chicken farm they owned somewhere out in the country. The Shays took a liking to me and hired me to deliver small grocery orders in my little red wagon. One day they took me to their farm. Mr. Shay gave me a bucket of chicken feed and showed me how to throw it out for the flock. Immediately, about two million chickens rushed me. Mr. and Mrs. Shay just laughed as I ran screaming from the squawking beasts. Of course, as I ran, I was spilling chicken feed so those nasty creatures kept pursuing me. I never went back, and whenever I ate fried chicken, I pictured myself taking revenge for the "Attack of the Monster Chickens."

Lee's Floral Shop on Centre Avenue was the place to go when flowers were required for a special function. All the employees were Black, which was true of the other Black-owned businesses. A huge drive-in hot dog shop was located behind Central Baptist Church. I have no idea who owned it, but it employed Black and White workers and didn't discriminate between the customers they served. Further down Centre Avenue was All Pro Chicken which served fried chicken. Although I wasn't into football at the time, I knew it was owned by some Black Pittsburgh Steelers who I saw around the shop.

13.2: All-Pro Chicken Restaurant between Plaza Beauty Salon &
Silver Sea Seafood restaurant (c. 1965-1975)

Health and Medical Services

Drug stores were essential to the well-being of a community, and pharmacists were highly regarded. In my neighborhood, at least six drug stores were within walking distance, and all but one was Black-owned. R-Star Drugs was run by Henry Bridges. Whether he was actually a physician really doesn't matter; to all of us he was Doc Bridges, and we turned to him for help when we were ill. For less severe problems, he'd fix us up with a non-prescription cure. For serious conditions, he'd contact Dr. Robinson, whose offices were just above his drugstore.[27] At his soda fountain, we could buy all kinds of fantastic ice cream-based treats—either to take home or to enjoy at the counter while spinning around on stools.

When he was not tending to our ailments, selling the vast array of merchandise in the store, or dishing out ice cream, Doc Bridges sat at the counter with his nose buried in the newspaper section displaying columns of numbers. When I was older, I asked him what he was looking at. "Checking my stocks," he explained. Later I realized that he was the only person I knew who invested his money in the stock market. I was impressed, because I had been led to believe that only White folks did that. How little I knew!

Doc Bridges was also my mentor, quietly guiding my footsteps without letting me know. I was puzzled when I heard him tell another adult, "That's young Ralph; he is smart as a whistle. If we take care of him, he will show people what our kids can do. He is going to be somebody."

Displayed on a rack at the front of the store were all sorts of magazines and comic books. I was fond of the "art magazines" with their carefully-posed images of naked females. Occasionally I stole a five cent comic book. As I grew older, I felt ashamed about stealing from this kind man and began leaving a few extra cents on the counter. "Oh look, Doc," I would say. "Somebody forgot their change." Still suffering from a guilty conscience after getting out of the Army and enrolling at Pitt, I felt I had to "man up" to my criminal past. I went to Doc Bridges and said, "I need to come clean and confess to stealing from you when I was a kid. I'm so sorry and am willing to do whatever you feel is right to make up for it."

Doc just smiled. "I know. Everyone who worked for me knew. We hoped you'd come in on a slow day so we could watch you. Sometimes you took so long to steal one of those books we wanted to come over and say, 'Here, take the damn thing and go home.' You'd take about a half hour to steal one magazine. Sometimes we'd bet on how long it would take you."

So much for being a master criminal! Mortified, I stammered, "If you knew, why did you let me get away with it? Why didn't you call the cops?"

"You showed that you were smart; all the folks liked you. You had a bright future, but were the most inept thief we'd ever seen. No way would that be your profession. Besides, why would I risk giving you a juvenile record and stop you from becoming what we knew you were destined to be? We still believe in you."

I have spent my life trying to pay forward his generosity as well as debts of kindness owed to so many people in this remarkable community. Thanks, Doc Bridges.

---

27 Other Black doctors lived and practiced in The Hill; they even made "home visits." We also had dentists and psychologists. Unfortunately, there were also "snake oil salesmen" who sat at little sidewalk tables and sold "magic elixirs" to the gullible.

Goode's pharmacy was a favorite stopping place for students coming home from Herron Hill Junior High and Schenley High. The long soda fountain counter had fake red-leather, revolving stools. A few cents bought a club soda, milk shake, banana split, or other special treat that could be enjoyed at the counter while trying to "hook up" with a date. In the corner of the store was a broadcast studio belonging to radio station WHOD where the most famous female dee jay in history, Mary Dee, spun platters, talked about important issues, and even waved at on-lookers. Goode's sold "walking sundaes," ice cream packed in a conical paper container along with a plastic spoon. We could enjoy them as we watched Mary Dee perform or on our walk home.

13.3: Goode's Pharmacy at the Corner of Centre & Herron Avenues

Of course drug stores took on a greater importance when boys became sexually active. Unfortunately the condoms were kept behind the counter, not out in the open as they are now. Having been taught sex was "dirty," buying condoms signaled "*I am doing it.*" Awkward! Certainly we didn't want to purchase them at a drugstore near home, which meant walking as far away as possible to hide this dastardly deed. Equally awkward was having to ask a female clerk or pharmacist for the condoms. So that required finding a drugstore where no women would wait on you.

The pharmacists knew what was going on and enjoyed torturing us. We would wait until no other customers were in the store, then pick up a candy bar and place it on the counter. The pharmacist would ask, "Do you want anything else?" Making our voice as deep as possible to sound grown up," we would mumble, "Yes, I would like a box of condoms." The pharmacist turned to the woman in the medicine area and screamed at the top of his lungs, "Mable, the boy wants some RUBBERS." Mortified, we'd shove the incriminating purchase into a deep pocket, creep towards the door, and check the street to make certain no one we knew was in sight. Girls had it so much easier. If condoms were meant to keep girls from becoming pregnant, why didn't they have to go through the torturous process of buying the damned things?

As I said, pharmacists played an important role in providing health care for minor problems. More serious conditions were treated by Black physicians who lived in The Hill. At times, however, these physicians felt it necessary to refer us to specialists in the health care centers beyond The Hill where all too often we faced discrimination. One small example from my own experience occurred when I was about 5 or 6 years old and, in my family's telling and retelling of the incident, it became known as the story of "Ralph's Ear Infection." My parents called Dr. Robinson whose office was a block from our house and told him I was "burning up." He determined I had an ear infection which had happened before, but this time he was concerned about my exceptionally high fever. Upon his advice, my parents took me to Children's Hospital where we waited a very long time before a White doctor entered the exam room. My parents explained our family doctor's concern, but after taking a cursory look at me, the hospital doctor said in so many words, "Take the boy home. You shouldn't be wasting my time on something as common as an ear ache."

When we arrived home, Mom took my temperature again, and it was well above 100. Alarmed, she called Dr. Robinson, and suddenly I found myself naked in a bathtub filled with ice water. Doc Robinson arrived, and as sick as I was, I could see he was angry. I thought I had done something wrong and that's why I was freezing my ass off. Doc and Mom were trying to calm down my dad who was threatening to head back to the hospital and beat the shit out of the doctor. My temperature had spiked around 104 degrees, and without the ice bath, I could have died.

Throughout elementary school, I was always seated at the front of the class because I had a hearing problem. Dr. Robinson explained in words I did not understand at the time that the massive infection had damaged my inner ear. How much of this incident I remember myself and how much I recollect from hearing the story retold, I can't say. I do know the hearing in my left ear was permanently damaged because of the White doctor's callous indifference.

Lest you think this was an isolated case by a single prejudiced practitioner, the following anecdote illustrates the institutionalized racism of the times. This took place in the early 1960s when, as president of the University of Pittsburgh's student chapter of the NAACP, I received a call from a nurse who said the University's hospital kept separate stores of White and Negro blood. Thinking this surely couldn't be true, I met with the director who casually acknowledged the policy, then added, "Now Mr. Proctor, you probably think that we believe that Negro blood is inferior. Well, that is not so. You see, we know that Negro blood is stronger than White blood. Since White blood is weaker, it would be dangerous for Negroes to receive more than two pints of White blood, because the White blood could make them sicker and they could even die. But Negro blood is so strong that Whites can benefit from unlimited pints of Negro blood."

Flabbergasted, I finally managed to say, "Okay, when the White folks get all this Negro blood do they become 'Colored,' since in some parts of our country they say that two drops of Negro blood makes you Negro?"

This time the hospital administrator was left speechless.

Eventually the Hospital blood bank's racist policy was rescinded, but that was only one change in a widespread disregard for the health of Blacks. The Tuskegee Experiment serves as a chilling example of the institutionalized dehumanization of Blacks. White medical researchers under the auspices of the United States Surgeon General wanted to understand the way in which syphilis progressed from infection to death. Accounts vary as to whether hundreds of Black men were deliberately infected with the disease or were simply not treated when they came for care. In any event, these men, and the women they infected, were allowed to die even after penicillin was proven to be an effective treatment. Discovery of this inhumane and immoral research led to the creation of review boards to assure the ethical treatment of research subjects. Today's "informed consent forms" are a result of the Tuskegee experiment. The other result is a pervasive mistrust of the medical community among Blacks, often causing them to avoid or reject sound medical care.

Discriminatory practices in routine health care were mirrored by the lack of ambulance service when an emergency arose. In those days, the idea of providing on-the-scene care had not yet been conceived. The idea was to transport the ill or injured person to the hospital as fast as possible, hoping they would still be alive upon arrival. This rapid transport was typically provided by the police, which led to problems for folks on The Hill. Response to calls from the Black community was often slow. I am still haunted by a scene I witnessed when I was about nine years old:

> Sitting on a small porch attached to the candy store/numbers joint was a Black woman, who had been stabbed in the chest. The hilt of the knife protruded from the wound which was spurting bright red blood. "Shit, look at that. She ain't gonna last long, spurting out blood like that!" Another person asked, "Did somebody call the cops?"

> "It don't make no damn difference. Y'all know damn well that they don't hurry to pick up Colored folks. You bet your sweet ass she'll be dead long before them sons of bitches show up!"

> Right before my eyes, she was dying. Her eyes rolled back in her head, leaving only the whites visible. She moaned softly, her breath sounded like she was breathing under water. She became incontinent and urinated on herself. The smell of blood, urine, and feces filled the air.

"Damn, where the hell is the cops?"

"Don't make no difference now; she gonna die right there. Somebody get a sheet or something to cover her up!"

No one moved. The woman let out one last moan and cried out, "Jesus, Jesus!" Then she stopped breathing. In the distance I could hear the faint wail of a siren.

In the 1960s, the United Negro Protest Committee (a civil rights group in Pittsburgh) founded Freedom House Ambulance Services to address medical emergencies. This was a bold and innovative initiative in which unemployed Black men were given 300 hours of intensive training in life-saving first aid measures. With help from The Falk Foundation and several physicians at Presbyterian University Hospital, a well-equipped ambulance was provided and history was made. Freedom House became a nationally recognized model for the provision of pre-hospital emergency care and the training became a standard for the preparation of emergency medical technicians. This is one more example of the ways in which the Black community responded creatively to discriminatory practices.[28]

Entrepreneurs in The Hill

When Black folks had successful businesses they were often looked upon as leaders in the community. One such leader was Mr. Purnell, the proprietor of Purnell's Print Shop at the corner of Wylie Avenue and Chauncey Street. His shop was big, impressive, clean, and busy. This was the place to go for signs, posters, church programs, wedding invitations, or business cards. As one of the most successful Black businessmen in The Hill, he was often consulted on a range of matters having little to do with printing.

Two successful businesses in The Middle Hill were owned by Robert Lavelle. He challenged the racist real estate practices of the Pittsburgh Multi-list Corporation and won, forcing them to open up the real estate market to Blacks. Thus, Lavelle Real Estate Company made it possible for Black folks to buy homes, at first in The Hill and later in any community.[29] Lavelle also purchased Dwelling House Savings and Loan Association, moved the office next to his real estate firm, and began providing mortgages to Blacks who were denied financing by Mellon Bank, Pittsburgh National Bank, and other White banks. This gentle giant of a man, with the assistance of a young Black Attorney, Byrd R. Brown, changed the lives of many Blacks who had been locked out of the decent housing market in Pittsburgh. Hats off to my old friend, the late Robert Lavelle who lived to the ripe old age of 94, granted long life by the creator for the magnificent work of this true hero.

---

28 Unfortunately, the story of Freedom House Ambulance Service is also an example of how Whites appropriated the accomplishments of Blacks. After Freedom House had operated successfully for a number of years, Mayor Peter Flaherty cancelled Pittsburgh's contract with the service and established a city-based service. Almost all of the original crew members were let go, because they could not pass the written examinations the city imposed—this after having responded to over 45,000 cases during the service's years of operation.

29 Because of the lawsuit that Lavelle filed and won against the Pittsburgh Multi-list Corporation, the national organization also had to end discriminatory practices.

*13.4: Lavelle Real Estate and Insurance & Dwelling House Building and Loan
Association at the corner of Herron & Centre Avenues (c. 1968)*

*13.5: Employees of the Pittsburgh District office of North Carolina Mutual Life
Insurance Company on Centre (c. 1930-1950)*

We had at least two Black owned gas stations in The Hill. One, on the corner of Centre and Kirkpatrick Streets, was owned by Herbert Bean. He was very involved in the community and was regarded as a fine example of what a determined Black could accomplish.

The second station was owned and operated by Mr. Hawthorne and his sons. Located on Wylie Avenue near Morgan Street, it was a full-service station, offering car repairs as well as selling gasoline. While none of Hawthorne's sons took over the station, the training they got at their father's hands led them to successful careers. The station earned enough to allow all the boys to attend college.

In addition to gas stations there were a number of locally owned, independent car repair shops in The Hill. They arose because of the outlandishly high prices and poor service at White-owned shops. Many of the shops on The Hill allowed customers to buy parts elsewhere and bring them for installation. In fact, my brother-in-law operated such a shop out of our backyard. These places were a vital part of The Hill's economic fabric and allowed folks to have their vehicles fixed without worrying about fairness and disrespect.

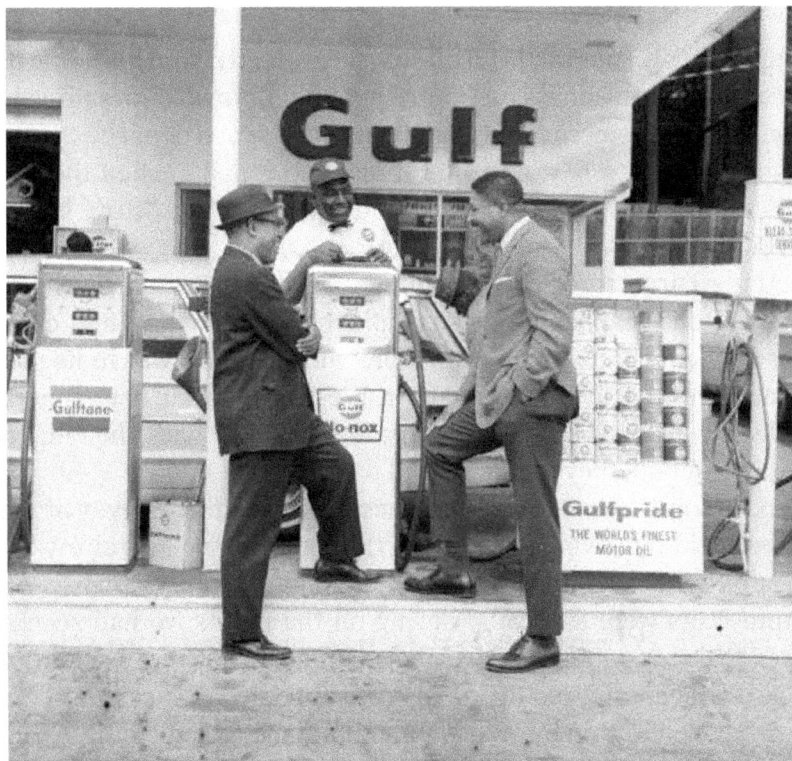

13.6: Herbert Bean's Gulf Station at Centre & Kirkpatick,
a well-known and respected establishment.

13.7: Miller Auto Parts store at intersection of Centre Avenue & Dinwiddie and Devilliers Streets (c. 1939-1945)

Two furriers operated in The Hill. Mr. Hill sold furs directly from his home on Junilla Street. Mr. Pryor had a commercial business on Centre Avenue. Both sold furs directly to consumers, but a large portion of their business came from the White-owned department stores. Customers thought that in-store tailors were doing alterations and repairs, when the work was actually done by Mr. Hill and Mr. Pryor. These gentlemen also made the "store brand" furs worn by many well-to-do Pittsburghers.

The Wests and the Turners were two prominent, well-to-do families who operated funeral homes in The Hill. Their establishments were plush, and they had fine cars. Later another funeral home was opened by Mr. Jones. However, when The Hill was in its prime, it was most likely that our relatives were laid out either at Mr. West's or Mr. Turner's funeral homes. While death is inevitable, most folks I knew had very few dealings with the "funeral men" unless absolutely essential. After all, they touched dead people.

My friends and I sometimes stopped by these establishments even if we did not know the people who were laid out. We never did anything disruptive and always acted respectful, because we were afraid the dead folks would rise up and grab us, or their ghosts would haunt us. Our impromptu visits were especially daring on the nights we had seen a horror movie. One evening, after seeing a double feature about Dracula, we were "talking bad" about how tough we would be if Dracula showed up in *our* town and tried to suck *our* necks. To prove how tough we were, we decided to stop by West's funeral home and look at the dead folks. We were laughing and joking as we approached the front door, but just as Stanford grabbed the knob, the door ever so slowly creaked open until it swung wide. A man was leaning over one of the caskets. As he straightened and looked at us, somebody let out a shrill scream of pure terror, and we turned and raced up Centre Avenue. In quick succession, each of us peeled off from the pack, fled through our front door, and clicked the lock shut. Later we were able to laugh at our encounter with Dracula, but not that night; it's too hard to speak when your heart is in your mouth.

13.8: West Funeral Home

13.9: Clyde Davis Funeral Home

There were at least three photography studios in The Hill. Albert Johnson provided pretty much the standard photographic fare; Charles "Teenie" Harris specialized in photos of individuals. Some clients were aware of Mr. Harris' connection to *The Pittsburgh Courier* and came to the studio in the hopes of becoming famous—or at least being photographed by the famous photographer. Arrington's studio, owned by the dad of one of my gang members, Donnie, was located on Watt Street across from Robert L. Vann Elementary School. Mr. Arrington was the exclusive photographer for the official photos at Vann School.

13.10: Charles "Teenie" Harris (with foot on window ledge)
in front of his studio on Centre Avenue (c. 1940-1945)

In addition to these studios, a number of freelance photographers plied their trade in The Hill and other Black communities. Fred Henderson was a commercial photographer who specialized in photographing industrial sites and products. Bill Goins specialized at photographing women as well as patrons of local night clubs and bars. Frank Hightower, and later his son, were also freelance photographers. Wally Dubois was a freelancer, who also owned a studio in Downtown Pittsburgh. When I took over Wally's studio, I joined the ranks of the Black professional photographers.

Barbers and Beauty Salons

When I was a youngster, Black-owned beauty and barber shops were located throughout The Hill. *Your House of Beauty* was affiliated with a famous Black female millionaire. Boyd's Barber Shop was located on Centre Avenue; Macedonia was on Wylie Avenue. I remember George Coles, Dozier Frazier, a dude called Hamm, and a host of others too numerous to mention. My point is that they proudly served us for many years when White establishments would not.[30]

13.11: La Salle Beauty Salon

13.12: Interior Crystal Barber Shop (c. 1942)

---

30 Had it not been for rampant discrimination, Black barbers and beauticians could have served White clients. Our establishments were just as nice, just as clean as those in White neighborhoods.

13.13: Exterior of Crystal Barber Shop and Billiard Parlor on Wylie Avenue
(c. 1950-1960)

13.14: Crystal Barber Shop & Billiard Parlor being demolished during
Urban "Renewal" (c. 1961)

Whether they straightened, dyed or cut our hair, barber and beauty shops were an important element in The Hill. They were sources of companionship as well as news of the neighborhood and the rest of the world. Many of the shops' owners had a bit of money and often helped less fortunate members of the community. They provided employment for hundreds of Black men and women. Some were leaders in the community.

We did not need White barbers and beauticians. In fact, Pittsburgh's pervasive Jim Crow culture denied us access to establishments beyond The Hill. Many salons in East Liberty, Shadyside, Oakland, and Downtown Pittsburgh made it quite clear that they did not wish to serve Blacks, often claiming they did not know how to "do Black hair." Yet, many Blacks had hair that was very much like so-called "White" hair. Further, if Black barbers and beauticians knew how to work with both Black and White hair, why weren't White hair specialists similarly trained?

Many times I heard residents in The Hill complain about lousy haircuts and other service at White-owned establishments. One major complaint was the White establishments' insistence on washing Black clients' hair before cutting or styling it. The results were often disastrous, because curly hair looks quite different after it dries. Some shops claimed that State regulation required this initial hair washing. If that were true, why were Black shops not required to follow the same practice? Could it be Whites considered Black hair to be dirty? My point is that Black barbers and beauticians could work with all kinds of hair. So, why weren't Whites similarly capable? Simply put, White barber shops and salons *could have* served Blacks if they had wished to do so.

The silver lining in that discriminatory cloud was that Black dollars stayed in the community. The barber shops and beauty salons, like so many other Black owned businesses, contributed to the economic vitality of The Hill and a growing Black middle class. Yet over time, we abandoned these establishments. As hair styles changed, shops that specialized in hair straightening were forced to adapt or close. Two additional forces contributed to the demise of barber shops and beauty salons in The Hill. One was the success of Pittsburgh's civil rights movement that broke many legal, if not cultural, barriers to services beyond The Hill. We abandoned Black-owned businesses, as we exercised our rights to patronize any establishment. The other was the destruction of many businesses during the misguided Urban "Renewal" project. Looking back, I believe we would have been much better off had we remained loyal to those who lived and worked right there in The Hill. The grass was definitely not greener elsewhere. The loss of these establishments was not good for my beloved Hill.

In addition to the store-front businesses, many enterprising people set up retail spaces in their homes (a fact kept well-hidden from the authorities). These home-based businesses ran the gamut from candy stores to speakeasy bars.

Traveling Vendors

When describing living arrangements, I mentioned the end of the horse-drawn huckster wagons. Later, some enterprising folks carried on the huckster tradition with a "store bus." They purchased old, yellow school buses, stripped out all but the driver's seat, and installed a counter top, a refrigerator, some bins and shelves, a meat counter, and some kind of cooking device. The drivers circulated through the housing projects, stopped at locations throughout the community, and honked their horns. People lined up to buy soft drinks, fruit, vegetables, cigarettes, eggs, milk—almost any item found at today's convenience stores. The vendors typically charged more than larger retail stores, which could be seen as exploitation of a captured customer base. But this would be too simplistic. Some residents in the housing projects did not have cars. City buses ran through the neighborhood, albeit infrequently, and jitneys were available to take folks shopping. But the store buses were not only convenient because they were readily accessible, but also because they sold small quantities like two eggs or one cigarette, or two slices of bread. This allowed folks to spread their money a bit further.

I recall watching in awe as a guy worked this system to his advantage. He would follow a store bus on foot. As people entered or exited, he would bum a few cents until he had accumulated enough to buy two cigarettes. He smoked them and started the whole process again. I asked him why he didn't just keep begging until he had enough for a pack. "Man, it could take most of the day to bum enough for a pack and while you doin that you ain't got no smokes. This way I can bum a bit and smoke a bit all day. If I gets a bit more I cin git a pop and a sandwich."

When I got older, some of us tried to organize against the exploitation of the store buses by providing weekly shopping trips to the supermarket. That worked for some folks; others told us to mind our own business. I think there was a line or two from an old Bill Withers song that said, "My friends tell me you are using me. Well baby, if it feels this good being used, then keep on using me till you use me up."

These modern hucksters were not the only White vendors who traveled freely through The Hill. One man drove a nice-looking car and carried a huge loose-leaf catalogue showing all kinds of merchandise from small appliances, to jewelry, to toys and games. People picked out items they wanted, made a small down payment, made another each week until the bill was fully paid. Then the man delivered the product.

In addition to the hucksters and merchandise sellers, other White people were very common in the neighborhood, including the mailman, the milkman, and the insurance salesmen. The latter sold burial insurance policies, paid for in weekly installments of 25 to 50 cents. Each payment was marked in a small "payment book," and when the policy matured, it could be cashed in for a few hundred bucks. If a person died before adulthood, the family had some money to defray the cost of the funeral. More often than not, parents gave the matured policy to the children on whom the policies were drawn. When Mom gave mine to me, I immediately cashed it in and returned the money so she could spend it on something she enjoyed. She accepted only after I assured her I had enough to put my sorry ass in the ground. I did not tell her I was going to be cremated. Folks in her generation did not think too kindly of that practice; they wanted a body to visit. Were these policies a good buy? Probably not, since most of the weekly payment went to cover the cost of collection.

Shopping beyond The Hill

Beyond The Hill were major department stores—Kaufmanns, Joseph Hornes, Gimbels, Frank & Seder's, and Rosenbaums. The precursors to indoor malls, these multi-story, ornate buildings housed departments for shoes, clothing, appliances, electronics, housewares, and home furnishing. "Going shopping" was often a daylong event for which one dressed up. When a break was needed, there were bakeries and restaurants. Needless to say, department stores did not employ Blacks, except as janitors or stock boys. Black customers were treated badly in spite of the fact they were spending hard-earned money in the establishment.

Department store merchandise was also very expensive. Fortunately, Five and Dime stores like G.C. Murphy, Kresges, and Woolworths were available for less-wealthy shoppers. *Five and Dimes* or *Five and Ten Cent Stores* were smaller, less upscale versions of department stores, Instead of a department occupying a whole floor, one or two counters featured the merchandise. They even had restaurants of a sort; actually lunch counters, although later a few tables, chairs, and booths were added. When Whites purchased food, they were welcome to sit and eat. Blacks had to place their order at the *take out* end of the counter where they were handed their food in a brown paper bag. The message was clear; *"You can spend your money here, but you cannot eat here."* It took national demonstrations and picketing during the Civil Rights Movement to stop this racist practice. Fortunately, Hill dwellers had our own Five and Dime Store, called *Diamonds* located on Centre Avenue in the Middle Hill. It was Jewish owned, but had Black as well as White employees. We were not treated as badly there.

13.15: Jean's Alterations

13.16: Gordon's Shoes

13.17: C. McEvoy Jeweler

13.18: Herron Hill Five and Dime, Castle Bar & Specks Market (1958)

I have read reports saying that most public housing developments were constructed at the top of hills with limited access to retail shops. I am convinced this was done to keep "undesirable" people away from "normal" folks. While partially true, that does not tell the story of people determined to live as normal a life as possible despite their circumstances. Bedford Dwellings, for example, was located along Bedford Avenue, the last street in The Hill before the terrain changed to sloping hillsides that overlooked the Eastern part of Pittsburgh. The planners of this public housing project did not include retail establishments, but right across Bedford Avenue was a regular residential community, complete with all manner of retail stores.

Post-Script

As I look back, the expectations placed on most of us Hill kids were about getting an education and going to work for "The Man." Even though we saw successful Black entrepreneurs, most of our education was focused on getting a job rather than setting up our own business. Parents took pride in their children who worked for a big, White-owned firm; less pride was accorded a son or daughter who set up their own business. My friends and classmates talked about becoming professionals in a major corporation and rarely discussed the option of opening our own businesses.

Years later, when I hosted a radio show, I would receive calls from listeners who were very negative about the possibility of owning a business. Some angry young people said that stores opened by Asians in the Black community should be burned out. When I remarked that a better solution would be to open their own stores, they would say things like, "We can't open our own businesses, because the banks won't lend us the money." Most of these callers were totally unaware of the history of Black-owned businesses in The Hill. Skeptically they asked, "So what banks loaned them the money?"

"No banks were involved," I'd reply. "Black Numbers Barons were our banks." Also, people saved their money, some pooled their money, and they started small. They did without televisions, cars, and credit cards until they got their businesses started. Then the successful ones helped the next one and the next one. In this way, they grew the number of stores in the community and were able to provide jobs for one another.

Sadly, when Urban "Renewal" fractured the fabric of the community, this type of trust and mutual aid was destroyed. That lack of trust keeps us down. I wonder, now, if Blacks might have fared better had as much emphasis and pride been placed on opening a business as on going to college and securing a corporate job. Nonetheless, I and many of my peers did follow our parents' dreams and went on to college.

CHAPTER 14

Getting Around

Public Transportation

Among the iconic images of Pittsburgh are the inclines that traverse Mt. Washington on the south side of the Monongahela and Ohio Rivers. Many Pittsburgh natives and visitors don't realize, however, that at one time an incline operated on the steep bluff between the Strip District and Bedford Avenue in The Hill. This, of course, went by the wayside in the name of progress.

Streetcars or trolleys were an important means of transportation throughout Pittsburgh and surrounding communities. But for those who lived in The Hill and other Black communities, these electric powered "buses" were vital since few residents owned a car. The original trolleys were painted red and yellow, and we dubbed them *Big Red*. They were powered through a long, flexible pole attached to the top of the car and connected through a grooved spindle to an overhead electric cable. If the cable slipped out of the groove, the driver had to put on a pair of heavy, insulated gloves, and manipulate the pole until it was reconnected to the cable. Until the city decided to "modernize" its public transit system, tracks were embedded in the streets along designated trolley routes.[31] Two routes served The Hill.

The route of the 85 Bedford trolley began at Herron Avenue, connected to Wylie Avenue, and continued down Wylie to Fifth and Liberty Avenues in downtown where it connected to the lower end of Bedford Avenue for the return leg of its circuit. Unlike most trolley lines that had two parallel tracks, the 85 Bedford as a loop route needed only one. Automobiles parked on either side of the street, which presented a problem only when the occasional car or truck came nose-to-nose with a trolley and the car's driver couldn't figure out how to navigate around the trolley. In spite of lots of cursing and shouting, "Big Red" always won the faceoff.

---

31 The city planners decided that the trolley system should be replaced by gasoline powered buses which allowed for the removal of "unsightly" overhead wires and paving over the tracks. Ironically, today electric-powered vehicles are seen as far more environmentally friendly, and modern, rapid-transit systems include electric trams. Also ironic is the adoption of imitation trolleys to transport visitors on sight-seeing trips around the city. Today, an original trolley is on display at the Heinz History Center.

14.1: 85 Bedford Trolley

14.2: 82 Lincoln Trolley

The 82 Lincoln line also served The Hill. The route began and ended at a "turn around" located at the top of Lincoln Avenue in the eastern part of the city. At the turn around, the driver got out and with the help of another person manually turned the car until it faced the direction for its next run. From the Lincoln Avenue turn around, the trolley travelled down Centre Avenue through East Liberty, skirted Shadyside, entered The Hill, and continued into downtown Pittsburgh.

Because the 82 Lincoln ran through several prosperous White neighborhoods, it served both Black and White passengers. Until the 1960s, all the drivers were White. For the most part, riding the streetcars was uneventful, but not particularly enjoyable. White passengers made it quite clear that they did not wish to sit next to Negros. Even if a vacant seat was right in front of them, they would search for an empty next to a White passenger. Sometimes, White riders would spread their packages across a whole seat to keep Blacks from sitting next to them.

Although there were no official Jim Crow laws, Black passengers tended to sit in the back of the bus. I preferred walking whenever I could.

Jitneys

One day, Cedric rubbed his eyes, blinked, and said, "Damn. I got to lay off that cheap wine."

"Why" I asked.

"Man, Ralph. I must be having a hallucination, because I could have sworn I just saw a *Yellow Cab* coming down the street."

We all laughed, and Stanford chimed in, "Whatever you been smoking, I want some, cause that had to be some good shit for you to see a Yellow Cab on Wylie Avenue."

Jimmy added, "Next you gonna be saying you saw a *People's Cab* drop off a fare on Junilla Street."

I chimed in, "How fast was the dude driving, cause as soon as he saw a Black face he knew his ass was lost."

We laughed like a pack of hyenas at our witticisms. Yet, it wasn't funny at all. Neither Pittsburgh cab company picked up or dropped off Black people in downtown. Unlike many major cities, hailing a cab on the street was not a Pittsburgh custom. White folks could hire a cab by going to a designated cab stand at the airport, bus station, or major downtown hotel, or they could call and ask for a cab to come to their doorstep. This service was not available to Blacks. As soon as cab drivers (they were all White) saw an approaching brown face, the "OFF DUTY" sign magically lit up, and they would stare straight ahead pretending no one was there. Reporting this to the Public Utilities Commission was an exercise in futility, because everyone knew that cabs did not and would not serve the Black community.

An enterprising former jitney driver, Silas Knox saw this slap in our collective faces as a business opportunity. He and several other investors started The Owl Cab Company in the early 1950s. It was completely Black owned and had Black drivers, mechanics, and dispatchers. The drivers had to dress professionally, including a jaunty Black hat. When I was asked to write something about the company for the Vann Elementary School newspaper, here is what I penned:

YELLOW CAB THOUGHT
THEY WERE BIG AND BAD
OWL CAB CAME
NOW THEY'RE SAD.

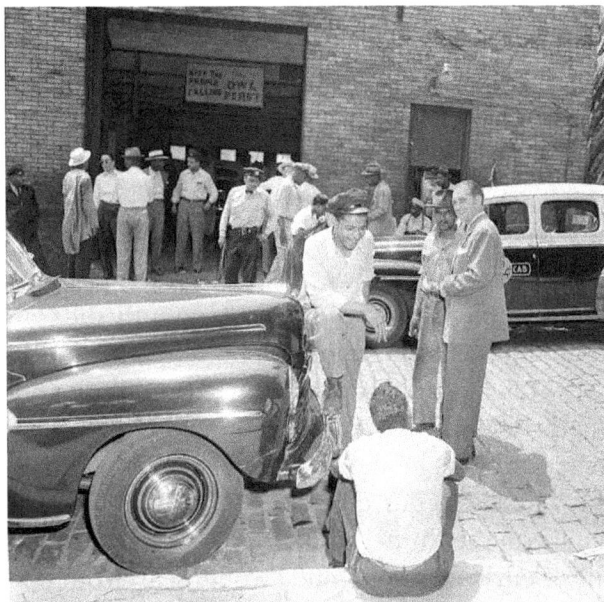

14.3: Scene in front of Owl Cab garage; sign in background reads
"Keep the people calling the Owl first" (c. 1945-1950)

Unfortunately, the company did not last long, but for a time, it was a shining example that we did not need the White-owned cab companies. To be honest, however, the Black community had long ago shunned the racist cab companies. We had Jitneys.

Think of jitneys as a low-tech forerunner of Uber and Lyft. They were privately owned and operated cars and could be hired at places where a "Car Service" sign was displayed in the storefront window. These were jitney stations, and the drivers paid rent and furnished them sparsely with a few chairs, maybe a desk, and in those days a rotary phone. Sometimes there was a television. In addition to operating out of stations, many jitney drivers simply hung around supermarket parking lots where people hired them to get home—much more convenient than lugging bags of groceries on a crowded bus.

The Jitney drivers charged slightly less than cab drivers, but of course the system was illegal. Several times, when I was young, some of the drivers applied for approval through proper channels, but were turned down. The "illegal" status of jitneys was of no concern in the Black community, where they were a welcome and necessary alternative to discrimination perpetuated by the "officially licensed" White cab companies.

One year in the late 1950s, public transit workers went on strike during the Christmas shopping season. At that time, before shopping malls, most families traveled by bus or trolley to department stores in downtown Pittsburgh. The strike left would-be shoppers searching desperately for a transit solution. Jitney drivers to the rescue! Drivers would just follow the trolley routes, pick up riders at every stop, and drop them at their destinations. A return trip was even better than riding a trolley, because the jitney driver would go right to your door for a little more money. The jitneys were more comfortable than the trolley cars as well. Even after the strike ended, the jitney drivers continued this service.

Private Transportation

Back when I was in high school, parents did not chauffer us around. We were expected to take a trolley or walk. In the city, most students did not drive to school. Even so, we had cars. Well, at least *one*. My best buddy, James Tyler, had a smoke-spitting 1938 Dodge with an iffy transmission that was still operable in 1955—sort of. Frequently the transmission locked the car in reverse. We'd all pile out and rock this behemoth back and forth till Jimmy could get it back into forward gear. This car weighed as much as an armored tank and seemed indestructible. One time we were driving through the Armstrong Tunnel between Forbes Avenue and the 10th Street Bridge. Jimmy lost control of the monster and side-swiped the tunnel. When we could finally stop to inspect the damage to our chariot, all we found were a few minor scratches; I admit to no damage inflicted on the tunnel walls.

In the evenings, Jimmy, Cedric, Stanford, and I would search our pockets and check between the seat cushions until we had enough change to buy a buck's worth of gas at about 39 cents per gallon. (Because I had a job selling lunch tickets in the school cafeteria, I was expected to kick in a few more pennies.) Once we were fueled up, we were off on an adventure. Often our adventures consisted of cruising around to impress girls and invite them for a ride. Most girls took one look at us and just laughed. Well a guy can dream, and *we* still thought we were cool.

Unlike Jimmy's old rattle-trap, the cars owned by many Hill residents were quite nice, as illustrated in the photographs throughout this book. This may be surprising to those who assumed that only pimps, preachers, undertakers, and numbers racketeers drove fancy vehicles, while ordinary citizens could afford only dilapidated cars, if they could afford any at all. This was not the case.

Even though banks would not lend money to Blacks for mortgages and personal loans, car financing companies saw a huge market. These companies were all too eager to take a financial risk and lend to Black folks, albeit at higher (often predatory) rates. This is how my dad was always able to have nice cars, even if they had been "pre-owned." Thus, car dealers may not have given Blacks the same kind of "deals" they gave White folks, but they did sell us cars.

14.4: Chevrolet Special Deluxe Station Wagon (c. 1948)

Cars—new or used—were status symbols as long as they were big and expensive. Although you might not be able to move to a "nicer" neighborhood or have a prestigious job, owning a fancy car proved you were SOMEBODY. Cadillacs were the preferred "ride"; followed by Chryslers, Buicks and Pontiacs. Car dealers cared nothing about race if the buyer could pay cash or finance it. With financing, it was possible to buy a car, pay it off in three years, trade it in for the newest model, and repeat the process in another three years. With this approach, the car was always under warranty. Car payments were a way of life, but worth it in order to avoid buying used cars with very short or worthless warranties.

Folks took pride in their cars and often admonished children not to lean on, play ball around, or touch vehicles. This norm was not necessarily understood by those outside "The Hood." At one time, I was director of a social service agency in East Liberty that ran a summer camp in Valencia, Pa. As many as 125 kids would board buses in our parking lot for the trip to the camp. Camp counselors were constantly reminded to keep the campers away from any cars parked in the lot. One day a vehicle owner complained that a youngster had placed a gym bag on the hood of his vehicle, resulting in some deep scratches in the paint. Naturally, we paid for the repairs. However, I called the White counselor into my office and asked her why she had not followed my directives about protecting vehicles. Her response was "What's the big deal. It's only some metal with wheels." When I reported the incident to the child's mother, she said, "Who the Hell let him put his damn bag on somebody's car. He knows better than that. I tell him all the time to stay the Hell away from people's cars, because they will hurt you if you mess up their cars." The difference in these responses illustrates the White counselor's lack of understanding of a cultural norm that, if violated, could have very bad results in the communities from which our campers came.

Keeping the family car sparkling clean and shiny was important in a neighborhood with few garages and the car would be on display for all to see. A neighborhood honor system kept residents from "poaching" parking spots. Reserving the space with chairs was unnecessary, because everyone knew whose car belonged with which house. Outsiders were admonished if they parked in someone's space, as was the case with a White woman who parked in front of a house occupied by an elderly person and her adult son. She ignored the neighborhood kids when they told her, "You can't park there." Then the son came out and explained, "I have to keep the space open for unloading groceries, because my mother can't walk very far. A friend who borrowed my car will be back soon and will be looking for my space to be open." The woman replied nastily, "*Your* space? I can park anywhere I want to. Nobody owns the street." As she locked her car and started to walk away, the man said, "Well, you're right, I don't own the street, so you just go on and leave your car here. By the way, you probably will not recognize it when you get back, what with all the broken glass, dents, and scratches. It might be a little hard to drive with all those flat tires. Have a nice day!" She moved her car.

Dad always had big cars and took great pride in keeping them looking sharp. When Dad got out the buckets and began washing his car, my sisters and I would try to sneak away before we could be drafted to help. Washing, rinsing, and drying was bad enough, but the "polishing" was sheer torture. As the only male child, I had the task of "Simonizing" the car. This entailed rubbing a stiff paste over the entire body of the car. After it dried to a haze, I had to rub it off and wait for Dad's inspection before rubbing it a second time with another rag. By now more than an hour of rubbing, polishing, and cussing had passed and my arm felt like it was about to fall off. But I still wasn't done—it had to be buffed again! Next came the dreaded windows that were cleaned by using old newspapers soaked in a mixture of vinegar and water. Because this vile smelling concoction worked on house windows, it was considered essential for car windows as well. Still not done! In the days before hand-held vacuum cleaners, the interior was swept with a small short-handled whisk broom.

Finally, I received the payment for my labors—a bottle of pop. Hey, Dad, isn't forced child labor illegal?

To be honest, however, I shared my dad's pride in those big shiny cars. Neighbors admired our car as we set out on Sunday drives around Pittsburgh. Nice cars were a great boost to self-esteem. They STILL are!

CHAPTER 15

The Family Road Trip

In order to be a "man" in The Hill, one had to abide by some pretty macho rules. Rule #1: "A man ain't supposed to cry." When Dad impaled his thumb with a fishing hook, he never uttered a word. He simply pushed the hook all the way through, cut off the barb with a tin snipper, and poured iodine into the open wound. Once he got lead in his eye when making sinkers for his fishing lines. Again he did not say a word; did not cry out; drove himself to the hospital, and just lay down on the couch when he came home. The only time I saw Dad cry was when his mother died; the pain of that loss must have been excruciating.

I knew I was supposed to emulate his strength. All of my friends got the same message from their fathers. So, when an unfeeling White doctor dumped a bottle of iodine into an open dog bite on my back, I did not utter a word even though I was mentally screaming. At nine years of age, I was a *Man*. Males had to grow up rapidly in my neighborhood; no time to be a *Boy*.

Rule #2: No "man" ran from a fight. The games we boys played were designed to show physical strength. No mound of dirt could be passed without playing *"King of the Hill."* All the boys grabbed, pushed, shoved, and wrestled for the right to stand on top of the dirt mound and declare yourself to be *King*. We played another, even dumber game. A boy had to stand with his arms out to his sides and allow anyone to punch him in the stomach. After being slugged, he'd say, "Is that the *best* you can do? My sister hits harder than that." Many days, I went home, holding back tears and clutching my aching, throbbing stomach. Stupid? Of course! But a boy had to show his toughness.

Rule #3: Sticks and stones may break my bones, but names will never hurt me. To demonstrate verbal power and impunity to insults, boys in The Hill played cruel word games called "snapping," "capping," "cracking," and "The Dozens." All the games except "The Dozens" had no real rules except to insult others while remaining impassive to insults directed to you. Of course, on occasion, a fist fight broke out. "The Dozens" was another story entirely. In that game, you insulted one another's *mothers*. That is dangerous ground, and fights often broke out during this game. Supposedly the games dated back to Africa.

Rule #4: Never let your opponents know that they hurt you. Developing emotionless expressions was considered a strength. I have been told that I have the ability to mask my emotions so well that no one can "read" me by facial expression, body posture, or looking in my eyes. I guess that means I have been well-trained. Sometimes that is not a good thing.

Rule #5: Don't let anybody take away your pride. I and all the guys I knew heard the message, *"Die first. You hear me, boy?"* There were times when I should have run from a confrontation, but could not because I did not want to shame my dad. My father was more adamant than most dads about my being a man. Stand up straight; shoulders back; chin up. Sometimes he pushed me so hard I wanted to fight him. I longed for the day when I would grow taller and stronger so I could beat him up. Why was he pushing me so hard? Why was he so relentless? Why was standing tall so important? My first clue came on a fateful summer visit to family.

We were near Hoffman, North Carolina but were running low on fuel so Dad pulled into a roadside filling station. A White man came out and as he began to fill the tank, I looked through the huge plate glass window at the front of the filling station. It was not like the places that sold gas back home in Pittsburgh. There was an eating place attached to it; not fancy like the restaurants in Downtown Pittsburgh. Rather it resembled Ray's Dairy bar up on Wylie. Through the window, I could see people sitting at the long counter or in one of the few booths.

"Dad," I piped up, "can we go inside to get a hot dog and some pop?" When Dad did not respond, I thought he had not heard me, so I spoke more loudly. Without looking at me, he remained silent. Mom asked me to be quiet, but there was no stopping me. My sisters and I were hungry and thirsty, and there was food and pop just a few feet away. I tried again.

Then I noticed something strange. My father was not standing tall. In fact, he was slumped over a little and not looking directly at the White man who was pumping gas. I thought maybe he was looking at the ground to find something he had dropped. By now the man had finished filling the car, and as Dad was paying him, they exchanged a few words. Mom was still fussing at me to keep my mouth shut. What the hell was going on?

I settled back in my seat, still mumbling about hot dogs and pop. Dad got back in the car, not looking at me or saying a word as he started the car. Instead of heading back toward the main road, we pulled around to the back of the establishment. Now I was really confused. What were we doing back there? Why was Dad parking the car?

As I was pondering this strange turn of events, the back door of the station opened and the man who had filled the gas tank walked toward us carrying a cardboard box full of sandwiches and pop. Now I had more questions: Why were we going to eat in the hot crowded car? Why was Dad still not talking to me? We ate in silence. I knew something was wrong. I just did not know what.

Not long after we were back on the road, my sisters and I started complaining that we were thirsty again. Dad must have been tired of our complaining, and soon pulled over to the side of the road by a small house. As he walked to the front door and knocked, I noticed that unusual posture again. An older White lady answered his knocking. After she and Dad exchanged a few words, she closed the door, and Dad motioned us to follow him to the back of the house.

The White woman met us in the backyard and handed Dad a scoop with a long handle, which Dad handed to my mother. Then he walked to a big round thing—a well—which I had never actually seen before. He began cranking a strange contraption and soon the bucket filled with water reappeared. We each drank cool, fresh well water from the ladle until we were full. I have to admit the water tasted better than the stuff that came out of the spigot back on Wylie Avenue. Mom and Dad thanked the lady for her kindness and instructed my sisters and me to do the same.

For the next several miles Mom and Dad spoke in glowing terms about the kindness of the White woman and how "special" she was. I was confused; why all the fuss about some old White lady who gave us a damn drink of water? What's the big deal? It wasn't like she invited us in for a glass of pop or lemonade. We had to take turns drinking from that damn metal scoop. Of course, as I grew older I came to realize that the woman was, indeed, special. Most southern Whites would never have allowed "Nigger lips" to touch the ladle she used for her own family. Many southern Whites would not have even allowed us to drink from the same well. I was learning the hard lessons of racism beyond The Hill.[32]

During the visit with our relatives, I continued to puzzle over Dad's strange behavior. Was he sick? What was wrong? He was not behaving in a fashion that was consistent with what he was beating into my head. This was not the Dad who let me challenge him when I did not believe something he said. He allowed me to take a sip of beer and a puff on his cigar. He even allowed me to prove, years ago, that there was no Santa Claus. This slumped over man who ignored me was perplexing, so I decided to watch him more closely.

Among his and Mom's kinfolks, his demeanor returned to normal, so obviously he was not ill—making the scenarios at the filling station and the White woman's house all the more mystifying. When Dad took me to a meeting near his old home in Asheville, I again saw him resume that slightly bent posture; he did not lock gazes with the White men. Our next meeting was with a Black man. Dad was his usual *stand tall* self. I started making mental notes as he interacted with various southern people to test my developing theory. I pulled up memories from all our trips to North Carolina. I started to pay attention to the body posture, the position of the hands, the positioning of the eyes. It was very different when these southern Black men interacted with one another than when they interacted with White men.

At last I had broken the code. My father had reverted to survival mode from the time he had lived down South. He and the other Black men I saw were assuming a "non-threatening" posture when around White men. Their eyes held a wariness, as if they were scanning the situation for signs of trouble. In the presence of their children or female relatives, the behavior was even more docile, more passive, and more non-threatening—a way of protecting the family from harm. When the White man left you could almost feel the defiance welling up and radiating from the Black men.

Now I understood what I had seen at that filling station. My Dad swallowed his pride to protect his family. Now I understood his admonition, "You don't let no man take away your pride. You die first. You hear me, Boy?"

I did hear you Dad. On one of my overseas trips, I was being blessed by the head monk of a monastery in China. When I asked my guide to translate his words, she said, "He knows that the White people in America treat you badly, but you should know that in the eyes of Buddha, you are as good as anyone. Do not let them make you feel inferior." I thanked him for his

---

32 It was dangerous for Blacks to travel by automobile throughout the United States. They could not be certain where they could safely eat, sleep, use restrooms, or buy gasoline. Some folks relied on the Green Book, a guide to safe places to frequent published by Victor Green. Dad didn't have one of those so we usually packed enough food and drinks to last for the trip to North Carolina. When Dad was tired, we pulled into a secluded spot, and Dad slept while we took turns watching for danger, although when I was young, I had no idea what the danger was. I was surprised we when we stopped at the filling station, but Dad must have known it was a safe place to buy gas.

blessing. Then with the help of my guide, I asked if my spirit told him that I felt inferior. He smiled and said, "No, not you. You may even have TOO much pride."

So, Dad, you see the lessons I learned from you, the sense of self-worth I gained in The Hill, helped me to reject those images of inferiority the world projected onto me. I am so sorry for all the times you had to swallow your pride to keep us safe as we traveled through the South. Thank you. I am your son, and I have *Stood Tall*. I have retained and guarded your manhood. It is *intact*.

CHAPTER 16

The Cost of Pride

Toughness is a two-sided sword. At a certain age, Black men in The Hill felt it was necessary to stop showing affection for their sons. This sudden change was confusing; so confusing I asked my mother why Dad no longer loved me. Her words of reassurance did not erase the hurt. Apparently, this lack of outward expression of emotion had something to do with not wanting his son to grow up to be a sissy. In speaking with my friends, they also remember the same hurt and confusion.

At one level, I knew Dad loved me. He took care of me when I was too young to care for myself. He worked long hours every day to make sure I had food in my belly and a warm, safe home. He took me places with him. He gave me piggyback rides and even held me on his shoulders when we viewed parades. Still, I never heard him say, "I love you, Son." I was hurt and confused when I could no longer kiss him goodbye. I never quite understood that, and no father would talk about it.

When I grew up and had sons of my own, I did not want them to experience that same pain. I told them every time I saw them that I loved them. They are grown men today, and I still say it. They are comfortable saying that to me as well. But Dad expressed his love obliquely; as did I.

I gave him gifts and the appropriate cards on birthdays and holidays. When he could no longer work, I "loaned" him money. That was a strange process. He would call and say something like, "Your Mom and I are going fishing, and I'm a little short. Can you lend me fifty, and I'll pay you back?" One day he called to say his car battery needed a charge and asked if I could take care of it. I said, "Sure, Dad. Take it to Shelley; he'll charge it for you." Then I called my friend who owned the gas station and said, "When my dad arrives, tell him the battery is too old to charge and install the best battery you have. Tell him it costs only $30 because it's on sale."

We played this "lending game" for a long while until one day Dad asked how much I owed him. I said, "Dad, you don't owe me anything. I make pretty good money. I can afford to do things for you and Mom. You took care of me when I was young. Now it is my turn. I can't take money from you." I thought that would make him happy, but he seemed a bit angry and said, "I told you all that was a loan, and I will pay you back as soon as I can. So just figure out how much I owe you. I know you try to trick me like when I asked you to have my watch fixed and you gave me a new one. You have a family of your own. I don't want to be a burden. I'll pay you back as soon as I get another job."

I was totally confused and asked a psychologist friend what I had done wrong. She told me that, even though I was trying to be a kind, good son, I had stripped my Dad of his pride. He needed me to know that he was still the father; that it was not my role to take care of him. He needed me to believe that he still had the ability to be a *man* and the ability to pay me back.

I understood. I called and said, "Hey, Dad, I found the slip where I keep track of what you owe me. It's about $300."

He said, "You sure? I think it was more than that."

"No, Dad. Don't you remember? You gave some of it back last November, just before Thanksgiving." Of course I was lying. I had no idea of how much he had borrowed. I was counting on his not remembering either.

"Well okay, Son. You know I'm gonna pay you back. Now that we got that settled, I need another hundred to buy your Mom an anniversary gift. You pick it out because you always seem to know what will make her happy."

"No problem, Dad. I'll stop over this weekend and give you the hundred in case you run into something you think you might want her to have. And I'll keep looking in case I find something, too. If I do you can just give back the $100." He went for it. I bought the gift for Mom.

When I gave it to him he told me he had to spend a "little" of the hundred, but I could put it on his "tab." We kept this little charade going until he passed away. That was okay because that was the way men needed to behave back in the day.

When I was about forty years old, I decided that I did not want my father to die without hearing me say, "I love you." I called and when he picked up the phone, I said, "Hi, Dad, I just called to say I love you." There was a long pause, and he finally said, "Good to hear from you, Son. How's them boys?" "They're fine, Dad."

Dad simply could not bring himself to utter those words to me. In the eyes of his generation, saying, "I love you," would somehow make both him and me seem weak or feminine. To the end, he held fast to his training about "being a MAN!" I don't judge my dad and other Black fathers harshly. They were doing their best to equip their sons with the tools needed to survive in a world that was harsh and cruel to Black boys. I wish they had had the words to explain those intentions, but they did not. It resulted in some confusion around child rearing for some families. My mother was trying to raise a gentleman by seeing that I got Emily Post manners and could play the piano. My father was raising a roughneck warrior who could protect himself and those he loved. Unfortunately, they did not know how to communicate those disparate goals. So they raised a boy who would beat your ass, if necessary, and then apologize profusely for the damage to your face.

LOVE YA DAD

CHAPTER 17

Looking Good, Fitting In, and Racial Pride

R esidents of The Hill lived by the mantra: *"When in public, you must look good."* This was, however, an issue fraught with complexity of acceptance by White society, Black identity, and self-respect. Looking Good was not only a matter of appearance, but also of behavior, especially in public where Whites were all too ready to see Blacks as uncivilized or as criminals. Even when treated badly, we couldn't respond with outrage. For example, my mother dressed up when she went shopping in downtown Pittsburgh. Yet, she was treated poorly by White clerks who always waited on her after all White patrons were served. If the clerks started to wait on my mother and a White person came up, the clerk stopped waiting on Mom and served the White person. All my neighbors felt the same sting of humiliation outside our beloved Hill, but our behavior still had to make us "Look Good."

Looking Good was not simply a matter of personal style. It was a way to fight against stereotypes that we were dirty, ugly savages. Whites would point to a filthy, homeless derelict to confirm their biases. "See, all Niggers are like THAT." A White student I knew at Pitt shared a story of the brainwashing she had received as a child. She was in the kitchen eating cupcakes. As she dived into the third, she said, "Mom, these are the best cupcakes I've ever eaten. Where did you get them?" When my friend heard the name of the baker, she spat out the mouthful of cupcake she was chomping on. "But she's a Negro and you've always said all Negros are dirty. Why would you feed me dirty food?" She was shocked to learn she had been eating treats prepared by this woman for years. Our parents were determined that we would not add to this degrading stereotype. If we ventured anywhere outside The Hill, we were subjected to careful inspection. Knowing that any one of us could be viewed as representative of our entire race added a heavy emotional burden to our childhood years.

My family was neither abjectly poor nor upper middle-class, but Mom and Dad made certain that my sisters and I were always scrubbed clean, had no holes in our clothes, and that everything but jeans was ironed stiff. Mom was a very good mender. She did most of the mending by hand, but when some heavy duty sewing had to be done, she walked to 638 Chauncey Street and used my aunt's treadle sewing machine. My mother would be appalled to see the current fashion of torn jeans and ragged cutoffs. We never had holes in our jeans because Mom always covered the worn spots with colorfully embroidered patches. When the slightest shiny spot showed on our jeans, out came Mom's sewing kit and a patch. Of course, patched clothes were worn only at home or while playing. Because I liked my soccer uniform to be clean, starched, and in good repair, Mom insisted I learn to wash, iron, and mend it, including sewing on buttons.

We all joked that "no matter how poor your ass is, there were two times each year when you got new outfits; Christmas and Easter. Don't matter if you are poor or if God don't care about outward appearance, when you put your hands together in prayer in a Black Hill District Church, you had to *look good*." So everyone had special Go-To-Meeting clothes.

17.1: Children at Birthday Party (March 1945)

17.2: Well-dressed woman

We bought most of our clothes at Hankin's Outlet in East Liberty. Mom could take a few bucks and buy enough slightly used clothes for the whole family to look good. Shopping there was an adventure for my sisters and me. That's where I always got my real, navy-issued pea-coats. On occasion I was able to find a real navy cap. I thought I was the coolest dude on the planet. When I was in the 9th grade, I was given a job selling lunch checks to students in the cafeteria. I loved that job, because my folks no longer had to give me an allowance. I could buy my own jeans at the Army/Navy store on Centre Avenue. I was given the same type of job when I entered Schenley High School; now I could buy my own jeans and sweatshirts. I was RICH.

Hats were a big thing in my community, and nearly all men wore hats in public. When passing women on the street, men touched the tip of the brim as a sign of respect. When wearing a suit, men were expected to have on a nice fedora hat. Baseball caps were for casual wear only. Indoors, hats were to be removed, and many a young kid got smacked upside the head for breaking that rule. I have to say, the one thing I hated about getting a new suit for Easter was the dumb, wide-brimmed hat that accompanied the outfit. Off it came as soon as I was out of my parents' eyesight.

Dressing well was the more benign connotation of *Looking Good*. Far more malignant was the cultural assumption that Blacks' natural features—dark skin, prominent lips, wide noses and tightly curled hair—are repugnant. Never mind that these looks were a standard of beauty in the area of Africa from which many Black slaves came. Never mind that Black appearance was apparently attractive enough to the masters who raped thousands upon thousands of their female slaves. Standards of beauty were synonymous with White features. I grew up in a society where getting a good job, marrying a "better" spouse, living in a "better" neighborhood, getting a better job, and receiving more civil treatment was based on "looking white." Succumbing to these social and cultural prejudices resulted in Blacks spending a great deal of time, effort, and money on trying to approximate "white beauty." In 1963, anger and frustration over the denigration of Black looks led me to write the following poem.

AND MY LOOKS ARE WRONG

Folks in the dominant American society
Say that White skin, blue eyes, thin lips
Long noses and a flat behind are the most desirable
Physical characteristics
And my looks are wrong
Images like that scream out at me from
Television, movies and magazines
Promising fame and fortune, sex and romance
If I look like these images
And my looks are wrong
Flesh colored Band-Aids are not meant for me
I cannot get blue jeans made for White folks
Over my ample hips
Cause my looks are wrong
But If my looks are wrong
Why do White folks
Stake themselves out in the sun
Risking skin cancer to
Brown down, just like me
Why do White folks pay good money to
Get their hair kinked
Just like mine
Get their lips enlarged
Just like mine
And why does Fredericks of Hollywood
Make a small fortune
Selling fake behinds that look
Just like mine
If MY looks are wrong?

The ironies catalogued in my poem underscore two aspects of appearance that Blacks tried to camouflage—hair and skin tone. At a young age, we got the message. Straight hair is *good* hair; kinky hair is *bad* hair. Derogatory terms like *nappy*, *BB shots*, and *cornbread knots* were used to describe our tightly curled hair. Therefore, to *look good*, we went to great lengths to straighten our "ugly" hair.

Sadly, tools and techniques used by Africans to groom hair for centuries were long ago lost in slavery. When I was growing up, the only readily available grooming tools were a very stiff brush and fine-toothed comb—suitable for White but not Black hair. My mother kept these torture devices in the lower, right-hand drawer of her dressing table. When I saw her reaching for that drawer I ran, trying to escape this dreaded process.

First, Mom literally had to catch me and clamp a leg around me to hold me on a stool. Next, the brush from hell was used to smooth out some of the tighter curls. This was followed by the application of a generous coating of Dixie Peach, a gel-like lubricant. Now came the *comb of pain*. Even when well-lubricated, Black hair does not yield easily to combs designed for straight White hair. Accompanied by screams and tears, Mom alternately combed vigorously and then brushed straight back. Mom would admonish me, "Stop fidgeting, sit still, and stop that crying, or I will give you something to cry about for real." Once I told Mom, "I *already* have something to cry about. You're *killing* me." She was not amused. A trip to the barber evoked the hope I could convince him to cut off all my hair. Being bald would have been a small price to pay to escape the torture of hair grooming. Naturally, he never granted my wish.

Once the torture was over, Mom would say, "My how handsome you look now!" All of this was done so we might come closer to meeting a standard that was beyond our reach. Think about the implications of this entire experience. If someone you love and who professes to love you is willing to inflict pain and humiliation to make you look good, *you must have been REALLY ugly*. Yet, nothing could change the fact that our ancestors in Africa had curly hair. There we would have been considered handsome and beautiful without all this pain and embarrassment.

When my sisters were young, their hair was braided very tightly into several "pigtails."

17.3: Young girls with typical hairstyles and attire at Madison Elementary School (1957)

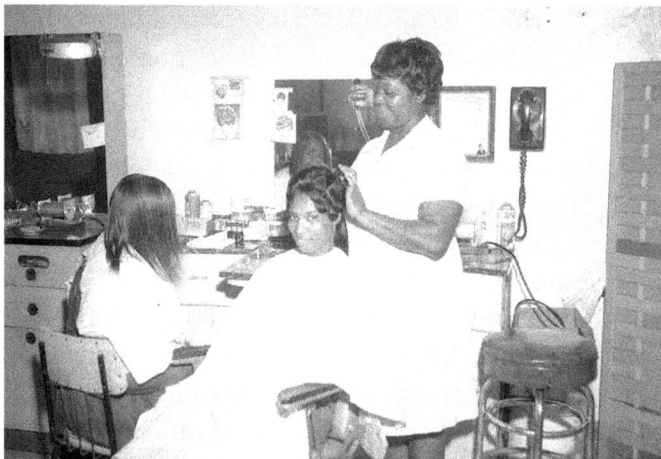

17.4: Woman in beauty shop having her hair straightened.

As they got older, looking *good* for girls meant straightening their hair. In the early days, this was done with heated iron straightening combs and curling irons. Before electric versions, these devices were heated on the open flame of a kitchen stove. This was particularly torturous in summer as most homes in The Hill were not air-conditioned. Liberal amounts of Vaseline were smeared on the hairlines of the face, forehead, and neck to protect against burns. This was never 100% effective. Screams of protest were generally met with retorts like, "Well, if you would have sat still, I wouldn't have burned your ear."

17.5: Example of women's straightened hair style (c. 1947)

As boys got older and became responsible for their own grooming, "hair pomade" entered the scene. This chemical concoction came in a can or jar of "grease" that, when applied to curly hair, along with vigorous combing and brushing produced hair that was partly straight, partly wavy, and partly curly. After the proper amount of pomade application, combing, and brushing, came the "Stocking-Cap." In the days before pantyhose, a guy had to convince a woman to give up a stocking. That was not as easy as it seems. When a pair of stockings got a snag," women put a dab of clear nail polish on either end of the "run." Although the repaired stocking could not be worn with skirts or dresses, they were fine for slacks. So, most women separated stockings into two different drawers; one for undamaged stockings; the other for those with repaired "runs." Typically the latter were donated for "stocking caps." The man took the stocking; pulled it over his hair; carefully tied a knot in the stocking at the top of his head; then cut off the foot. The cap was worn long enough for the pomade to dry in place. Unfortunately, if a stocking run turned into a hole, hair could escape and dry like a stiff spike. The solution to this problem entailed taking a wash rag, soaking it with hot water, wringing it out, and slapping it on the protruding hair spike. Once the grease melted, the wayward hair could be forced to join the rest of the bunch. After this treatment, a tornado could pick a dude up, fly him five miles, smash him against a building, and break every bone in his body. But when the ambulance arrived, not one hair would be out of place. Of course, with a head full of grease, these sharp-looking dudes got hassled for leaving slimy splotches on couches and pillow cases. A similar problem arose with another hair style called (for reasons I can't fathom) the Gerry or Geri curl. In this variation, the hair was styled into hundreds of exaggerated, long curls, and involved the generous application of a heavy oil to make the hair shiny. You could tell when someone with a Gerry was in the house, so the joke went, because they always left a "head print" on the sofa.

Another hair-straightening approach was the application of a toxic, lye-based chemical called Conk. A Conk Job began by smearing Vaseline wherever the hair and skin met. The shoulders and neck were covered with a cloth or tarp. Then the conk was applied to the hair, and after a suitable amount of time passed, great quantities of water were used to rinse the hair. A neutralizer was worked into the hair to stop the chemical process from causing further damage. Once this was over, your hair had been conked; you had a conk or a conk job. Because the hair was literally *burned* straight, many men had to be treated for skin burns. One unfortunate aftermath of conking was that it often turned the hair a reddish color. If you did not want red hair, you had to have black dye handy; thereby, further damaging your hair. *This was dangerous.*[33]

Ironically, this attempt to emulate White beauty could result in stigmatizing men and limiting their access to jobs. The biased view was that only pimps, punks, preachers, entertainers, and athletes conked their hair. When I once told my Dad that I was going to have my hair conked, he replied, "Son, there's no need to buy the product, because I'm going to conk you upside the head." Interestingly, the same sort of bias did not apply to women who used this product.

---

33 In his autobiography, Malcolm X tells an anecdote about when he was called Detroit Red. He had conked his own hair, but when it was time to wash out the lye, he discovered that the water pipes in his bathroom sink had frozen. In order to save his head and possibly his life, he was forced to remove the chemical mess by repeatedly flushing his head in the toilet.

Shortly after conk jobs became popular the next harmful practice raised its ugly head (no pun intended). In a "process" or a "Marcell," the straightened hair was styled into giant, seasick-inducing waves. Many hair salons specializing in this technique popped up in The Hill. The most famous one was Process Pete's, located on Centre Avenue in the Middle Hill. Both men and women had their hair styled in this fashion, and once again, this style could lead to the same stigmas associated with conked hair.

Moisture was the deadly enemy of all these hair-straightening efforts. Once the hair got wet, it tended to "go home," which meant reverting to its natural, tightly-curled state. Rain was an absolute disaster. Both men and women had to wear swim caps when in a pool. Men, of course, were then ridiculed as sissies. Most disconcerting was hair "going home" during amorous encounters. Vigorous love-making causes heat; heat causes sweat; sweat is moisture; moisture makes artificially straightened hair revert to its naturally curly state. Get my point?

17.6: Two men with conked and processed hair style (May 1956)

During the Civil Rights revolution in the 1960s, some Blacks started to abandon the emphasis on straight hair in favor of an untreated and curly style as would be worn in Africa. At first there was some resistance to this "back to nature" movement, but gradually it began to catch on. Soon "natural" morphed into the *Afro*, loosely based on African hair styles. Hair was grown longer; the kinkier, the better. The pendulum had swung. I, like most males who were in the public eye of political change, stopped using any sort of chemical or pomade. However, my mix of African and European genes resulted in a weird mix of straight and curly hair. Still, the act of "going natural" was liberating, even as it freaked out some of my White co-workers.

17.7: The photograph was taken c. 1970-1975. By that time the natural Afro hair style had become widely accepted as illustrated by the students in the pictured classroom.

This was a confusing time. Because the new hair style was associated with the emerging, free African nations, a new self-identity was also emerging for Blacks in the United States. Arguments arose over the use of terns like "Black" and "African American." Tension was mounting as a new, often anti-White militancy emerged in The Hill and other Black communities. Many people who had their hair straightened were ridiculed as "Uncle Toms." For the first time, lighter-skinned, straighter-haired Blacks were less admired.

Not everyone, however, embraced the new terms for self-identification. Rejection of the terms *Negro* or *Colored* caused confusion and consternation. My parents, like many older residents of The Hill, did not mind being called Colored. They did not understand that in a White-dominated society, "colored" meant you were neither Black nor White. This relegated us to an unspecified group, somewhat like calling a dog a "mongrel." There was no land to which "colored" people were tied. There was even an uncomplimentary ditty—*Colored* people; they were *Light, Bright and Almost White*—to describe our status as "human mongrels."

The descriptor "African American" was also a source of discomfort. For example, one prominent, light-skinned, Colored man who lived in the Sugar Top section of The Hill said he did not like my television show, *Black Horizons*, because I was always pushing to *Africanize* Black folks. I acknowledged that I was, in fact, trying to inform listeners of our heritage. Human civilization emerged in Africa, and Africans created civilizations about which we should be proud. He protested, "BUT, WE DID NOT ALL COME FROM AFRICA."

I asked, "Then please tell me where we came from."

"Well" he said, "Don't you know that some of us came from Jamaica or Haiti or Cuba."

"What you say is true, but don't you know that the Black people in the countries you named and some you didn't, were brought there as *slaves* by European colonizers? We are *all* from Africa." Obviously, this *Negro* leader had no notion about our past.

I felt a little sorry as he walked away, obviously confused. Yet many Blacks were confused during the turbulent rise of the Black pride movement. In Pittsburgh, African history was not taught in the public schools until well into the 1960s. On two separate occasions, I was hired by the School Board to help create and later re-write the curriculum for African American History. I was even contracted to teach White teachers how to approach the subject with Black children.

Others opposed the emerging trend of calling ourselves *Black* because of the negative connotations of this adjective. Of 200+ references to Black, all but one has negative connotations. Here are just a few examples:

- Extorting money is *blackmailing*;
- Individuals barred from employment or other activities are *blacklisted*;
- The plague was the *Black Death*;
- A family failure is a *Black Sheep*;
- Damaging someone's reputation is giving them a *Black Eye*;
- Failing to keep up is being behind the black 8 ball;
- Good cowboys/guys wore *white hats*; villains wore *black hats*;
- *Devil's food cake is black*; Angel-food cake is white;
- A small, inconsequential untruth is a *white* lie; so by default, a serious lie must be black;
- If a white cat crosses your path, you might reach out to pet it. Black cats are to be avoided as bad luck;
- White magic is *good*; Black magic is *evil*, and
- When racists really wanted to insult Negros, they didn't just call them Niggers; they called them *Black* Niggers.

Interestingly, the only positive connotation for Black in standard English is in the field of business where being "in the black" is far more preferable than being "in the red."

Given these pervasive, yet taken-for-granted expressions, it is understandable why some folks vehemently resisted identifying as "Black." Yet, when I would ask what name would make them more comfortable, most would say, "I want to be called *Negro*."

"Well I hate to tell you this, but you have been called *Black* all your life since *negro* is the Spanish word for black. That's what the Spanish slave traders called us, and the rest of the world simply adopted the name."

Not only Blacks resisted using that descriptor. During a Civil Rights meeting, several White friends said with a smile, "I'm sorry, Ralph. I just can't call you *Black*. That is such a negative term. Besides, you're not Black; you're brown."

In response I asked, "Do you have any problem calling yourself *White*?" If you are *Pink* and call yourself White, why can't I be Brown and call myself *Black*? These aren't simply descriptive words; they make a political statement. You can no longer *hurt* me by calling me *Black*, because now I embrace the term. We can now focus on inequality. I'm afraid this issue is not yet solved, but I stand before you not as a *Colored* man or a *Negro*. I am proudly a BLACK man who is also a descendant of the *Motherland* called Africa. Most certainly people have a right to call themselves by any name they choose, but I will fight to preserve that right. You already know my preference."

The issue of "colorism" or "shade-ism" complicated the quest to look good. Some women could "tone down" the darkness with a lighter shade of makeup. But that was a mere approximation of whiteness. Some individuals adopted the far more extreme measure of using skin bleaching creams. Magazines and newspapers aimed at Black communities featured many advertisements for such products. Some were euphemistically called "Skin Toners" or "Skin Enhancers." All promised to lighten dark skin; many were dangerous. Fortunately, over time, these products have all but vanished in the United States.[34]

Dark skin tone was not the only feature considered less than beautiful. The standard of White beauty also included thin lips. Africans were taught that our large, fleshy lips were ugly. My sisters and other women never wore red lipstick, because that would draw attention to their lips. Some Black women even applied lipstick only to part of their lips to minimize attention to their big lips. Women with large, puffy lips were often ridiculed. The entire time I was in high school, one girl was teased unmercifully, being called *liver lips* and *Ubangi lips*.

Many years later, as several guests entered the studio for my television show, I recognized the woman as the target of that constant torment. When I asked if she remembered me from high school, she did and thanked me for always being so kind. I then said, "Good to see you after all these years. Did you ever think the day would come when people would actually spend *money* to get lips like yours?"

She snapped back, "See, there you go, after all this time, still making fun of my lips."

I was taken aback. I had never done that; in fact, I had attempted to keep others from bothering her. Before I could say anything, another woman spoke up, "Girl, why are you attacking this man. Did you even hear what he was saying? He paid you a damn compliment, but you want to snap his head off. Don't you know what he's talking about? Don't you read? Don't you know that White people are spending a whole bunch of *money* to make their lips look like the ones you were born with? You need to let go of that shit from a long time ago. The man said you are beautiful, and you want to bite his damn head off." She then extended her hand to me and said, "I'm Marie. You can tell me I'm beautiful anytime you want. I promise I will not bite you; unless of course, you like to be bitten."

WOW! Slapped down by one and flirted with by the other.

---

34 During my travels from 1958 to 2001, I discovered that a great many of these products were still being used in India and the Philippines. A recent CNN article called "Fairness Mania" indicates that many in India are still risking serious health issues by using a steroid-based cream to "lighten their faces." Dark-skinned women are afraid that they will never find a man.

By now my former classmate had considered my comment and apologized. Of course, she had never been ugly. She, like so many of us, had been a victim of vicious brainwashing. This incident took place more than 30 years ago. For the most part, we have recovered from these biases about what counts as beauty. We invest less in trying to look like poor versions of Whites. But the effects still linger. At the community college where I currently teach, I overhear comments about "good hair, bad hair." Female students tell me they are treated badly because of their darkness, or they are insulted because they wear a natural hair style. Even more unfortunate was an incident occurring when I visited my newborn granddaughter. In the corner of my daughter-in-law's hospital room was a group of older women who were examining the back of my grandchild's ear and the beds of her fingernails. According to a widespread belief, these areas indicate whether a baby will "Brown Down" or remain light-skinned as they grow older. The very term means that getting darker is bad. Outraged, I declared, "She will be beautiful no matter what shade she turns out to be. I will not have you damaging her mind before she realizes how beautiful she is."

Interestingly, the Proctor family, like many other Black families, has been racially mixed for centuries.

Many Blacks, including my family, claimed to have Native American ancestry. No one knew for sure to which tribe we belonged. Some said we were Cherokee; others said the Blackfoot tribe. At some point, I decided to trace my family history, starting with my dad's people. Since Dad was very light-skinned with wavy hair, I surmised that somewhere in the not too distant past we had European ancestors. Because my Aunt Mazie was the family genealogy expert, I asked her, "Who were the White folks in the family?"

Clearly uncomfortable, Mazie reared back and asserted. "There weren't any."

"Aunt Mazie, how can you say that, when both you and Dad are damn-near as White as anybody I have ever seen. You stand there with long, straight, black hair, long nose, and thin lips. I can see your veins through your skin. And you're going to tell me there ain't no White folks in the family? How do you explain the way you, Dad and some of your brothers and sisters look?"

Without missing a beat, Maizie exclaimed, "Oh that's our Indian blood"

Many years later I successfully traced my Dad's roots and found we are African and Irish. *No "Indian" blood whatsoever.* Still, I had yet to finish my mother's side of the family. Maybe I'd find my Indian ancestors in that part of the family tree. In the interim I took one of those DNA tests, which reported that I'm primarily African, with a 16% splotch of Irish, and about 3% "other" European. Damn! I guess I'll have to sell those Cherokee war bonnets I'd bought in honor of my Indian roots. As I write this book, the host of a genealogy show airing on Public Television laughs at the myth of "Indian" Blood. According to his research, only 5% of Blacks have Native American ancestors.

In my parents' generation many Blacks disavowed any White heritage. Claiming Native American ancestry helped to deny the painful truth that our mothers, grandmothers, great-grandmothers on back through time had been raped with impunity by White victimizers. Then, too, they could avoid the shameful thought that some of our ancestors had fallen in love with Whites and had allied themselves with those who oppressed our race.

When I was a teenager, two men appeared at my home one day. Their purpose was to update the Proctor clan list. First they asked for the names of all family members; then for family photos. When they began separating the photos into two stacks, I looked more closely and saw that my father and my sister, Carol, were in one pile; the rest of us were in the other, with my mother being at the bottom of the stack and my image at the top. Suddenly it dawned on me that we were being divided on the basis of our skin tone. I was just light-skinned enough to be included in the census. My mother was not. In marrying a dark-hued woman, Dad had "married down." The Proctor clan was interested in only lighter skinned Proctors in order to emphasize the clan's *White* heritage. I threw them out of the house.

Because my father was very light skinned and my mother a bit darker, my sisters and I ran the gamut from very light to medium reddish brown. Because I am medium-brown in color, I have sometimes been considered "too dark" and sometimes "too light." This fixation on skin tone has been damaging when used as a basis for accepting or rejecting one another. Here are two experiences of colorism from my dating years.

During the summer before we left for college some friends and I worked in a laundry. One day, I noticed an exceptionally beautiful co-worker. My friends knew this woman, but when I asked them to introduce me, they refused. I laughed and said, "Okay, so you both want her, and you can't stand the competition."

Frowning they replied, "Hell no, Man. We don't want no parts of her."

How could that be? My horny, young friends were usually trying to have sex with any female who moved. They looked at the object of my fascination with utter distain.

As I was about to launch a physical confrontation, one friend said, "Man, Ralph, look at her."

"I AM looking at her; that's why I want to meet her. She is fine, like good wine."

My other friend chimed in, "No, Ralph; *really* look at her. She's as Black as your shoes."

"So what. My shoes look *Good*."

"Ralph, why would someone of your color want to deal with *coal*?

Still missing their intent because I didn't judge people based on color, I declared, "You two can go to Hell. I'm going to go across the room and meet her. She is a double *Fine Fox*."

Working up my courage, I approached the woman who was chatting with some friends. She was even prettier close up. When she smiled, I made my voice as deep as possible and said, "Hi. My name is Ralph." Mind you, I was only 16 years old and knew *nothing* about picking up women. When she returned my smile and asked, "What can I do for you, Ralph?" I said, "You're so pretty, I would like to get to know you better."

Her smile vanished. "What for, Ralph? Why do *you* want to get to know *me*?"

Okay, fair enough. I didn't realize I needed a ready rationale for wanting to get to know her. As I stood there looking stupid, she continued, "There's only one reason someone as *light* as you wants to meet a girl as *dark* as I am. You just want to get in my *pants*."

I was dumbfounded. My friends were rolling around, laughing their asses off. One of them said. "Look at him. He doesn't have any idea what the hell is going on."

The woman continued her onslaught. "My mother and my aunts warned me about light-skinned, pretty-boys like you. They told me you won't take me home to meet your *mother*. You won't *marry* me. All you want is in my pants."

I suppose there was some truth to what she was saying. I certainly was not going to marry her or anyone else. I was only *sixteen*! But why wouldn't I take her to meet Mom? As far as the "inside of her pants" were concerned, I suppose there may have been an element of that, but I really just wanted to be with someone that beautiful. She did not buy that and told me to go "find someone my own color to mess with."

My friends laughed for days, but I was still confused. Why would someone that pretty think she was not acceptable to any man? I truly did not understand the psychological damage that had been inflicted on her by people who loved her but did not teach her to be proud of who she was. What a shame.

Well, I gave up on that quest, went to college, dropped out of college, went to the Army, served three years, came back home, and enrolled in the University of Pittsburgh. As fate would have it, I soon met another quite beautiful woman. I really liked her; we dated a few times; I even took her home to meet my mother. One day she asked, "Ralph, are you gay?"

Shocked, I asked why she would think that.

"We've been out four times now, and you haven't asked for *any* yet. So I'm wondering if you prefer men."

Apparently I was moving too slowly. I assured her I found her very attractive and admitted I wasn't sure when it was the right time to ask for sex. Smiling, she said, "Let's be real. I'm very attracted to you. You're attracted to me. So I figure we are going to have sex soon."

HALLALUJAH. This beautify woman was offering me sex! I calmed down and said, "I hope so."

"Okay. We have that out of the way, but before we get started, I need to tell you something. We can have all the sex you want, but I cannot have children by you."

YES! I must be in HEAVEN.

"Did you hear me?" she asked.

"Oh yes. I think I understand the contract. As much sex as I want, *no children*. I am *cool* with THAT. When do we get started?"

"No," she said. I need you to REALLY understand. If we get married, I may get pregnant. When the baby comes, and I am pushing the baby down the street in a stroller, I don't want someone coming up and asking me 'whose baby is that?"

"Why would somebody ask you that?" I asked in complete confusion.

"Ralph, I'm much darker than you. You're light enough that we could produce a White skinned baby. Some nosy woman may look at the baby, look at me, and ask whose baby that is. I'd probably smack her and go to jail for assault."

Once again I was dumbfounded. Here was an absolutely beautiful woman who was badly affected by the fact that she was dark skinned. What the fuck!?!

A line from a detective movie with an all-Black cast concisely stated the prejudices of colorism, "If you White, you alright; if you Brown, stick around; If you BLACK, git BACK." From the earliest days of slavery, we were brainwashed into believing that lighter skinned

Colored people were more acceptable to Whites. By extension, White skin is beautiful; dark skin is ugly—even if millions throughout the world in Africa, India, The Philippines, Australia, New Zealand, Mexico, and Central and South America are dark-skinned and beautiful.

All-too-often, decisions about who to befriend, date, and marry were based on the pigmentation of one's skin. Sadly, such prejudice caused rifts between lighter skinned and darker skinned Blacks as well as resistance to identifying as "Black."

When Blacks accepted a White standard of beauty, we hurt ourselves and one another. We chose friends, relatives, and life partners in an effort to be more acceptable in White Society. One version of this aim of "fitting in" took a toll on what has been called a lost generation of Black professional men. These highly educated individuals had done what White society told them they had to do in order to become successful.

Whites told them they would be accepted if they had the proper education. So they went to college and earned "proper" degrees. When hired by corporate America, they were told that dressing properly was necessary to fit in. So they went to Brooks Brothers and brought proper professional clothes. Reading the right paper was important, so they traded their subscription to *The Pittsburgh Courier* for the *Wall Street Journal*. Fitting-in meant abandoning Jazz in favor of classical music. Fried chicken, bar-b-que ribs and sweet potato pie were replaced by "proper" White cuisine. In these and other ways, these Black professionals became chocolate versions of White people in order to "fit in." But something was wrong. They had conformed to White expectations, yet were still not accepted. At the same time they were called "Uncle Tom" or "Aunt Jemima" by other Blacks. Malcolm X mocked them by saying, "What do White folks call a Nigger with a Ph.D.?" After pausing he said, "NIGGER." Understandably, they were angry after playing by the rules, only to realize the game had been rigged from the beginning.[35]

While some Blacks did go through these machinations in order to be accepted in the White culture of corporate America, many of us did not. It did not matter, however, because no matter what our backgrounds, Blacks were all-to-often treated as undesirable interlopers. Illustrative of this point is the treatment that my friend Matt Nelson and I were subjected to as professionals working at the University of Pittsburgh in the 1960s. In terms of background, Matt and I came from different social circumstances. As mentioned in earlier chapters, I came from a working-class family which, while not abjectly poor, was not well-off financially. Matt on the other hand came from an upper-class, well-to-do Nashville, Tennessee family. Despite these differences, we both worked hard to achieve our goals. Matt graduated at the top of his class at a highly respected, Black medical school.[36] I was educated primarily at top-notch White universities. As we pursued our education and professional goals, neither of us gave up our cultural background in order to "fit in" We enjoyed Jazz, ate fried chicken and ribs, and read newspapers and periodicals from both our own culture and the dominant one.

As a dental pathologist at Pitt, Matt wore the traditional white lab coat of medical professionals. As an academic dean, I never wore a suit, but dressed similarly to other male

---

35 For a more detailed account, see: Ellis Cose, *The Rage of a Privileged Class: Why Are Middle-Class Blacks Angry? Why Should America Care?* (HarperCollins, 2009).

36 Despite the excellent reputation of Matt's alma mater, graduates back then encountered difficulty when seeking positions in White health care institutions. In recent years, graduates of that school do not have any problems finding lucrative jobs.

deans. Without giving up our cultural roots, we certainly appeared to "fit in" to the professional, academic culture of the University. Yet, after working late one evening in the Dental Clinic, Matt was walking to his car when a White janitor accosted him and challenged his right to be in the building. As Matt related this incident, his eyes filled with tears of anger. I could relate, having been subjected to similar bias by parents of a White student. The parents had been told to make an appointment with me to discuss some difficulties their daughter was having. When I answered the knock on my office door, they said, "We're here to see the Dean." I introduced myself, yet they responded, "No, we're here to see the REAL Dean."

These are simply two examples of the myriad instances of being judged instantly on the color of our skin. Whether Blacks worked to achieve some approximation of "ideal" White beauty, or abandoned our culture to fit a corporate norm, or remained true to our inner, authentic self, we were, in the eyes of so many Whites, the "alien other."

More than 40 years have passed since these incidents occurred to Matt and me. Yet, even now, I feel compelled to ask, "Are we free from the burden of Looking Good according to some idealized version of White beauty?" Can we accept that we are good looking regardless of how curly or straight our hair; regardless of how light or dark our skin; no matter how big or small our lips? Although chains no longer bind our wrists and ankles, we still suffer from a condition I call "CHAINS ON THE BRAIN." This was caused by a "beauty game." Even as we tried to master the rules so we could gain acceptance, the rules changed, often leaving us confused, hurt, angry, and hating our own appearance.

Yet, despite the constant bombardment of messages telling us we were ugly, we still managed to look in the mirror and on occasion say, "Not bad, baby, not bad." We were not beaten down so badly that we could not function. We still managed to live fairly good lives as long as we were in The Hill among our own people who showed us love and respect. *Looking Good* took a lot of time, effort, and money. Once again, my people showed their resiliency in dealing with a well-hidden but dangerous practice directed at them by White society. We took the blows and still we rose.

CHAPTER 18

Mental Health—
Still We Endure and Rise

Two questions can be asked about the mental health of residents in The Hill.

1. To what degree did Blacks in The Hill suffer from mental illness?

2. Given all we went through, why was there not MORE mental illness in the Black community?

Both are complicated to consider. When I lived in The Hill, little research had been conducted and not much has been done since then to answer the first question. Where such research exists, one has to wonder about what assumptions and qualifications the researchers brought to the task. Undoubtedly some Blacks suffered from mild to severe mental disabilities. Yet questions still linger. Whose norms—what societal assumptions—are the basis for diagnosing mental illness in a Black person? Are the feelings and behaviors exhibited normal or abnormal among Blacks? What misperceptions and misinterpretations arise when diagnosticians have no understanding of Black lives and cultural norms?

As I contemplate the second question, I think of the indignities and injustices to which Blacks have been subjected since their forced arrival in America. It is one thing for an individual to be psychologically traumatized, but what are the implications of an entire racial group being systematically and continually treated as inferior? The term "micro-aggressions" had not been coined when I was living in The Hill. But I, like all members of my community, lived in a perpetually hostile social environment:

> ...being treated as scum...being robbed of the truth about their ancestry...never hearing that Black people made important contributions to society...learning only White, never Black, history...being forced to address Whites as "mister, miss, or other formal titles, while being call by one's first name, or "boy," or "nigger"...hearing that our natural looks are ugly and we should try to look like White folks...seeing white images of God and Jesus...hearing false claims that most welfare recipients are Black...fearing that applying for a job, trying to get a mortgage or attempting to use a public bathroom might lead to arrest... fearing that driving a nice car might result in your own death or the death of a

> loved one...having to be twice as good as Whites to get a decent job...biting your
> tongue while watching your mother being disrespected by store clerks

Such psychic insults – both large and small – cause an anguish so deep, it is hard to fathom how any Black person enjoys mental health. Still many of us raised in The Hill flourished. We still stood tall and proud. How can we account for this?

From my perspective, it is important to make a distinction between life in The Hill as I experienced it and life on The Hill after the devastation of Urban "Renewal." It is also crucial to factor in the stories emphasized by White folks and those told among Blacks.

There is no doubt that poverty leads to mental illness, and there is no doubt that many Hill residents were poor because of racism in the society at large. Yet, before the devastation of "Urban Renewal," residents of The Hill included many blue collar workers of comparable economic status as their White contemporaries. Also among the residents were middle- and upper-class business owners and professionals. While chronic unemployment can contribute to mental illness, and it is true Blacks had a hard time getting jobs in the White community, in The Hill itself thousands of jobs were available. Some psychologists think that overcrowding contributes to mental illness, and certainly parts of The Hill were overcrowded. Experts agree that exposure to violence can lead to mental illness, and like all communities, we had our share of domestic abuse. Gangs became more prevalent as the social fabric of The Hill was ripped apart. Crime, too, happened in The Hill. But these negative images of poverty, overcrowding, violence, and crime received constant attention. Less acknowledged was the suffering caused by police brutality or economic and medical violence perpetrated by White society on Blacks. (And waiting each day for the next bad thing to happen – with the certainty that it will – has got to undermine sanity.)

Even with all this, the role of racism in mental illness is not clear cut. As I indicate elsewhere throughout the book, most of the racism I encountered took place outside The Hill; this was not true for me alone. Many Hill residents were born, raised, went to school, got a job, married, raised children, and died in The Hill. This community buffered many from the harshest aspects of racism. Seen from this perspective, I can understand how my mother could endure the racist treatment she encountered at the hands of clerks in downtown stores. Knowing she would shortly return to the sheltering arms of a community that loved her, she could endure the temporary racist insults.

Spirituality and the church also helped forestall the emotionally damaging effects of racism. Many Black folks viewed church as a "filling station." When the world beat you down and drained your battery during the week, you could come to church on Sunday and God would recharge your battery and refill your courage. Black church services were about redemption and salvation; about the better life that waited when God called you home. I was raised in the Methodist Church and even though I had my doubts about Heaven and Hell, I left church services feeling renewed and, like Sampson, ready to kick some Philistine asses.

Contributing to the complex picture of mental health and illness was the stigma attached to seeking professional help. From a young age, Black children are taught to be strong both physically and mentally.

Don't let them see you cry. I overheard a physician from India tell his Black colleague, in reference to a racist incident. "Man, don't ever let them know they got to you. Don't *ever* let them see you sweat."

We were expected to hold our own against all that Whites did to bring us down. Mommy, daddy, uncles, aunts, sisters, brothers, preachers, friends and enemies respected you if you were tough. Going "crazy" was a sign of weakness. *A man ain't supposed to cry. Sticks and stones will break my bones but words will never hurt me.* "Hey Ralph, I know you just dislocated your thumb on that last play. No problem. Here, I'll just snap it back in place and you can go back on the field." Stop that crying; people will think you're a sissy. You cut off your little toe? No problem; you got *nine* more.

We were taught how to scan situations for potential danger. If we were in trouble, extended family was always there to help. If we could survive slavery, we were told, "this little bit of racist shit ain't nothing." Being prepared for trouble and mistreatment can sometimes soften the blow. Expecting little from Whites can blunt the force of racism.

In addition to the "be strong" messages, Blacks in my community tended to avoid mental health assistance because of racism in that system. Stories abounded of dangerous or bad treatment in one of those "Looney bins." It was highly unlikely that Blacks would receive treatment from a Black professional. After all, at that time, less than two percent of the American Psychological Association members were Black. Most Blacks were skeptical that a White person could offer answers when they could not really understand the questions.

In fact, the word "treatment" sends chills down my spine. I had recently helped the Community College of Allegheny County (CCAC) establish a program to increase the likelihood that young Black males would stay in school long enough to consider college. My research had indicated that a number of factors caused young Black males to drop out of school well before it was time to consider a college education.

One factor was the disproportionate number of Black males who were in so-called "special education" classes. These classes were taught with the assumption that Black males lacked the mental capacity to attend college. They were, consequently, never exposed to the courses college-bound students were expected to take. Another issue was the disproportionate prescribing of Ritalin, a drug to handle the alleged "aggressive tendencies." Statistics show that Black males are placed on "detention" or expelled from school at a rate far greater than White Males. Black males engaging in normal behavior for their culture are often seen as aggressive and dangerous and are sent to the principal's office for "corrective action." As a result of all this negative attention and "labeling," many Black males are turned off to education by the time they reached the third grade.

Illustrative of the problem is an incident that occurred when a teacher asked for my advice on handling an "overly aggressive" student. I met the teacher just before the class headed out to the playground for recess. I asked her not to gaze too long on this negative behavior, because I wanted no clues as to what behavior she considered aberrant. As the students returned to the classroom, a substitute teacher took charge, allowing the teacher and me time to discuss the situation. I asked her to identify the behavior she saw.

"Did you see those boys on top of that mound of sand? Did you see them pushing and shoving and yelling at one another? It was so hard for me not to go over and get them to behave." Apparently she had been chastising these boys every time she saw their "overly aggressive behavior."

"I did see a group of boys playing King of the Hill. I saw them laughing, arm-in-arm as they debated who had won the game."

Seeing her confused expression, I explained, "They're friends, playing a game that is very common in African American, inner-city communities. They're not aggressive. They're not pathologically violent. They are just proving they are tough "men." It is all part of the effort to prepare our youngsters for the onslaught of negativity they will certainly encounter when they leave their own communities. They are normal kids from a normal Black community. Can you imagine how they feel when their behaviors are constantly labeled as 'bad,' and they're criticized or punished for what they consider fun?"

As we continued to talk, her skepticism and concern gradually gave way to a new understanding that her expectations of behavior had been shaped by the cultural norms of *her* community while the boys' behaviors had been shaped by the norms of *theirs*. All-too-often, such ingrained, cultural bias shapes educational policies that drive young Black males from school. Sadly, these same types of biases often underpin research studies designed by White researchers to study the mental health of Black communities.[37]

In both therapy and education, trust forms a basis for healing and learning. Yet, if Whites perceive Blacks as dangerous, then trusting relations cannot be established. Studies have shown that Whites overestimate the size and danger of Black males, thereby triggering a fear reaction.

I personally experienced this size bias when I entered a room in which some of my White colleagues were so deeply involved in an animated conversation, they did not hear me arrive. One colleague said, "He's at least 6'3"." Another said, "No. He's only six feet." Still a third disagreed, arguing that the person was even taller and must weigh about 250 pounds. Finally, I interrupted them, "Wow, you folks sure can't agree about this person's size. Why don't you just ask him? Who are you talking about?"

Everyone turned to me and said, "Hey, Ralph. We were arguing about you." I was shocked and said, "You've got to be kidding. I'm 5'9" and weigh an even 190 pounds. I'm nowhere near the size you folks are estimating."

I was dumbfounded when they argued with me about my own size. Finally I asked, "Linda, you're about the same height as me. How tall are you?" "Five, nine," she replied. No one believed we were the same, but when Linda and I stood back to back, we were, indeed, exactly the same height. There was complete silence until someone said, "Damn, I never would have believed that. Even though I see that with my own eyes, as soon as you stepped away from Linda, I would have bet you were at least six feet tall." As we continued to talk, they all admitted that they had been afraid of my perceived power when they first met me. They were surprised that I was a gentle human being.

---

37 The same problem has been rampant in medical research where conclusions about diseases and treatments have been based on studies of White males. Increasingly, the validity of such studies for Blacks and women of any race is being called into question.

Another instance occurred when I worked at the University of Pittsburgh. One of my supervisors asked me to help introduce some controversial educational changes. I suggested that he would be better suited for the task than I, because of his higher degree and higher rank. He said, "No, it will get done faster if you do it. Nobody is going to fuck with you because of your size."

On a trip to China, I got sick after being drenched in a day-long downpour. The Chinese guide expressed surprise, because, "You are the strongest one in the group." Understand that I was far from the biggest man in the group. A recent study said that Whites in America, routinely overestimate the size and danger potential of Black American men. It is my contention that this tendency may well lead to an overestimation of the mental pathology of Black men.

The over-estimation of size and potential danger of Black males can lead school personnel (like the teacher mentioned above) to perceive normal behaviors as problematic, anti-social or pathological.

Consequently, Black students, far more than Whites, are referred for psychological evaluation and alternative educational placements as well as being over-medicated with mood-altering drugs. These actions can lead to a lifelong stigmatization, creating a negatively reinforcing feedback loop. Could this explain why Black males are frequently turned off to education by the third grade?

Taking all of these issues into consideration, it is not surprising that I and other Blacks view the mental health system and the research on the mental health status of Blacks with suspicion. I am grateful for my time in The Hill and the mental and emotional strength imbued by my caring parents, extended family, and community.

CHAPTER 19

The End of The Hill

What Went Wrong?

During the mid-1950s and into the 1960s, two forces converged and destroyed The Hill that I knew and loved. One was perpetrated by city leaders under the guise of "urban renewal." The second was precipitated by the fight for civil rights. By 1968, The Hill was already in decline. The final blow came with the riots following the assassination of Martin Luther King, Jr.

Prior to these forces, approximately 8,000 people lived harmoniously in The Hill; about 67% were Black; 33% White. About 400 businesses, many owned by Blacks, provided goods and services. A growing middle class was creating a robust economic base for Black and White residents. Like two decks of cards that had been shuffled together, each ethnic and racial group kept its identity and culture while treating differences with tolerance and respect. This mixed community was the vision of integration that I had assimilated while growing up in The Hill. This was the vision I had hoped to extend to communities beyond The Hill. What went wrong?

What Went Wrong with Urban "Renewal"?

Dinwiddie, a short street running between Centre and Fifth Avenues, was lined with beautiful old Brownstone houses. As I walked past these castle-like residences on my way to the small butcher shop where Dad worked, I fantasized about living on Dinwiddie. I even picked out the house I wanted to occupy and vowed to own it one day.

I left for the Army in 1958 with my dream intact. By the time I returned in 1960, many of the old Brownstones including my dream house were gone—casualties of Pittsburgh's Urban "Renewal" of The Hill. Throughout this book I have placed "Renewal" in quotation marks to underscore the discrepancy between the idealized vision promulgated by city leaders and the devastating results of their flawed plan.

By the time Urban "Renewal" began in the mid-1950s, The Hill, especially the lower section, unquestionably needed attention. The housing stock was aging and many of the stately old homes had been carved into cramped apartments. City government blamed The Hill residents for the deplorable conditions, but the City had been complicit in the deterioration.[38] The code enforcement agency had continually turned a blind eye to building violations in rental properties owned by White landlords, many of whom did not live in Pittsburgh, let alone The Hill. Because of willful neglect, buildings were condemned and demolished.

Please do not get the wrong impression. Thousands of good people still lived in the Hill. Many of them were employed; many others would have loved to work but could not for a variety of reasons. Many lived in decent homes and drove nice cars. Some of the old churches still served the people. What I am trying to convey is that The Hill of my youth was gone, along with many of the businesses that served us.[39]

When plans for Urban "Renewal" first began, City fathers promised to involve the Black community; Black contractors and construction workers were to be hired to do renovations or, when necessary, demolition and rebuilding. These promises were not kept. Nor was the promise of one-for-one replacement of housing units. Assistance with interim housing and a promise that residents could return to their beloved community never happened. As wholesale destruction of homes and businesses proceeded, the social, cultural, and economic fabric of The Hill was torn apart.

In the name of Urban "Renewal," the Right of Eminent Domain was exercised in a way that destroyed well-maintained, middle-income areas. While this may have been technically legal (although there is room for doubt about that), it certainly wasn't moral or ethical. For example, Whiteside Road was located off Bedford Avenue adjacent to the Ammon Recreational Center. In this *cul du sac* were lovely, two-story houses with nicely manicured lawns owned by middle-class Blacks. The city tore them down and replaced them with low-income housing. In another abuse of Eminent Domain, very nice houses in the prestigious Sugar Top area were destroyed to accommodate the University of Pittsburgh's desire to create a buffer between The Hill and its newly constructed athletic complex. In another area between Downtown Pittsburgh and Fullerton Street, bulldozers destroyed Bedford Avenue, a long, wide boulevard lined by nice houses and divided by a center island planted with stately trees. Because of these actions, stable, middle-class areas from one end of The Hill to the other were gutted. Changing demographics changed the economic base of the community as well as the traditions that comprised its rich, multi-faceted culture.

Because of restrictive housing covenants, displaced Hill inhabitants moved to neighborhoods where they would be accepted. Many Italians moved to the East End; Jewish residents moved to the East End or Squirrel Hill; middle- to upper-class Whites moved to Mount Washington, Mount Lebanon and Beechview (all places where Blacks were not welcome). Blacks migrated

---

38 Following riots that took place in 1967, President Lyndon Johnson created the 11-member Kerner Commission to determine the root causes and to suggest remedies to prevent their recurrence. Many officials, including the President, privately expressed the belief that the cause for the riots rested in the pathology of Blacks and the Black communities. They were shocked by the Commission's conclusion that, "White society is deeply implicated in the ghetto. White society created the ghetto; white society condones the ghetto, and white society maintains the ghetto."

39 Even today, areas in The Lower Hill could be revitalized, but whether that happens or how that happens depends not on the Black community, but on those who control the development rights to the site of the now demolished Civic Arena. Until the fall of 2021, these rights were owned by the Pittsburgh Penguins Hockey organization that claimed people of The Hill would be involved in the planning and development process. We'll never know if they would have honored that commitment, because the team is being sold to the Fenway Sports Group, a sports conglomerate based in Boston.

toward East End areas where Blacks already resided. But the influx of so many Blacks caused problems with Italians already established in those neighborhoods. This fracturing of a multi-ethnic community created homogenous enclaves where racist ideologies could take root. As more and more generations of people lived surrounded by people like themselves, there were fewer people who could respond to racist comments with something like, "Hey, wait a minute, what you just said about Blacks (Jew, Italians, Indians, etc.) isn't true. I live, work, and worship with them; what you said just is not true." I do not mean to paint The Hill as a multi-ethnic utopia. But I do contend that The Hill offered a vibrant model of peaceful and respectful relationships among different ethnic groups.

If urban *renewal* had truly been the goal of city government, blighted areas could have been revitalized while good areas could have been preserved. That wide swaths of The Hill were swept away with no regard for the quality of housing, the vitality of businesses, and the cohesiveness of the community raises the question, "What was the true intent of what has come to be known as a case study in failed urban planning?" I believe from the bottom of my heart Urban "Renewal" was a euphemism for "Negro Removal"—i.e., ridding the area of Blacks and poor to middle-class Whites for the benefit of well-to-do Whites. This view may seem extreme and biased. Perhaps it would be if government officials and urban planners had learned valuable lessons to prevent such devastation from recurring. Yet, destruction of The Hill was followed in short order by the similar destruction of East Liberty and the North Side— two other predominately Black enclaves.

In recent decades, millions of dollars have flowed into East Liberty, the Northside, and The Hill in an effort to undo the damage caused by Urban "Renewal." While it is possible to repair the physical scars left behind by the wrecking balls, recreating communities that had evolved over several hundred years is impossible. And therein lies one purpose in recounting my life in The Hill. Once I left its sheltering environment, I encountered virulent racism in Pittsburgh, in cities throughout the United States, and in countries around the world. Had it not been for those early years of nurturing, I might have collapsed and given up in the face of such hatred. Instead, I had the strength to fight back.

19.1: Intersection of Wylie Avenue & Washington Place, looking toward downtown (c. 1958-1960). Before the wholesale demolition of The Lower Hill, the area housed a number of businesses like Hayes Drugs & Tambelli's Restaurant featured in this picture.

19.2: Wylie Avenue near Townsend Street, looking toward downtown Pittsburgh (c. 1955-1957). Buildings have been razed to make way for the Civic Arena.

19.3: Example of wholesale demolition of areas in The Hill

19.4: Intersection of Webster Avenue and Crawford Street, looking toward downtown Pittsburgh. Civic Arena construction in background (c. 1959)

19.5: Civic Arena under construction; Connelley Trade School on right (c. 1960-1961)

Fighting Back

The Civil Rights Movement was beginning to coalesce as I neared adulthood and was gaining force by the time I left the Army. In the 1960s, two different philosophies began to shape resistance to long-standing injustices. One philosophy was advocated by the southern Baptist minister, Reverend Martin Luther King, Jr., who preached love and peaceful confrontation of the racist system of American Apartheid perpetuated through Jim Crow laws and customs. King argued for non-violent resistance and full integration across all social levels and institutions.[40]

The other philosophy, advocated by Malcom X, focused on self-reliance, self-respect, self-protection, and separation from White society. Groups including The Black Panthers, The Deacons for Self Defense, and the so-called Black Muslims argued that Blacks would never be accepted by Whites. They endorsed the use of *any* means necessary to achieve freedom, believed in self-defense, and argued for the creation of Black-controlled schools where their children could learn the truth about history. Marcus Garvey, another proponent of separation,

---

40 Martin Luther King, Jr. an admirer of Mahatma Gandhi, was the leader of The Southern Christian Leadership Conference. Other groups espousing King's philosophy of integration through non-violent resistance included The National Association for the Advancement of Colored People (NAACP) and The Congress of Racial Equality (CORE) in the North, and The Student Non-Violent Coordinating Committee (SNCC) in the South. In addition to these nationally known groups were many smaller groups throughout the United States.

said that depending on Whites to help Blacks attain equality would be like leaning on a broken stick... we would soon be consigned to the ground.

As I became involved in the Civil Rights Movement, I was torn between these two radically different approaches. My heart and soul drew me to King's vision of a nation living in harmony where all people were judged by the content of their character and not by the color of their skin. My mother's quiet strength probably contributed to my attraction to non-violent confrontation. As she would say, "Remember, honey, there is great strength in gentleness." I was, however, a product of my father's training to fight those who would hurt me and my loved ones. Those early lessons, coupled with my training in the Army, drew me toward the Black Power philosophy. In the end, I found a middle ground, vowing to use physical force only when others assaulted me or loved ones. Perhaps it was this middle ground that allowed me to become an observer and a student of the struggle for social justice. From the vantage point of an activist, teacher, researcher, historian, and world traveler, I have pondered both the peaceful integration and independent self-determination approaches to equality. In this way, I have fulfilled both my mother's and father's hopes that I would work with my mind and not with my hands.

As I look back on my efforts in the Civil Rights movement and the two philosophies that drove the actions of different groups, I realize that a critical element was missing. To those of us in The Civil Rights Movement, integration meant that America would become a seamless society where Blacks would be welcomed at all levels. Our best minds would work next to their best minds. Everyone would have an equal chance at the American Dream. We naively assumed this was a shared vision. We should have known better.

I can recall listening to a well-known White liberal advocating for integration. He spoke enthusiastically about Blacks going to White Schools, worshiping in White churches, holding government seats, and fitting into the totality of *White* society. Slowly it dawned on me that never once did he utter a word about the Black communities or the institutions we had built. He was talking about abandoning them and moving into White society. At the time, I didn't think of it as cultural genocide and, in all likelihood, neither did he. Yet, this was the 20th century equivalent of White colonists and Christian missionaries "civilizing" Native Americans. In both cases, Whites operated from the assumption that the traditions, customs, mores, and lifestyle of non-European cultures were inferior—as were the people of those cultures.

We wanted our humanity and culture to be acknowledged and respected. Neither integration nor the separatist philosophy achieved this aim.

What Went Wrong with the Separate-But-Equal Philosophy?

On the outskirts of Tulsa, Oklahoma, lay a Black community derisively called "Little Afrika." "Black or Negro Wall Street" was the other unofficial name for this Tulsa community, because its residents were said to have amassed money equal to the wealth of Wall Street in New York City. The actual name of the neighborhood was Greenwood, and it was founded by a Black man named J.B. Stadford. Like so many Blacks leaving the South after the Civil War, Stadford headed west into what had been designated "Indian Territory." When gold and oil were discovered in this territory, the U.S. government broke its treaty with the Native American tribes,[41] and White fortune-seekers flowed into the area. By the time Stadford arrived, the established White citizens made it clear that Blacks were not welcome; they told him to go live on the other side of the railroad tracks. J.B. Stadford did just that. Around 1890, he purchased several acres of land, subdivided his purchase, and sold smaller plots to other Blacks. He was later joined by D.W. Gurley who also purchased and sub-divided several acres. Together the two began to build a new city and named the main street "Greenwood" after a town in Mississippi.

Because Blacks were prohibited from using public and private facilities in Tulsa, they began to create an infrastructure of necessary services. As occurred in Pittsburgh's Hill, the residents of Greenwood built their own schools, banks, libraries, theaters, shops, churches, and restaurants. They formed their own police force. Some of the wealthiest Blacks even owned airplanes in the early 1900s when flying was a very new adventure. It was said that a dollar turned over a hundred times before it left the community, making Greenwood one of the richest communities in America.

Discriminatory laws and customs, however, are only the outward manifestation of racism rooted in fear and hatred of Blacks. Such hatred does not tolerate self-sufficient separation. Falsely alleging that a Black man had raped a White woman, a mob of White townspeople and the KKK attacked Greenwood. Tulsa police and the U.S. Army joined in the frenzy; dropping incendiary bombs and burning the town to the ground—but not before the banks and stores had been thoroughly looted. The official death toll varies depending on the time and evidence used, but about 40 people died. About 800 were hospitalized. As many as 6,000 Black residents were confined for several days before being released.

In the aftermath of this massive destruction, Whites brought in heavy equipment, bulldozed the town, and covered the rubble with soil. Grass was planted, and all signs of the town's existence vanished. Until the truth was discovered in the 1960s, Oklahoma's official position was that Greenwood had never existed.

By the 1960s, Greenwood had made somewhat of a comeback, albeit as a mere shadow of its former self. This is when a second assault was launched—not by an angry mob wearing KKK robes or badges or firearms—but by men in business suits armed with briefcases carrying the weapon of Eminent Domain. In the name of Urban "Renewal" the federal and local governments seized private property legally owned by Blacks. The "suits" were followed by construction workers in hard hats and driving earth-moving equipment. Soon four highways were constructed through the center of Black Wall Street. Once again, Greenwood was destroyed; this time in the name of progress.[42]

Thus, as was the case with The Hill, the economic foundation that allowed a vibrant community to flourish was gone. The initial decimation of Greenwood was swift, vicious, and complete. Whether fueled by fear, jealousy, or hatred, the racist motivation for the attack is

---

41 Scholars of Oklahoma history debate whether the discovery of gold or oil precipitated the influx of fortune seekers. Regardless of the cause, the result was the expulsion of Native Americans from the land they had been promised. A more detailed account of broken treaties is provided by Clifford E. Trafzer's book, *As Long as the Grass Shall Grow and Rivers Flow: A History of Native Americans* (Fort Worth: Harcourt College Publishers, 2000).

42 The use of Eminent Domain to seize property was used in many communities throughout the United States. Although the rationale of "urban renewal" was the reason given for exercising this governmental power, the result was often the displacement of urban poor, both Black and White, in areas targeted for gentrification by young White professionals.

undeniable. The destruction of "Little Hayti" (as The Hill was derisively called in bygone years) was slower, more subtle, but just as devastating.

Because of Pittsburgh topography, there was little room for expansion and development within the city boundaries. Because the Lower Hill was adjacent to Pittsburgh's city center, Black-owned homes and businesses were situated on some of the most valuable land in Pittsburgh. As indicated above, the land was systematically seized, the buildings destroyed, and the residents displaced under the guise of urban planning. Just as surely as the mob in Tulsa destroyed Greenwood, the Pittsburgh city planners brought an end to a self-sufficient, vibrant Black community. Could the architects of Pittsburgh's Urban "Renewal" foresee the consequences of their actions? Were these consequences what they had, in fact, intended from the outset? I cannot see into their hearts to know the truth. Suffice it to say, from the moment that White, male Europeans set foot on American soil, they saw this land as theirs and anything in it ripe for the taking.[43] This historically and culturally pervasive sense of entitlement and privilege played out both virulently and subtly as self-sufficient Black communities were destroyed.

What Went Wrong with Integration?

From my early life in The Hill, I carry a vision of how different racial cultures can co-exist with mutual respect. This vision has made me a devoted seeker of integration. Looking back, however, I can see that those of us who fought to bring down the barriers of discrimination did not pay close enough attention to the risks. We were so busy fighting for the right to work with, eat with, go to school with, worship with Whites that we did not consider what might be lost in that effort.

In the 1990s, I undertook a research project on the Pittsburgh Civil Rights Movement, and I asked each person I interviewed whether it had been worth the effort. Except for one man who gave an unequivocal "No," the others felt that gains had been made, but the Movement stopped too soon. From the perspective of those then retired warriors, many of the changes were superficial. My interviewees acknowledged that we had not fully understood the degree to which fundamental institutional change had never been achieved. This perspective was vividly brought home to me when I was an administrator at the University of Pittsburgh.

> A colleague who held me in low regard said that I and tens of thousands of other Blacks (and women) had been hired for positions because of federal funding for the Poverty Program. Our qualifications, he contended, were not comparable to those of Whites in similar positions. After some investigation, I discovered his assertion was true. I was the only administrator in my division who did not hold a doctoral degree.

---

43 For an account of a similarly racist destruction of a Black community see: *Banished from Johnstown: A Racist Backlash in Pennsylvania* by Cody McDivitt (2020).

At first, I thought that was not a big deal, because I was as intelligent as my White counterparts. When I told my antagonist this, he retorted, "Intelligence has nothing to do with it. You and others have been employed in good positions because institutions have been given special grants to hire you. You're considered "para-professionals," which means sub-professionals. You and others will have jobs only as long as the Poverty Program money flows freely. When it dries up, so will your jobs. Pitt and other White-controlled institutions will return to business as usual."

The Poverty Program had included a requirement for "Maximum Feasible Participation of the Poor." Institutions that wanted to reap the benefit of this federal windfall had to hire Blacks and also appoint poor individuals to organizational boards. That should have been a game-changer in terms of fundamental restructuring of institutions, but sadly my colleague's predictions came true. Special "Poverty Program Boards" were created, and when the money ran out, the boards were dissolved and the employees let go.

This is merely one example of the ways in which organizational power remained in White hands. Had institutions truly valued the intent of the Poverty Program legislation, temporary grant funds would have been used as a bridge to permanent positions supported by on-going, operating budgets. Rather than creating "token" boards, corporate charters would have been revised so that the composition of their boards would always include representation of Blacks and other minorities.

Another example of how Whites retain power comes from the world of music. Prior to the gains of the Civil Rights Movement, there had been two musician unions in Pittsburgh—one White, one Black. The former controlled which performers were hired for various jobs and unsurprisingly most went to White musicians. The latter, however, worked to secure jobs for Black musicians. With integration, the two unions merged with the alleged intent of assuring more equitable access to jobs. All officers of the merged union were White, further entrenching the preferential access to jobs, and Black musicians no longer had a strong voice to advocate for them. How disgraceful that when Nancy Wilson, one of the greatest Black singers of all time, performed in Pittsburgh, my friend Dr. Nelson Harrison was the only Black musician in the orchestra. And he would not have been there if a White musician hadn't been sick and personally asked Nelson to fill in for him. Full integration should have meant an equal right to work, not reliance on opportunities to do a favor for a friend.

Across a range of industries and institutions—media, education, transportation, entertainment, business, government—Blacks were able to find employment as a result of civil rights legislation. Yet ultimate decision-making power remained primarily in the hands of White owners and governing bodies. This remains true today, and proposed measures to prevent (non-existent) voter fraud will create barriers for Blacks to elect candidates who represent their concerns. Thus, the individuals who make the rules will most likely be White males, and as history has proven, those who make the rules do so to their own benefit.

As discussed above, the other issue we did not fully comprehend was the meaning of "integration." Since colonial times, Blacks were denied access to the goods and services in White communities. Although many necessities for daily living were available in The Hill, others, including colleges, medical centers, and other specialty goods and services, were available only in White communities. And they were designated for the exclusive use of Whites. When such inequalities were no longer tolerable, we fought for and won the legal right of equal access. This felt like a win. What we hadn't foreseen was the one-way migration out of Black communities and the resulting consequences.

What Was Lost?

Much was lost because of this exodus of Blacks from The Hill. Blacks began to patronize White establishments that had previously scorned them (and all-too-often still provided poor service). Needless to say, Whites did not begin to shop in The Hill. Black-owned stores, restaurants, bars, hotels, and other community-based businesses lost revenue. Those owners who could relocate did; those who couldn't, closed. (Figure 3 lists the range of businesses that were lost.) White business owners who now benefited from the influx of Black consumers had no reason to open establishments in The Hill, especially because Urban "Renewal" had failed to create the attractive, vital community it had promised. Famous musicians lost performance venues as major nightclubs were shuttered. Less visible, but just as devastating, was the loss of smaller dance venues and bars that featured live music by less renowned performers or Black performers who simply wanted to remain in Pittsburgh. Scores of small clubs no longer needed the bartenders, cooks, servers, and valet car parkers. Money that had previously flowed into, circulated through, and remained in The Hill now flowed out to White communities. As businesses closed, jobs for Black residents were lost. Tax revenues decreased leaving little money for infrastructure repairs and upgrades.

Exacerbating The Hill's economic decline was the loss of professionals and middle-class working families who could now move into previously all-White neighborhoods. Although no one should be denied the right to choose where to live, the migration of professionals to the suburbs left The Hill bereft of its leaders. As physicians, dentists, lawyers, teachers, social workers, etc. found housing and employment outside The Hill, few were left who could mobilize

Figure 3: Black-Owned Businesses Lost

Hotels
Motels
Elegant Night Clubs
Jazz clubs
Mom & Pop Restaurants
Bar B-Que Businesses
High-end Restaurants
Caterers
Bakeries
Clothing & Shoe Stores
Furriers
Tailors
Cleaners
Florists
Pool Halls
Movie Theaters
Car Washes
Cab Companies
Real Estate Agencies
Record & Video Rental Stores
Painting Companies
Convenience Stores
TV Repair Shops
Printing Companies
Photography Studies
Hair Product Manufacturers
Ball Parks
Baseball Teams

citizens, lobby for changes in legislation, or resist detrimental government policies. The loss of population also meant less voting power, and in turn, less political influence.

With integration, parents began to send their children to previously segregated colleges and universities. Just as business enterprises suffered from the loss of patrons, so did Black institutions of higher education. Falling enrollment and falling revenue threatened their sustainability. Lost, too, was the opportunity for students to study Black history and culture. At the level of primary and secondary education, forced busing typically meant Black children were transported to schools in unfamiliar White surroundings. Here, they found little in the curriculum that acknowledged, let alone honored, the contributions of Blacks to society. Money to support integration most often went to schools in White communities; rarely, if ever, did money go to Black communities to improve facilities or administrative and teaching staff.

Already deeply wounded by the outward migration of residents and the destruction wrought by Urban "Renewal," the riots in the aftermath of Martin Luther King's assassination dealt the community its final blow.

The Final Blow—The Riots

The morning after King's death, I and many Hill residents came together to comfort one another and to decide how to respond to this tragedy. Younger, angry voices called for retaliation. Older voices argued for calm. Community leaders reached out to the Governor and police pleading for interventions that would forestall violence. As these went unheeded, vandalism and looting began. Although some businesses were burned, "Black-owned Business" signs appeared in windows and Black residents moved to protect White merchants who had always treated them fairly. Still, fires occurred, mostly along the lower end of Centre Avenue, where several grocery stores and bars, at least one pharmacy, and a variety of other stores were destroyed. Also destroyed was the business owners' sense of safety and security.

Before the riots, a glimmer of hope for restoring The Hill remained. Although many businesses were gone, a few remained, including The Crawford Grill Number 2. In the aftermath of the riots, I spoke with many White Pittsburghers who were shocked that Blacks were so angry. Destroyed once and for all was the illusion that Blacks were content (even happy) with their treatment as second-class citizens. Loss of this illusion brought to the surface long-standing racial fears, and Whites stopped patronizing the few remaining music venues and restaurants.[44]

By the 1970s, The Hill had become a ghost town. Gone were the homes, the stores, the leaders, the middle class. Gone was the vibrant night life and the sound of music. Gone was the community where we protected one another and lifted each other up. Into the empty spaces, crept poverty, drugs, and crime.

---

44 I offer a more detailed account of the riot that occurred in The Hill in my book, *Voices from the Firing Line: A Personal Account of Pittsburgh Civil Rights Movement* (Learning Moments Press, 2022).

19.6. National Guard soldiers deployed in Lower Hill during riot of April 1968. St. Benedict The Moor Church is in the background.

What If?

During an interview with Byrd Brown, one of the most important civil rights leaders in Pittsburgh, we reflected on the bitter lessons of integration. As Byrd Brown succinctly put it, "If you were a conscious Black person in Pittsburgh, you could not live for one day without encountering blatant racism. In the old days, we could live in blissful ignorance of the pain that lay just outside the imaginary lines that delineated The Hill. We should have fought to hold on to that life."

Byrd's words haunt me as do the ruins of The Hill. Certainly the fight for integration had helped many Blacks achieve their individual goals. Just as many, perhaps more, were left behind with no supportive community to help lift them up. In retrospect, we should have paid as much attention to strengthening our own communities and institutions as we did to integrating into White society. I cannot help but wonder where we might be today if we had used our resources and our gains of civil rights to:

> ...build good, new housing along Herron Avenue and Sugar Top...

> ...make it possible for Black entrepreneurs to erect new businesses in the areas just beyond the Civic Arena...

> ...improve municipal services...

> ...relocate the Aurora Club, the Loendi Club, the Hurricane Club, and the famous Crawford Grill...

> ...remain loyal to Black colleges and universities and provide financial assistance to assure educational opportunities for more of our young people...

...celebrate both White and Black cultures every day rather than on "Token Tolerance Day/Week/Month...

...retain excellent teachers, principals, counselors, athletic coaches, and other school-based professionals in our community-based public schools...

...continue to live and work in the Hill.

What if we had paused in our headlong flight to White society and asked, "How can we preserve a community built on the dreams and sacrifices of our elders.

19.7. Lower Hill District clearance near completion, 1957.
(Photo by John R. Shrader, Allegheny Conference on Community Development
Photographs, Detre Library and Archives, Heinz History Center)

Dreams destroyed, not deferred. The Lower Hill lies devastated as if a
victim of war, but this war was conceived and executed by men with
briefcases, plans and maps from the Urban Redevelopment Authority of
Pittsburgh. Complicit were the Mayor, City Council and Pittsburgh business
leaders, willing to destroy lives, homes, minority businesses and houses of
worship in order to provide entertainment to affluent White folks.

CHAPTER 20

The Loss of Place

As I've explained, The Hill was a Black enclave surrounded by a White city. Each had its own distinctive culture characterized by a myriad of tangible and intangible qualities. This, in itself, was not problematic. What was problematic was the overt and covert assumption that White culture was inherently superior to Black culture. In fact, this assumption was so strong, that aspects of Black culture were assumed to be flawed versions of White standards resulting from Blacks' lack of intelligence or moral character. In short, Blacks were assumed to have no culture worth considering.

Pushed out of The Hill by Urban "Renewal" and granted the right to equal access by Civil Rights laws, Blacks faced the challenge of being accepted by White society. As I look back on more than 65 years of struggle to meet this challenge, I have come to several profoundly sad (even tragic) realizations.

First is the realization that Whites never truly valued the inclusion of Blacks in "their" society. While laws forced admittance, the dominant White culture remained unwelcoming. To this day, centuries-old animosities, mistrust, fear, and guilt have never been truly put to rest.

Second is the realization that Whites did not (could not) comprehend that Blacks had a rich culture worthy of understanding and respect.

Third, and most painful, is the realization that as Blacks lost their connections to The Hill, they lost their sense of community and their own culture. Far too often, they succumbed to the same assumptions of White superiority that had enslaved them. Consequently, fitting-in seemed to be the only path toward acceptance and equality. And fitting-in meant trying to be as White as possible. This belief was validated by a White society that was most accepting of Blacks whose looks and mannerisms were approximations of Whiteness. Yet, no matter how hard we tried, no matter how far we rose, no matter how noteworthy our accomplishments, in the end too many Whites still saw us as "black," along with every prejudice that connoted.

Can We Understand Each Other's Culture?

I have been a lifelong student of White culture. I had to be if I wanted to avoid harm, if I wanted a measure of professional and financial success. Whites on the other hand have no need to understand the culture I assimilated from the moment I was born and brought to my home in The Hill. Throughout my adult life, I have looked for ways—through activism, research, advocacy, and teaching—to bridge the divides between these two cultures. Always, my aim is to convey two fundamental points. (1) Blacks do have a culture. (2) That culture is different, but it is not inferior. Try as I might, this goal always seems just beyond my reach. In part, this is to be expected, because culture comprises thousands upon thousands of thoughts, feelings, mannerisms, customs, styles, norms, etc. we assimilate from the moment of birth.

The term "culture shock" was coined to describe the feeling of total disorientation when suddenly plunged into completely new surroundings. Unfamiliar sounds, smells, sights, language, clothes, food, social proprieties, music, dance—everything is strange. I contend that when Blacks were pushed from The Hill by Urban "Renewal" or left voluntarily because barriers were struck down, they experienced a disconnection from a place in which they felt safe and accepted. At virtually every turn, they encountered the message, "You are not good enough. Your way of speaking and walking are substandard. Your food is "common." You're ill-mannered, uneducated, and uncultured. To be accepted, turn your back on your inferior ways and adopt ours." The toxicity of this message erodes one's identity and raises the question, "Just where *do* I belong?" With the loss of community comes the loss of those who can push back and say, "Hey, wait a minute. We're just as okay as you are."

As a youngster in The Hill, I assimilated a Black style of walking which I still exhibit when among other Blacks. It's a carefree way of "bopping" down the street with a nonchalant air and a bit of a swagger that conveys, "Yeah, I'm cool. I'm okay." For men, there was a "bounce" in their step; for women, a sway of the hips. When I watched Barack Obama walking to a podium or striding to meet a visiting dignitary, I'd think, "Has this dude ever lived in a Black community?" His gait was constrained; his posture stiff. Then one day I caught the briefest glimpse of him walking away from a news conference in which he had announced the success of an initiative. Halfway down the hall (probably when he thought the cameras were no longer on him), I saw the little telltale, bop and sway. "Yeah, the dude is a brother." I mention this seemingly innocuous incident, because it is emblematic of a struggle many professional Blacks had to conform to a White standard of acceptable walking.

The humorist STEVE ALLEN used to make fun of White men, saying they could dance with rhythm only when drunk. This erroneously ascribed a sense of rhythm to genetics, when it was actually a part of Black culture. One evening, I attended a dance with the same White anthropologist friend who had asked about my speech patterns when we visited my parents. He was incredulous when I casually pointed to a young White woman on the dance floor and remarked:

"She's been spending a lot of time among Black folks."

"How could you possibly know that?" he asked.

"Because the only way she could learn to dance like that is by hanging out with Black folks."

Determined to prove I was wrong, my friend called the young lady over and said, "My friend here says, without any evidence, that you have spent a lot of time among Negroes. What do YOU have to say about that?

As she barely stopped moving to the music, she replied "Of course. I go to Morgan State [a Black college]. Where do you think I learned to dance?" With that, she held out her hand to me and said, "Wanna dance?"

Before I could respond, some kid practically yanked her onto the floor. "Got to go," she laughed as she sped off to dance.

Just as a manner of walking and dancing can identify one's cultural affiliations, so too can one's speech patterns. As I mentioned earlier in the book, Mrs. Donahue gently taught me how to speak more formal English. I became so fluent in this "second" language, those who have only heard, but not seen me, are surprised I'm Black.

Years ago, I found myself unexpectedly thrust into the role of producing a television show on Black affairs and culture. I had no idea of what I was doing, so in desperation, I called the two Black producers who were responsible for the first such show on American television. Let's just say they were not forthcoming with useful advice. Thinking I wasn't using the correct technical terms, I apologized for my ignorance and tried again. Still no information. I tried once more with the same results. I was so frustrated and angry, I let out a stream of profanity-laced sentences, only to hear the two producers laughing. "Damn man, we are so fuckin' sorry. We thought you were some White dude trying to milk us for Black secrets."

"Well, what the fuck changed your mind?"

Laughing even harder, they gasped out, "Dude, Only a brother could have cussed us out the way you just did!"

As amusing as this incident turned out to be, it illustrates an important point about cultural belonging. If I "speak Black" among Whites, I'm likely to be judged uneducated or stupid. If I "speak White" among Blacks, I may be seen as an outsider, as uppity, or as putting on airs.

Even the rhythms of speech can signal an insider from an outsider. This was brought home to me when I arrived at the apartment of a White friend. Holding a phone in her hand, she beckoned me in, motioned for me to have a seat, and signaled that I should remain silent. For the next ten minutes, she sat holding the phone, not uttering a sound, making no gestures, never changing her facial expression. Finally she said, "Okay, I'll call you tomorrow."

Confused, I asked, "What were you doing? Were you on hold all that time?"

"Oh, no, I was having a conversation with my mother."

"Conversation? How could you be having a conversation, when you never uttered a word until you said 'goodbye!' How would your mother know that you didn't go make a sandwich or go to the bathroom?"

My friend now looked as puzzled as I had a moment earlier.

After this, I began to notice many other instances of this very different cultural concept of "conversation." Earlier I discussed the White minister who fell in love with a Black congregation. I mentioned the "call and response" pattern that is normal during worship. This pattern also shapes the way we Blacks talk among ourselves, frequently interjecting a word or phrase as a sign we are listening and actively participating in the conversation. Should a young Black woman remain so silent in a phone call with her mother, she would be considered rude, disrespectful, and defiant. Failure to give a response could elicit an "are you listening?" or "don't be sitting there sulking; you better say something!" or "Why you being so damn quiet? You better TALK to me!"

As I've reflected on the incident with my friend, I realized that this "call and response rhythm" would be considered rude by Whites who are more accustomed to listening silently until the other person finishes speaking. I also began to pay attention to the fact that Black folks abandoned the colorful way of communication when speaking with Whites.

I want to say a bit more about the issue of "trigger words" that I raised in the Prologue, because they can impede mutual understanding just as differences in conversational style can. Terms like "micro-aggression" and "White Privilege" are meant to call attention to the ways in which racism continues to permeate society. They are meant to raise consciousness as we would have said back in the 1960s. As well intended as these terms might be, they can, all too often, evoke negative and defensive reactions. This is what I mean by "trigger words." For example, when many White folks hear the term "White Privilege," they immediately become defensive and say things like, "I've worked hard for everything I've got. Nobody gave me anything." What follows can be a volley of accusations and counter accusations from minds that have been closed to the other's point of view.

Let's say we replaced "WHITE Privilege" with "UNEARNED Privilege." Again, defensive responses might come fast and furiously. "I went to school and studied hard." "I've worked two jobs since I was 21 to get where I am today." "Nobody's giving me a break because I come from a poor neighborhood or because I'm Black." "I've never taken a handout in my life. Whatever I have I scrimped and saved for. It's what I deserve for the sacrifices I've made." The truth of the matter is that everyone has "unearned privileges" based on gender, religion, last name, skin color, family status, or any number of other "categories" into which we are born. Those "givens" bestowed by the circumstances of our birth give us advantages in some ways and disadvantages in others. Buzz words like "White Privilege" and "micro-aggressions" are bandied about with such frequency, they lose any real power to engender greater awareness or understanding.

As I explored the definition of "micro-aggression," I was struck by the irony of "micro," which means "very small," and calls to mind synonyms like "tiny" and "insignificant." The words and deeds characterized as "micro-aggressions" are not small, tiny, or insignificant. They wound so deeply, meaningful conversation becomes nearly impossible. Let me give you some examples of so-called micro-aggressions that have occurred in my life and in the lives of others I know.

- A White woman who clutches her purse more tightly when I step on the elevator;
- Dog-walkers who stop and glare at me as I drive through a White neighborhood;
- Bosses and co-workers who call women girls;
- Saying "Some of my best friends are—Black...Gay...Muslim;
- Using terms like, "You People, THOSE people";
- Saying, "he is Gay...Black...Muslim, but HE is nice";
- You are pretty for a FAT person;
- She is the smartest Woman I know;
- Referring to or calling grown Black men and women "boys" or "girls";
- Using my first name without my permission or without our being friends;
- Being surprised that Black folks are "articulate";
- Asking me, "What do Black people think about that?" Would you ask a White person the same question about White folks?
- Saying, "I am not talking about YOU! You are so exceptional. I was talking about those OTHER colored people.
- Referring to Black folks as 'Colored" or Negro;
- Being surprised at my anger about racism or any other kind of oppression;
- Telling Black folks to "get over "slavery because it was a long time ago;
- Claiming you are not prejudiced because no one in your family ever owned slaves;
- Saying you are "color blind." That is impossible unless you really are blind.
- Thinking that all Black men are sexual predators;
- Thinking that all Black men would have sex with anything that moves;
- Believing that all Black men would prefer White women over Black women;
- Believing that all Black men have enormous genitals;
- Believing that Black athletes are better than White athletes because they are all "natural stars" and do not achieve because they work at becoming good at sports;
- Thinking everything White is good and everything Black is bad;
- Not understanding that you must always scan the environment for danger;
- Not realizing that I live my life waiting for the next bad thing to happen because I am a Black man;
- Assuming the failure of one Black person proves the inferiority of all Blacks

I could go on, but these few examples illustrate the ways in those who are not White, middle class, straight men are marginalized in American society. I can imagine someone thinking, "What's the big deal? Just get over it." While it is true that any one such micro-aggression may seem trivial, as they accumulate, day in and day out over a lifetime, they act like a death by a thousand cuts—the first cut hurts but isn't fatal; neither is the 5th or 6th cut. No one can know, however, when the last small cut, inflicted over a lifetime, leads to the death of your soul.

Non-verbal norms also come into play in communication. As mentioned earlier, in African culture it is considered rude to look an older or more important person in the eyes while speaking. This norm was carried to America and reinforced when slaves could incur the wrath of masters by daring to look them in the eye. Today, however, in White society, avoiding eye contact is often interpreted as a sign of disrespect, shiftiness, lying, or inattention.

In these and countless other ways, Blacks who want to be accepted in White society must follow White cultural norms. On the one-way street of integration, Whites have no need to adapt to Black culture. Unless, of course, it is an aspect of Black culture they want to appropriate.

When I was a child, I could always tell whether a singer was Black or White by their style of singing. Jazz, Rhythm and Blues, and gospel singing infused Black music with distinctive styles. So it was ironic that what had previously been scorned as "Race Music,"[45] suddenly became popular after Elvis Pressley became famous by imitating Black Blues singers. Now we suddenly had *White* rock and roll. As mentioned at the very outset of this book, White folks do not necessarily understand that Blacks had invented jazz.

When The Hill had thriving businesses, retail shops catered to the tastes and preferences of their Black customers. Men could easily find the Coogi sweaters and double-breasted suits favored by well-dressed men; women could find the brightly colored clothes and cosmetics they preferred. Shoe stores carried styles that fit the "the look" of Hill residents. Ribs, fried chicken, greens, sweet potato pie, and other Southern specialties were integral to a distinctive Black cuisine.

It may seem quaint now that almost anything one wants can be purchased via the Internet. But after integration, the stores that had served the Black community were gone and White retailers had no incentive to fill the gap. The emergence of national retailers homogenized everything from apparel to the skin tone of baby dolls. (The first black Barbie didn't hit the shelves until 1980.) "Soul food" was appropriated by fast food chains and upscale restaurants.

Perhaps these seem like petty complaints. After all, doesn't the appropriation of Black culture indicate an acceptance of the very culture I claim Whites disparaged? I contend that "appropriation"—claiming ownership of someone else's culture—is quite different from appreciating that culture and acknowledging its source. As The Hill withered, the community that passed Black culture from one generation to the next was lost.

---

45 The term "Race Music" was a derogatory term that really meant that "Vulgar, NIGGER music." It meant that Blacks showed too much emotion (other than sadness, which was acceptable). Black singers cried, yelped, shouted, shook their bodies, and showed no restraint. White performers were "Dignified," but Black singers were just too raw, too emotional. A White friend of mine, who listened to "Race Music" when she attended college in the 1960s recalled her classmates recoiled at her playing James Brown records. In fact, record stores outside of the Black community did not sell R&B, Jazz, or Gospel music. I recall that the National Record Mart was picketed, because they did not carry music performed by Blacks. When MTV first aired, it did not play music by Black artists; that is why BET was started. When Whites appropriated the rhythm part of Rhythm and Blues, they called it *New Music*. By claiming it was *new*, Whites could take credit for it and make money while denying Black writers and performers the chance to make money on the genre. It would take another book to detail the deceit and piracy of the White music world.

Is There a Way Forward?

Given the devastation of Greenwood and The Hill, it is likely that Malcolm X's separatist strategy would have failed to achieve his desired ends just as peaceful integration failed to achieve Martin Luther King's. If neither separation nor integration leads to a free and just society, what path is open to those who are fighting to end the marginalization, oppression, and exploitation of Blacks and other minorities? Is the United States forever doomed to be a society divided by race, class, and gender? Is there a way to move toward the form of integration I had imagined? I have no answer to these questions.

Can we reclaim and embrace a Black culture? This was certainly an aim of the Black Pride Movement and some gains were made. Yet, today we must post signs proclaiming, "Black Lives Matter," an indication that we have yet to realize Martin Luther King's dream "that one day this nation will rise up and live out the true meaning of its creed: We hold these truths to be self-evident, that all men are created equal."

I've heard Whites object to the "Black Lives Matter" signs saying that *all* lives matter. That is unquestionably true. However, the value of White lives is taken-for-granted; that of Black lives is not. Living among Whites is fraught with menace—from the emotional sting of micro-aggressions to the threat of death at the hands of police and citizen-vigilantes. I despair as I see so many symptoms of persistent racism:

...A blatantly racist President embraced by millions...

...Gerrymandering to assure the election of White legislators...

...Legislation to restrict voting rights...

...Backlashes to affirmative action by aggrieved White men...

...The incarceration of a disproportionately greater number of Black men...

...The shift of funding for public education to private, for-profit charter schools, often in the poorest communities...

...Tax laws that benefit the wealthy and further burden the poor...

...Substandard medical care...

...The virulent spread of hate speech through the Internet...

...Self-serving blindness to both individual and institutionalized White privilege...

...Homogeneous communities where no one has to encounter the "foreign Other"...

The list goes on and on, but I want to linger for a moment over the issue of homogeneous communities for it brings me back to my purpose in writing about The Hill.

I have already made the point that urban renewal did a grave disservice to the residents of The Hill. Even at my advanced age, I still meet others who grew up in The Hill when it was a multi-ethnic, multi-cultural community. Black or White, these individuals speak with wistful longing of what we had and what we lost. And in that longing is a story of hope that the city leaders failed to honor. In this, they did a grave disservice to the public they were meant to serve. The story of The Hill I knew growing up was one of possibility—the possibility that as we worked, laughed, cried, worshipped, struggled, lived, and died together, we saw our common humanity. Fear and hatred dissipate when we see ourselves in the face of "the other." Acceptance of our shared humanity allows for the possibility of compassion, understanding, respect, and dignity. This is the foundation upon which a just and equal society can be forged.

When we retreat to enclaves and surround ourselves with those who are like us, possibilities for shared understanding and mutual respect whither. Prejudice can take root and flourish. In destroying The Hill, the city planners destroyed a model for integration that our society desperately needs. I fear this model is lost. Yet, the memories of my childhood refuse to let go of hope. And so it is with hope that I have shared my story of a remarkable community and say with pride, I Am from The Hill.

Epilogue

As I come closer to the end of my life's journey, I ask "What do I make of my experiences?" Looking back over more than 80 years, I treasure all that I was given by my loving parents and nurturing community. Without them, none of my life's accomplishments would have been possible. Upon this foundation I built a life of striving to make lives better for others. Through activism, teaching, and research I have tried to contribute to a more just and inclusive society. For this, I have no regrets. That said, I do have some regrets, mostly about the people I have wounded and left behind on the many battlefields of life. Still, I had vowed to live without "what ifs" or "if only." To the best of my ability, I have fulfilled that vow and have been enriched beyond measure by the experiences and friendships of a lifetime.

The Hill of my youth is long-gone, along with a large part of my soul. In writing this book, I have tried to fulfill the promises made so long ago to those elders who guided and supported "this neighborhood brat." I have tried to counteract The Hill's reputation as a violent, crime-infested ghetto by commemorating its vitality prior to Urban "Renewal." Above all, I want to honor the people who, when denied equality, forged a community where young Black boys and girls were protected from racism and prepared to face the discrimination that awaited them beyond The Hill. We were once a triumphant, resilient community. We absorbed the blows of racism and still we rose. Still we sang—in our churches, in our streets, and in our homes. If you listen closely on a quiet day, the music is still carried ever so gently on the wings of hope and dreams that simply will not die. Do you hear it?

About the Author

Ralph Proctor, Jr., Ph.D. grew up in an extraordinary place and culture known as The Hill in Pittsburgh. He has drawn upon his memories to celebrate a vibrant way of life created by individuals who would not be defeated by racism. An expert on African-American History and African-American Art, Dr. Proctor continues to teach in higher education. Over the years he has served in professional and administrative capacities in academia, social service agencies, and business organizations. He pioneered the use of oral history at the University of Pittsburgh with his study, *Racial Discrimination against Black Teachers and Black Professionals in the Pittsburgh Public School System: 1934-1973*. In addition he has published *Voices from the Firing Line: A Personal Account of the Pittsburgh Civil Rights Movement*. In his personal and professional life Proctor has been and continues to be a tireless warrior in the battle for civil rights.

Index to Photographs

Learning Moments Press

Learning Moments Press is the publishing arm of the Scholar-Practitioner Nexus, an online community of individuals committed to the quality of education. Learning Moments Press features three series of books.

> The Wisdom of Practice Series showcases the work of individuals who illuminate the complexities of practice as they strive to fulfill the purpose of their profession.

> The Wisdom of Life Series offers insightful reflections on significant life events that challenge the meaning of one's life, one's sense of self, and one's place in the world.

> The Social Context Series showcases the work of individuals who illuminate the macro socio-economic-political contexts within which education policy and practice are enacted.

Cooligraphy artist Daniel Nie created the logo for Learning Moments Press by combining two symbol systems. Following the principles of ancient Asian symbolism, Daniel framed the logo with the initials of Learning Moments Press. Within this frame, he replicated the Adinkra symbol for *Sankofa* as interpreted by graphic artists at the Documents and Designs Company. As explained by Wikipedia, Adinkra is a writing system of the Akan culture of West Africa. *Sankofa* symbolizes taking from the past what is good and bringing it into the present in order to make positive progress through the benevolent use of knowledge. Inherent in this philosophy is the belief that the past illuminates the present and that the search for knowledge is a life-long process.

For other publications of Learning Moments Press, visit scholarpractitionernexus.com.